P9-EJJ-127

ANDREA IMMER ROBINSON'S

2006 WINE BUYING GUIDE

for Everyone

IRL.OAT

ANDREA IMMER ROBINSON'S

2006 WINE BUYING GUIDE

for Everyone

**FEATURING MORE THAN 700 TOP WINES
AVAILABLE IN STORES AND RESTAURANTS**

Andrea Immer Robinson

WITHDRAWN
CONTRA COSTA COUNTY LIBRARY

3 1901 04188 2095

BROADWAY

ANDREA IMMER ROBINSON'S 2006 WINE BUYING GUIDE FOR EVERYONE. Copyright © 2005 by Andrea Robinson. All rights reserved. No part of this book may be reproduced or transmitted in any form or by any means, electronic or mechanical, including photocopying, recording, or by any information storage and retrieval system, without written permission from the publisher. For information, address Broadway Books, a division of Random House, Inc.

PRINTED IN THE UNITED STATES OF AMERICA

BROADWAY BOOKS and its logo, a letter B bisected on the diagonal, are trademarks of Random House, Inc.

Visit our website at www.broadwaybooks.com

First edition published 2002

The Library of Congress has cataloged the first edition as follows:
Immer, Andrea
[Wine buying guide for everyone]
Andrea Immer's wine buying guide for everyone /
Andrea Immer; edited by Anthony Giglio.— 1st ed.
p. cm.
Includes index.
1. Wine and wine making. I. Title: Wine buying guide
for everyone. II. Giglio, Anthony. III. Title.

  TP548 .I4624 2002
  641.2'2—dc21   2002023077

ISBN 0-7679-1546-1

10 9 8 7 6 5 4

CONTRA COSTA COUNTY LIBRARY

CONTENTS

ANDREA IMMER ROBINSON'S

2006 WINE BUYING GUIDE
for Everyone

INTRODUCTION

Although enjoying a good glass of wine is easy, all the types, costs, and confusing labels can make *shopping* for a bottle pretty hard. For the typical wine consumer, buying guidance—in the form of critics' 100-point scores and elaborate tasting reports of rare and exclusive bottlings—isn't much help. That is why I wrote *Andrea Immer Robinson's Wine Buying Guide for Everyone*. It is your road map to the *real* world of wine buying—from restaurants and hotels to supermarkets, price clubs, wine shops, and Web sites. Here is what you'll find inside:

Real-World Wines

This guide showcases more than 700 of the most popular and available wines on the market. That includes everything from supermarket stalwarts to trade-up labels to superpremium "restaurant" brands (with plenty of boutique pedigree but without the you can't-get-it frustration). Putting it plainly, if the wine is in your favorite neighborhood shops and eateries, at your supermarket or Costco, Olive Garden or Walt Disney World, Marriott or Carnival Cruises, Delta Airlines or wine.com, it's probably in this book.

Wine Reviews from the Trenches

I am indebted to the many consumers and wine pros who helped assess, for each of the wines in this book, what really matters to buyers at the point of purchase—taste and value for the money. For each wine, you'll also see their real-world reactions, as well as my impressions of how the wine stacks up in its grape or style category and in the marketplace overall. My tasters also contributed write-in candidates to the list of wines, and I've included those that received the highest number of positive mentions and have decent availability. There's also space in each listing for your notes, so you can keep track of the wines you try. (I hope you'll share your impressions with me for the next edition—read on to see how.)

Other Helpful Buying Tools in the Guide

Throughout the *Guide,* I've included simple tools to address just about every major wine buying question I've ever been asked. They are:

Best-Of Lists—A quick reference to the top-performing wines in each grape or style category.

Andrea's Kitchen Fridge Survivor™ and Kitchen Countertop Survivor™ grades—"How long will a wine keep after it's opened?" Having heard this question more than any other from my restaurant customers and wine students, I decided several years ago that it was time to find out, so I started putting every wine I taste professionally to the "fridge/countertop test." The resulting report card should help both home wine drinkers and restaurateurs who pour wine by the glass make the most of the leftovers, by simply recorking and storing red wine on the kitchen countertop and storing recorked sparkling, white, and pink wines in the fridge.

Immer Robinson Best Bets—This is the book's "search engine" of instant recommendations for every common wine occasion and buying dilemma, from Thanksgiving wines to restaurant wine list best bets, party-crowd pleasers, blue chip bottles to impress the client, and more.

Wine List Decoder—This handy cross-reference chart will help you crack the code of different wine list terms, so you can quickly and easily find the styles you like.

Great Wine Made Simple Mini-Course—Mini-lessons covering wine styles, label terms, glassware, buying wine in stores and restaurants, and other housekeeping details to simplify buying and serving wine, so you can focus on enjoying it.

I had been in the restaurant wine business for more than a decade before I wrote my first book, *Great Wine Made Simple.* Having studied like crazy to pass the Master Sommelier exam (the hardest wine test you can imagine), I knew there were lots of great books out there. So why another? Because as I worked training waiters and budding sommeliers, I began to see that in practice those books weren't much help. Wine, like food, golf, the saxophone, and so many other sensory pursuits, is something you learn not by studying but by doing. So *Great Wine Made Simple* teaches wine not through memorization but the way I learned it—through tasting. It works, and it's fun, whether you are just a dabbler or a committed wine geek.

Similarly, I intend this guide to fill a gap. Most people around the country buy wine based on price and convenience. And whether it's restaurant guests, viewers of my *Simply Wine* show on Fine Living network, or visitors to andreaimmer.com, they all have the same questions: What are the good, cheap wines? And which wines are really worth the splurge? This buying guide is the first to answer those questions realistically, featuring wines and tastes in the broad marketplace, along with plenty of shrewd pro advice to help you make the most of every wine purchase. Food is one major way to do that, so as a professionally trained cook I've also included lots of pairing pointers.

What's New in This Year's Guide

First, lots of wines! With the re-launch of my Web site andreaimmer.com, I recruited lots of new palates to the Tasting Panel . . . and they worked hard! My panel has now rated literally thousands of wines, and culling that list for really worthy selections to include in the Guide resulted in two hundred new additions with impressive taste and value reviews. One note: you will not see the new additions included in the Best Of table rankings because they're so new to the book (but they'll be eligible next year if they continue to perform well with the panel). I hope you'll log on to andreaimmer.com, join the Tasting Panel, and contribute *your* reviews—it's free, and a great way to keep track of your tasting notes. While you're there you can check out my new interactive wine-tasting DVD, *Andrea's Complete Wine Course*, and my new wine club, the A-List™. Now for the trends:

Hurrahs for Shiraz and Pinot Grigio

These two grapes continue to see sizzling sales, prompting just about every major wine brand, from Beringer to Yellow Tail, to add them to their lineup if they weren't there already. That said, there's a lot of sameness in this sea of new sips, so I added only a handful—the best of them—to the *Guide*.

The Critters Are Coming!

Maybe someone should build an ark, because this wine market is awash in a flood of new wines sporting animals on the label—seriously! If you check out the supermarket or wine shop, you'll see wine shopping is starting to seem like visiting a zoo (maybe you already felt that way anyway!). Ever since Yellow Tail wines, with the kangaroo on the label, took the market by storm, cute creatures have crawled onto brand after brand. In those cases where the wine is as compelling as the label, I've included them in the *Guide*.

A Dream Come True

We wine geeks wondered if we'd ever see the day: Riesling and Pinot Noir, darlings of the sommelier set and my two favorite grapes in the world, have finally begun to catch the mainstream wine market's attention. Even before Pinot Noir made its big-screen debut in the movie *Sideways,* the world's most complex red grape had begun to see sales gains across every price point. Same with Riesling, and wineries are scrambling to source more to meet the demand. It might seem surprising that two of the most elegant grapes have come on so strong in a market generally dominated by big Chardonnays and strapping Shirazes, but I think it's a sign of the ever-growing sophistication of American wine consumers. While they're not abandoning the big go-to grapes, they are expanding their taste horizons.

Tasters Are Trading Up (and Down)

Since national sales trends have shown impressive sales gains in the super-premium ($15 and up) price sector, you'd expect my panel's contributions to emphasize more and more high-end wines, and in fact they did. The average price of the new wines added to the *Guide* was a whopping $29! Yet there were also scores of value-priced wines on the list. Perhaps that means that what I've hoped for all along is starting to happen: Americans are enjoying inexpensive, everyday wines on a more frequent basis, and then enjoying a bottle that's a little more special just a little more often (like once a month, or even once a week!). I sure hope so! If that describes you, then this edition of the *Guide* should be the most helpful yet. Enjoy!

HOW TO USE THIS BUYING GUIDE

Here is everything you need to know to get instant buying power from the *Guide*.

Looking Up Wine Recommendations—by Wine Category or Winery Name

Wine Category—Grape, Region, or Type
The wine reviews are grouped by major grape variety, region, or type. For example:

Review section headings look like this

> ### WHITE WINES
> *Sparkling/Champagne*

You'll probably recognize some of the main grape and style categories, because they lead the wine market in both quality and sales. These include what I call the Big Six grapes (the white grapes Riesling, Sauvignon Blanc, and Chardonnay; and the reds Pinot Noir, Merlot, and Cabernet Sauvignon), plus Pinot Grigio, Italian reds, Syrah/Shiraz, and some other popular categories. This is also the way most wine lists and many shops are set up. The "Other Whites" and "Other Reds" sections are used for less common grapes and proprietary blends.

Helpful to know: I've arranged all the wine categories from lightest to fullest in body, as a quick reference for when you are shopping or perusing a wine list. More and more, restaurant wine lists are being arranged by body style, too, because it helps both the guest and the server quickly determine which wines are lightest or heaviest, so they can match their personal preference or food choice if they wish.

Winery Name—Alphabetical Wine Listings
The wines in each category are in alphabetical order by winery name, so you can easily find the specific wine you're looking for. For example:

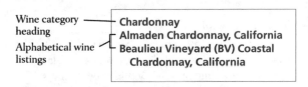

Wine category heading ——

Alphabetical wine listings

Chardonnay
Almaden Chardonnay, California
Beaulieu Vineyard (BV) Coastal
Chardonnay, California

Helpful to know: If you are looking for a specific winery name rather than a grape or style category, the Winery Index at the back of the book will show you which producers' wines were reviewed for the guide and the page number for each wine review.

Key to the Ratings and Symbols in Each Wine Entry

This sample entry identifies the components of each wine listing.

1. Wine name and provenance (country or state)
2. Price category
3. Taste and value ratings
4. Symbols: These identify wines rated as
   - ✓ best-of (rated most popular in their category) or
   - ✗ worthy write-ins in their respective categories.
   - ☺ An Andrea personal favorite

			②		③
❶	**Chateau Andrea Rose**		PC	T	V
	New York		$$	26	28

❹ ❺ ✗ Tasters marvel at its "amazing quality for a bag-in-the-box." Pro buyers (including me) find it "every bit as good as the finest Cold Duck ... and sometimes better!"

❻ *Kitchen Fridge/Countertop Survivor™ Grade:* A

❼ Your notes: _____

5. Reviewers' commentary, in quotation marks, along with my notes on the wine
6. My Kitchen Fridge/Countertop Survivor™ Grade
7. Space for your wine notes.

Price Category

Prices for the same wine can vary widely across the country. Here's why: individual states regulate the sale and taxation of wine within their borders, and sometimes local municipalities have further regulations and taxes. That means the price for any particular wine depends very much on where you live and shop. In general, wines are cheapest in large urban areas, where there's lots of retail competition. They are usually most expensive in so-called "control states," where there is zero competition because the state acts as the sole retailer (Pennsylvania is one example). In addition, some of the wines in the survey are available in a different size or in more than one size (e.g., half-bottles, standard 750 ml bottles, magnums, jugs, and larger). The price categories here, based on a standard 750 ml bottle, are intended as a guideline to help you compare relative prices of the different wines in the survey:

$ = up to $12
$$ = $12.01 to $20
$$$ = $20.01 to $35
$$$$ = above $35

NA indicates a wine not available in 750 ml bottles (sold only in jugs or bag-in-box format; prices for these are quite low).

Note: These are retail store prices, not restaurant wine list prices.

Taste and Value Ratings

Tasters (no pro credentials necessary, just an opinion) were asked to assess any of the listed wines that they'd tried in the past year on the following criteria:

- *Taste*—What did you think of the wine's taste?
- *Value for the Money*—Were you happy with what you got for the price you paid?

I kept the rating criteria simple, with scores listed on a scale of 0 to 30:

  0–9 = Poor
  10–15 = Fair
  16–19 = Good
  20–25 = Very good
  26–30 = Outstanding
  X = No data available (applies to write-in wines)

Certainly everyone has an opinion based on his or her own preferences and experience, and that is precisely what I sought to capture with this simple scale. I have also learned, from my years in the restaurant business and teaching wine classes, that most consumers can recognize inherent wine quality, regardless of their level of wine sophistication. I am pleased to say that the responses bore that out. Specifically, the wines that are consistently recognized by experts as quality and value leaders in their category were standouts among my tasters, too. Similarly, wines that have slipped, or whose price has risen unduly, were for the most part assessed accordingly. Other provocative attributes that influenced commentary and ratings included extreme prices (either high or low), an extreme reputation (either good or bad), and substantial inconsistency in the taste from one year to the next.

Symbols

Best-Of ✓—Identifies the top-rated wines in each category. (Rated "most popular" in the category—an average of the taste and value scores.)

Worthy Write-In X —Denotes that a wine was added to the book listings by popular demand (as noted earlier, only those write-ins with decent availability were included). Because most tasters gave their write-ins verbal endorsements rather than scores, I haven't included scores here but will do so in future editions of the guide.

Andrea Personal Favorite ☺ — Not always those with the highest scores!

Reviewers' Commentary and My Notes

Along with their taste and value assessments, reviewers were asked to include comments on the wines—not tasting descriptions per se but "buyers' notes" reflecting their gut reactions to the wine. If they felt a wine was overrated, underappreciated, delicious, awful, in a beautiful (or ugly) bottle, or whatever, I asked them to say so and have passed along those impressions, as well as my own based on working every day with myriad wines, wine servers, and wine drinkers.

Andrea's Kitchen Fridge Survivor™ and Kitchen Countertop Survivor™ Grades

I think a great many people hesitate to open wine for everyday meals because they won't know what to do with leftovers. No wonder! It's wildly expensive to pour out unfinished wine. And the frustration of wondering and worrying whether your wine's over the hill, *after* the intimidation of shopping for the wine, is more than most of us can be bothered with.

Since I couldn't stand the idea of people pretty much giving up on wine with dinner, and "How long will it keep after I open it?" is one of the most common wine questions I'm asked, I decided it was time to give some real answers.

I'm a bit embarrassed to admit that I began to test how long wines hold up in the everyday kitchen not because I was on a quest to answer these big-picture questions but because I kept tasting some impressive leftovers. In my sommelier and writing duties, I taste multiple wines often, and rarely with enough company to finish them the day they're opened, or even the next. In going back to the leftovers—to see if they were as good (or as disappointing) as I'd remembered—I got some amazing surprises. Far more often than you'd think, the good wines stayed that way for days. Even more astonishing, some of the wines that were initially underwhelming actually came around and started tasting better after being open for a while (in the same way that some cheeses need to sit out at room temperature to show their best flavor or a pot of chili can taste better after a day or two in the fridge).

And thus were born the Kitchen Fridge Survivor™ and Kitchen Countertop Survivor™ experiments. I hope the grades will give you confidence to enjoy wine with dinner more often, or even multiple wines with one meal (I frequently do), knowing that you can have tastes or just a glass of many wines, over several days, without the wines going "bad."

To test the wines' open-bottle longevity, I handled them as follows:

Whites—Recorked with the original cork (whether natural or synthetic). Placed in the fridge.

Reds—Recorked with the original cork. Placed on the kitchen counter.

Sparkling wines—Opened carefully without popping (popping depletes carbonation faster). Closed with a "clamshell" stopper designed for sparkling wines—sold in housewares departments and sometimes wine stores. Placed in the fridge.

Bag-in-box wines—These were not tested, because the airtight bag inside keeps the wine from oxidizing as it's consumed—one of the major virtues of this type of packaging.

The same process was repeated after each daily retaste, until the wine's taste declined noticeably. As I said, some wines actually taste better after a day or two. They were handled the same way.

There's no science to this. My kitchen is just a regular kitchen, probably much like yours. Hopefully these grades, which showed the wines' staying power in an everyday setting, will give you the confidence to enjoy wine more often with your everyday meals:

Avg = a "one-day wine," which tastes noticeably less fresh the next day. This doesn't mean the wine is less worthy, just less sturdy—so plan accordingly by inviting someone to share it with you.

B = holds its freshness for 2–3 days after opening

B+ = holds *and gets better* over 2–3 days after opening

A = has a 3- to 4-day "freshness window"

A+ = holds *and gets better* over 3–4 days

To learn how to lengthen the survival rate of your wine leftovers, see "Handling Wine Leftovers" in the *Great Wine Made Simple* Mini-Course chapter of this book.

Your Notes

Would you join my tasting panel? Of course, I would love for you to record your wine impressions and share them with me for the next edition of the *Immer Guide* (you may do so at *www.andreaimmer.com*). But even if you are not the survey type, do it for yourself. Whether you're at home or in a restaurant, the guide is a handy place to keep notes on what you drank, what you paid, what food you had with it, and what you thought. Don't you hate it when you've enjoyed a wine, then can't remember the name when you want to buy it again?

A Few Questions About the Wine Entries

How Were Wines Chosen for Inclusion in the Book?

The wines represented are top sellers in stores and restaurants nationally, in each style category. I featured mostly the top-selling premium, cork-finished wines because they outsell generics overall. However, I did include the dominant jug and bag-in-box wines, and my tasters did not ignore them. Don't see one of your favorite wines? Keep in mind that both popularity and availability of specific wines can vary a lot regionally, so a big brand in your area may not have the same sales and presence in other markets. This is especially true with local wines—for example, the Texas Chenin Blanc or New York Riesling that's on every table in your neck of the woods may not even be distributed in the next state. I also included worthy write-ins—those with decent availability that got the highest number of positive mentions from my tasters, although in some cases that availability may be skewed heavily to restaurants. Why? you ask. Many buyers have told me of their frustration at seeing the wines they'd like to purchase available only in restaurants. It's a phenomenon that became increasingly common in the wine boom of the 1990s. Simply put, wineries with a limited supply often concentrate on restaurant lists because of the image enhancement they can offer—good food, nice setting, and (usually) fewer competing selections than in a shop.

Why No Vintage Years?

This guide deals with the top-selling wines in the market, and so, for the most part, the year available in stores and restaurants is the winery's current release. But I am also making a philosophical statement about vintages for the wines in the guide, and it is this: I believe that the leading wines in the market *should* be fairly consistent from one year to the next so that consumers, and the retail and restaurant wine buyers who serve them, need not sweat the vintage, as long as it's current and fresh. There are certain wine categories where vintage is a bigger consideration—among them expensive California reds, French Bordeaux and Burgundy, and upscale Italian reds. But even with these, if you do not intend to cellar the wines (very few buyers do), vintage isn't so critical. A few of the tasters mentioned the vintage issue, but most were comfortable with my approach.

> **IMMER ROBINSON INSIGHT:** Ninety-five percent of the quality wines on the market are meant to be consumed within one to three years of the harvest (the vintage date on the label), while they are young, fresh, and in good condition. Most wines do not get better with age, so why wait?

Can You Really Define "Outstanding" Wine?

Indeed I can. We all can. Broadly, it is a wine that captures your attention. It could be the scent, the taste, the texture, or all three that make you say first, "Mmm. . . ," and then, "Wow" as your impressions register in the moment, in the context of all your prior experience and the price you paid. If it all sounds very personal and subjective, you're exactly right—it is. That is why I felt a guide like this, showcasing the impressions of real-world buyers, was so important. The fact that the wines herein are big sellers is already an endorsement. The details put each wine in context—of price, similar-style wines, occasion, and whatever else buyers feel is important. No other wine buying guide does that.

Who Are the Tasters? You

Over a six-month period in 2005 I collected tasting data on my Web site from thousands of American wine buyers—trade colleagues (retail and restaurant buyers, sommeliers, hoteliers, chefs, waiters, importers, and distributors). The trade buyers included most major chain restaurants and stores, chefs, and my master sommelier colleagues, among others. I also recruit tasters through my restaurant guests, my students at The French Culinary Institute, and of course the friends and family network, including family members I didn't even know I had until I found them on the e-mail trail. I originally thought consumers would be less keen than trade to share their wine opinions, but I was wrong. As noted previously, consumers account for more than seventy percent of the responses. Although I don't purposely exclude anyone, I do review every survey returned for signs of ballot stuffing from winery companies and eliminate all suspicious responses (there were literally just a couple).

Why Do These Tasters' Opinions Matter?

Clearly, this guide for everyone takes an utterly populist perspective that's different from every other wine publication on the market—and that is exactly what I intend. I think the honest assessments and perspective of consumers who have to pay their own money for wine (while wine journalists rarely do), and the restaurateurs and retailers who serve them, are extremely important and helpful—because they're the real world. (With so little of that perspective in the marketplace, can it be any wonder that wine is barely a blip on Americans' cultural radar screen?) I am not dismissing the value of, and expertise behind, the leading critics' scoring reports. But I do think they often further the notion that there are haves and have-nots in the wine world: the 90+–rated "good stuff" that none of us can afford; and the rest—the wines we see every day whose lower scores seem bad by comparison. That perspective is perhaps valuable to a tiny, elite group of luxury wine buyers. But for what I call the OTC (other than collectors) market, which comprises the bulk of the nation's buyers (including just about everyone I know), this dichotomy leaves us feeling utterly insecure about our own taste and budget, skeptical about the quality of the selection at the stores and restaurants we frequent, and self-conscious about our (legitimate) desire for value for the money—in the vernacular, good, cheap wine. If I've achieved my goal, this guide's real-world information will give you a renewed sense of confidence in your own taste and some great word-of-mouth guidance on new wines to try that are actually available where you shop and dine. Enjoy!

MOST POPULAR WINES—REFLECTING BOTH TASTE AND VALUE FOR THE MONEY

25 Most Popular Whites *
Based on Taste and Value

Name	Wtd. Avg. T/V Score**	Price Cate-gory
Mulderbosch Sauvignon Blanc	29	$$$
Nobilo Sauvignon Blanc	28	$
J. Lohr Bay Mist Riesling	27	$
Reichsgraf von Kesselstat Piesporter Goldtropfchen Riesling Kabinett	27	$$
Kim Crawford Sauvignon Blanc	27	$$
Mer Soleil Chardonnay	27	$$$$
Chalone Estate Chardonnay	26	$$$
Penfolds Rawson's Retreat Chardonnay	26	$
Columbia Winery Cellarmaster's Reserve Riesling	26	$
J. Lohr Riverstone Chardonnay	26	$$
Louis Jadot Pouilly-Fuisse	26	$$
Chateau Ste. Michelle Columbia Valley Chardonnay	25	$
St. Supery Sauvignon Blanc	26	$$
Kendall-Jackson Vintner's Reserve Riesling	26	$$
Fetzer Valley Oaks Gewurztraminer	26	$
Hirsch Gruner Veltliner	26	$$

*To find the complete tasting notes for each wine, refer to the alphabetical winery index in the back of the book.

**Scores were rounded off. Wines are listed in order of actual score ranking. The number of wines in each "Most Popular" listing reflects the overall number of wines in the category. So our "Top Whites" list numbers 25, while the Top Rieslings ranking shows just five entries. It's also a fairly close reflection of each category's sales and prominence in the fine wine market overall.

Name		
Conundrum by Caymus	26	$$$
Casa Lapostolle Sauvignon Blanc	26	$
Kenwood Sauvignon Blanc	25	$
Babich Sauvignon Blanc	25	$
Frog's Leap Sauvignon Blanc	25	$$
Ferrari-Carano Fume Blanc	25	$$
Fetzer Valley Oaks Riesling	25	$
Sonoma-Cutrer Russian River Ranches Chardonnay	25	$$$
Brancott Reserve Sauvignon Blanc	25	$$

25 Most Popular Reds
Based on Taste and Value

Name	Wtd. Avg. T/V Score*	Price Category
Selvapiana Chianti Rufina Riserva	28	$$$
Montecillo Rioja Crianza	27	$
Estancia Alexander Valley Meritage	27	$$$
Frescobaldi Chianti Rufina Riserva	27	$$$
Ferrari-Carano Siena	27	$$$$
Archery Summit Red Hills Estate Pinot Noir	27	$$$$
Lindemans Bin 50 Shiraz	26	$
D'Arenberg The Footbolt Shiraz	26	$$
Chateau St. Jean Cinq Cepages	26	$$$$
Concannon Petite Sirah	26	$
Franciscan Oakville Estate Merlot	26	$$
Osborne Solaz	26	$
Monte Antico Toscana	26	$
Ramsay Pinot Noir	26	$$
Hill of Content Grenache-Shiraz	26	$$
Francis Coppola Diamond Series Black Label Claret	26	$$
Casa Lapostolle Cuvee Alexandre Cabernet Sauvignon	26	$$
Gallo of Sonoma Merlot	25	$
Merry Edwards Russian River Valley Pinot Noir	25	$$$$
Ridge Geyserville Zinfandel	25	$$$
Columbia Crest Two Vines Merlot	25	$
Bogle Old Vines Zinfandel	25	$
Alice White Shiraz	25	$

*Scores were rounded off. Wines are listed in order of actual ranking.

Name	Wtd. Avg. T/V Score*	Price Category
Escudo Rojo Cabernet blend	25	$$
Stag's Leap Wine Cellars Merlot	25	$$$

Best of the Big 6 Grapes

Name	Wtd. Avg. T/V Score*	Price Category
5 Most Popular Rieslings		
Columbia Winery Cellarmaster's Reserve	26	$
Kendall-Jackson Vintner's Reserve	26	$$
Fetzer Valley Oaks	25	$
Eroica	25	$$$
J. Lohr Bay Mist	24	$
10 Most Popular Sauvignon/Fume Blancs		
Mulderbosch	29	$$$
Nobilo	28	$
Casa Lapostolle	28	$
Kim Crawford	27	$$
St. Supery	26	$$
Kenwood	25	$
Babich	25	$
Frog's Leap	25	$$
Ferrari-Carano Fume Blanc	25	$$
Brancott Reserve	25	$$
30 Most Popular Chardonnays		
Mer Soleil	27	$$$$
Penfolds Rawson's Retreat	26	$
J. Lohr Riverstone	26	$$
Louis Jadot Pouilly-Fuisse	26	$$
Chateau Ste. Michelle Columbia Valley	25	$
Sonoma-Cutrer Russian River Ranches	25	$$$
Talbott Sleepy Hollow Vineyard	25	$$$$
Gallo of Sonoma	24	$
Ferrari-Carano Napa-Sonoma	24	$$$
Edna Valley Vineyards Paragon	24	$
Acacia Carneros	24	$$$
R. H. Phillips Toasted Head	24	$$
La Crema	23	$$
R. H. Phillips California	23	$
Chateau Ste. Michelle Cold Creek	23	$$

Rombauer	23	$$
Casa Lapostolle Cuvee Alexandre	23	$$
Landmark Overlook	23	$$$
Cambria Katherine's Vineyard	23	$$
Columbia Crest Grand Estates	23	$
Estancia Pinnacles	23	$$
Clos du Bois	23	$$
Hess Select	23	$
Fetzer Valley Oaks	23	$
Beringer Founders' Estate	22	$
St. Francis	22	$
Rodney Strong Sonoma	22	$
Grgich Hills	22	$$$$
Lindemans Bin 65	22	$
Yellow Tail	22	$

15 Most Popular Pinot Noirs

Ramsay	26	$$
Merry Edwards Russian River Valley	25	$$$$
Etude Carneros	25	$$$$
Cristom	25	$$$$
Domaine Drouhin Oregon	25	$$$$
Elk Cove	24	$$
Robert Sinskey Los Carneros	24	$$$
MacMurray Ranch Sonoma Coast	24	$$
Rex Hill Willamette Valley	24	$$
J Wine Co. Russian River	24	$$$
Au Bon Climat	24	$$$
La Crema	24	$$
Domaine Carneros	24	$$$
Duck Pond	24	$
Echelon	24	$

20 Most Popular Merlots

Franciscan Oakville Estate	26	$$
Gallo of Sonoma	25	$
Columbia Crest Two Vines	25	$
Stag's Leap Wine Cellars	25	$$$
Chateau Souverain Alexander Valley	25	$$
Rodney Strong	24	$$
Beringer Founders' Estate	24	$
Shafer	24	$$$$
St. Francis	24	$$$
Fetzer Valley Oaks	24	$

*Scores were rounded off. Wines are listed in order of actual ranking.

Name	Wtd. Avg. T/V Score*	Price Category
Montes Alpha "M"	23	$$$$
Chateau Larose-Trintaudon	23	$$
Bogle	23	$
Duckhorn Napa	23	$$$$
Markham	23	$$$
Swanson	23	$$$
Stonestreet	23	$$$
Clos du Bois	22	$$
Blackstone	22	$
Christian Moueix	22	$

30 Most Popular Cabernet Sauvignons and Blends

Name	Wtd. Avg. T/V Score*	Price Category
Estancia Alexander Valley Meritage	27	$$$
Chateau St. Jean Cinq Cepages	26	$$$$
Francis Coppola Diamond Series Black Label Claret	26	$$
Casa Lapostolle Cuvee Alexandre	26	$$
Escudo Rojo Cabernet blend	25	$$
Penfolds Cabernet/Shiraz Bin 389	25	$$$
Pine Ridge Stag's Leap District	25	$$$
Los Vascos	25	$
Arrowood	25	$$$$
Simi	24	$$
Gallo of Sonoma	24	$
Columbia Crest Grand Estates	24	$
Rosemount Cabernet Merlot	24	$
Black Opal	24	$
J. Lohr Seven Oaks	24	$$
Joseph Phelps	24	$$$$
Franciscan Oakville Estate	24	$$$
Cain Cuvee Bordeaux Style Red	24	$$$
Chateau Gruaud-Larose	24	$$$$
Beringer Knights Valley	23	$$$
Groth	23	$$$$
Estancia	23	$$
Silver Oak Alexander Valley	23	$$$$
Jacob's Creek	23	$
Sterling Napa	23	$$$
Viader Napa Valley red blend	23	$$$$
Stag's Leap Wine Cellars Napa	23	$$$$
Heitz Napa	23	$$$$

| Beringer Founders' Estate | 23 | $ |
| Chateau Greysac | 23 | $$ |

Best of the Rest

Name	Wtd. Avg. T/V Score*	Price Category
10 Most Popular Champagnes and Sparkling Wines		
Domaine Chandon Riche	27	$$$
Iron Horse Wedding Cuvee Brut	26	$$
Krug Grande Cuvee Champagne	25	$$$$
Perrier-Jouet Grand Brut Champagne	24	$$$
Taittinger Brut La Francaise Champagne	24	$$$$
Piper-Heidsieck Brut Cuvee Champagne	23	$$$$
Domaine Chandon Brut Classic	23	$$
Moet & Chandon Brut Imperial	23	$$$$
J Wine Co. Brut	23	$$$
Domaine Ste. Michelle Brut	22	$$
10 Most Popular Pinot Grigio/Gris		
Livio Felluga Pinot Grigio	24	$$
Alois Lageder Pinot Grigio	24	$$
Folonari Pinot Grigio	23	$
Santa Margherita Pinot Grigio	23	$$$
Cavit Pinot Grigio	22	$
King Estate Pinot Gris	22	$$
Bolla Pinot Grigio	21	$
Zemmer Pinot Grigio	21	$$
Ecco Domani Pinot Grigio	19	$
Rancho Zabaco Pinot Grigio	18	$
5 Most Popular Other Whites		
Fetzer Valley Oaks Gewurztraminer	26	$
Hirsch Gruner Veltliner	26	$$
Conundrum by Caymus	26	$$$
Bolla Soave	25	$
Hugel Gewurztraminer	24	$$
10 Most Popular Italian and Spanish Reds		
Selvapiana Chianti Rufina Riserva	28	$$$
Montecillo Rioja Crianza	27	$
Taurino Salice Salentino	26	$$
Monte Antico Toscana	26	$
Osborne Solaz	26	$

*Scores were rounded off. Wines are listed in order of actual ranking.

Name	Wtd. Avg. T/V Score*	Price Category
Ruffino Chianti Classico Riserva Ducale Tan Label	25	$$
Nozzole Chianti Classico Riserva	24	$$$
Pesquera Ribera del Duero	24	$$$
Ruffino Chianti Classico Riserva Ducale Gold Label	24	$$$
Marques de Caceres Rioja Crianza	23	$

10 Most Popular Shiraz/Syrahs and Rhone-Style Reds

Name		
Lindemans Bin 50 Shiraz	26	$
D'Arenberg The Footbolt Shiraz	26	$$
Hill of Content Grenache-Shiraz	26	$$
Alice White Shiraz	25	$
Rosemount GSM (Grenache-Shiraz-Mourvedre)	25	$$$
Jaboulet Cotes du Rhone Parallele 45	25	$$
Jacob's Creek Shiraz Cabernet	25	$
Georges Duboeuf Cotes du Rhone Rouge	24	$$
Alain Graillot Crozes-Hermitage Rouge	24	$$$
Wynn's Coonawarra Estate Shiraz	24	$$$

10 Most Popular Red Zinfandels

Name		
Ridge Geyserville	25	$$$
Bogle Old Vines	25	$
Rancho Zabaco Dancing Bull	24	$
Seghesio Sonoma	24	$$
Woodbridge	24	$
Montevina Amador	24	$
Rancho Zabaco Dry Creek Valley	24	$$$
Laurel Glen Reds	23	$
St. Francis Old Vines	23	$$$
Rosenblum Vintners Cuvee	23	$

TOP TASTE RANKINGS

Top 30 White Wines by Taste

Name	Taste Score*	Price Category
Didier Dagueneau Pouilly-Fume Pur Sang	29	$$$$
Chalone Estate Chardonnay	29	$$$
Rombauer Chardonnay	28	$$
Nobilo Sauvignon Blanc	28	$
Kim Crawford Sauvignon Blanc	28	$$
Louis Jadot Pouilly-Fuisse	27	$$
Mer Soleil Chardonnay	27	$$$$
Lucien Crochet Sancerre Blanc	27	$$
J. Lohr Bay Mist Riesling	27	$
Hirsch Gruner Veltliner	27	$$
Grgich Hills Fume Blanc	27	$$$
Conundrum by Caymus	27	$$$
Chateau Ste. Michelle Late Harvest Riesling	27	$$
Ferrari-Carano Napa-Sonoma Chardonnay	27	$$$
Sonoma-Cutrer Russian River Ranches Chardonnay	27	$$$
Talbott Sleepy Hollow Vineyard Chardonnay	26	$$$$
St. Supery Sauvignon Blanc	26	$$
Eroica Riesling	26	$$$
Cakebread Sauvignon Blanc	26	$$
Grgich Hills Chardonnay	26	$$$$
J. Lohr Riverstone Chardonnay	26	$$
Brancott Reserve Sauvignon Blanc	26	$$
Kendall-Jackson Vintners Reserve Riesling	26	$$
Ferrari-Carano Fume Blanc	26	$$
Columbia Winery Cellarmaster's Reserve Riesling	26	$

*Scores were rounded off. Wines are listed in order of actual ranking.

Name	Taste Score*	Price Category
Casa Lapostolle Sauvignon Blanc	26	$
Cloudy Bay Sauvignon Blanc	25	$$$
Robert Mondavi Fume Blanc	25	$$
Frog's Leap Sauvignon Blanc	25	$$

Top 30 Red Wines by Taste

Name	Taste Score*	Price Category
Selvapiana Chianti Rufina Riserva	29	$$$
Viader Napa Valley red blend	28	$$$$
Heitz Napa Cabernet Sauvignon	28	$$$$
Ferrari-Carano Siena Sonoma County	28	$$$$
D'Arenberg The Footbolt Shiraz	28	$$
Chateau St. Jean Cinq Cepages	28	$$$$
Ridge Geyserville Zinfandel	28	$$$
Franciscan Oakville Estate Merlot	28	$$
Etude Carneros Pinot Noir	28	$$$$
Merry Edwards Russian River Valley Pinot Noir	28	$$$$
Silver Oak Alexander Valley Cabernet Sauvignon	27	$$$$
Swanson Merlot	27	$$$
Rosemount GSM (Grenache-Shiraz-Mourvedre)	27	$$$
Robert Mondavi Napa Cabernet Sauvignon	27	$$$
Rancho Zabaco Dry Creek Valley Zinfandel	27	$$$
Pine Ridge Cabernet Sauvignon Stag's Leap District	27	$$$
Penfolds Cabernet/Shiraz Bin 389	27	$$$
Opus One Cabernet Sauvignon blend	27	$$$$
Navarro Correas Malbec	27	$
Montecillo Rioja Crianza	27	$
Lindemans Bin 50 Shiraz	27	$
Joseph Phelps Cabernet Sauvignon	27	$$$$
Hill of Content Grenache-Shiraz	27	$$
Estancia Alexander Valley Meritage	27	$$$
Cristom Pinot Noir	27	$$$$
Alvaro Palacios Les Terrasses Priorat	27	$$$$
Shafer Merlot	27	$$$$

Williams-Selyem Pinot Noir Sonoma Coast	26	$$$$
Groth Cabernet Sauvignon	26	$$$$
Chateau Souverain Alexander Valley Merlot	26	$$

Best of the Big 6 Grapes

Name	Taste Score*	Price Category
Top 10 Rieslings by Taste		
Eroica	26	$$$
Kendall-Jackson Vintner's Reserve	26	$$
Columbia Winery Cellarmaster's Reserve	26	$
J. Lohr Bay Mist	24	$
Fetzer Valley Oaks	24	$
Jekel	24	$
Trimbach	24	$$
Bonny Doon Pacific Rim	23	$
Chateau Ste. Michelle	23	$
Hogue	22	$
Top 15 Sauvignon/Fume Blancs by Taste		
Didier Bagueneau Pouilly-Fume Pur Sang	29	$$$$
Kim Crawford	28	$$
Nobilo	28	$
Grgich Hills Fume Blanc	27	$$$
Lucien Crochet Sancerre Blanc	27	$$
Cakebread	26	$$
St. Supery	26	$$
Brancott Reserve	26	$$
Casa Lapostolle	26	$
Ferrari-Carano Fume Blanc	26	$$
Cloudy Bay	25	$$$
Frog's Leap	25	$$
Robert Mondavi Fume Blanc	25	$$
Villa Maria Private Bin	25	$$
Babich	24	$
Top 30 Chardonnays by Taste		
Chalone Estate	29	$$$
Rombauer	28	$$
Louis Jadot Pouilly-Fuisse	27	$$
Mer Soleil	27	$$$$

*Scores were rounded off. Wines are listed in order of actual ranking.

Name	Taste Score*	Price Category
Ferrari-Carano Napa-Sonoma	27	$$$
Sonoma-Cutrer Russian River Ranches	27	$$$
Talbott Sleepy Hollow Vineyard	26	$$$$
Grgich Hills	26	$$$$
J. Lohr Riverstone	26	$$
Cakebread	24	$$$
Acacia Carneros	24	$$$
Chateau Montelena	24	$$$$
Chateau Ste. Michelle Columbia Valley	24	$
Clos du Bois	24	$$
Edna Valley Vineyards Paragon	24	$
Fetzer Valley Oaks	24	$
Landmark Overlook	24	$$$
R. H. Phillips Toasted Head	24	$$
Trefethen	24	$$$
Gallo of Sonoma	24	$
Cambria Katherine's Vineyard	24	$$
La Crema	24	$$
Rodney Strong Sonoma	23	$
R. H. Phillips California	23	$
St. Francis Sonoma	23	$
Sterling	23	$$$
Chalk Hill	22	$$$$
Estancia Pinnacles	22	$$
Robert Mondavi Napa	22	$$
Simi	22	$$

Top 15 Pinot Noirs by Taste

Name	Taste Score*	Price Category
Etude Carneros	28	$$$$
Merry Edwards Russian River Valley	28	$$$$
Cristom	27	$$$$
Williams-Selyem Sonoma Coast	26	$$$$
Domaine Carneros	26	$$$
Domaine Drouhin Oregon	26	$$$$
J Wine Co. Russian River	26	$$$
Archery Summit Arcus Estate	26	$$$$
Au Bon Climat	26	$$$
Elk Cove	26	$$
Robert Sinskey Los Carneros	26	$$$
MacMurray Ranch Sonoma Coast	25	$$
Byron Santa Maria Estate	24	$$$
Cambria Julia's Vineyard	24	$$$
David Bruce Santa Cruz	24	$$

Top 20 Merlots by Taste

Franciscan Oakville Estate	28	$$
Swanson	27	$$$
Shafer	27	$$$$
Chateau Souverain Alexander Valley	26	$$
Stag's Leap	26	$$$
St. Francis	25	$$$
Duckhorn	25	$$$$
Montes Alpha "M"	25	$$$$
Sterling	25	$$$
Rodney Strong	25	$$
Chateau Larose-Trintaudon	24	$$
Gallo of Sonoma	24	$
Markham	24	$$$
Stonestreet	24	$$$
Beringer Founders' Estate	23	$
Fetzer Valley Oaks	23	$
Columbia Crest Two Vines	22	$
Bogle	22	$
Clos du Bois	22	$$$
Blackstone	21	$

Top 30 Cabernet Sauvignons and Blends by Taste

Chateau St. Jean Cinq Cepages	28	$$$$
Heitz Napa	28	$$$$
Viader Napa Valley red blend	28	$$$$
Silver Oak Alexander Valley	27	$$$$
Estancia Alexander Valley Meritage	27	$$$
Joseph Phelps	27	$$$$
Penfolds Cabernet/Shiraz Bin 389	27	$$$
Pine Ridge Stag's Leap District	27	$$$
Groth	26	$$$$
Cain Cuvee Bordeaux style red	26	$$$
Arrowood	26	$$$$
Chateau Gruaud-Larose	26	$$$$
Francis Coppola Diamond Series Black Label Claret	26	$$
Pahlmeyer Meritage	26	$$$$
Santa Rita 120	26	$
Stag's Leap Wine Cellars Napa	26	$$$$
Casa Lapostolle Cuvee Alexandre	26	$$
Far Niente	25	$$$$
Jordan	25	$$$$
Franciscan Oakville Estate	25	$$$

*Scores were rounded off. Wines are listed in order of actual ranking.

Name	Taste Score*	Price Category
Beaulieu (BV) Rutherford	24	$$$
Beringer Knights Valley	24	$$$
Cakebread	24	$$$$
Chateau Gloria	24	$$$
Dynamite	24	$$
Escudo Rojo Cabernet blend	24	$$
Frei Brothers Reserve	24	$$
J. Lohr Seven Oaks	24	$$
Laurel Glen Terra Rosa	24	$
Rosemount Cabernet Merlot	24	$

Best of the Rest

Name	Taste Score*	Price Category
Top 5 Champagnes and Sparkling Wines by Taste		
Perrier-Jouet Grand Brut Champagne	28	$$$
Billecart-Salmon Rose Champagne	28	$$$$
Gruet Brut St. Vincent	27	$$
Iron Horse Wedding Cuvee Brut	27	$$
Krug Grande Cuvee Champagne	27	$$$$
Top 10 Pinot Grigio/Gris by Taste		
Alois Lageder Pinot Grigio	24	$$
Livio Felluga Pinot Grigio	24	$$
Santa Margherita Pinot Grigio	24	$$$
Folonari Pinot Grigio	22	$
King Estate Pinot Gris	22	$$
Cavit Pinot Grigio	22	$
Bolla Pinot Grigio	21	$
Ecco Domani Pinot Grigio	18	$
Rancho Zabaco Pinot Grigio	18	$
Mezza Corona Pinot Grigio	18	$
Top 10 Other Whites by Taste		
Conundrum by Caymus	27	$$$
Hirsch Gruner Veltliner	27	$$
Fetzer Valley Oaks Gewurztraminer	25	$
Hugel Gewurztraminer	25	$$
Bolla Soave	24	$
Martin Codax Albarino	24	$$
Beringer Gewurztraminer	22	$
Hogue Gewurztraminer	22	$

| Columbia Crest Gewurztraminer | 20 | $ |
| Pepperwood Grove Viognier | 20 | $ |

Top 10 Italian and Spanish Reds by Taste

Selvapiana Chianti Rufina Riserva	29	$$$
Ferrari-Carano Siena Sonoma County	28	$$$$
Alvaro Palacios Les Terrasses Priorat	27	$$$$
Montecillo Rioja Crianza	27	$
Taurino Salice Salentino	26	$$
Ruffino Chianti Classico Riserva Ducale Gold Label	26	$$$
Ruffino Chianti Classico Riserva Ducale Tan Label	26	$$
Antinori (Marchesi) Chianti Classico Riserva	24	$$$
Felsina Chianti Classico	24	$$$
Marques de Caceres Rioja Crianza	24	$

Top 10 Shiraz/Syrahs and Rhone-Style Reds by Taste

D'Arenberg The Footbolt	28	$$
Hill of Content Grenache-Shiraz	27	$$
Lindemans Bin 50	27	$
Rosemount GSM (Grenache-Shiraz-Mourvedre)	27	$$$
Wolf Blass President's Selection	26	$$$
Penfolds Kalimna Bin 28	26	$$$
Alice White	25	$
Alain Graillot Crozes-Hermitage Rouge	24	$$$
Chapoutier La Bernardine Chateauneuf-du-Pape rouge	24	$$$
Chateau de Beaucastel Chateauneuf-du-Pape rouge	24	$$$$

Top 10 Red Zinfandels by Taste

Ridge Geyserville	28	$$$
Rancho Zabaco Dry Creek Valley	27	$$$
Seghesio Sonoma	25	$$
Bogle Old Vines	24	$
Fetzer Valley Oaks	24	$$
Montevina Amador	24	$
Rancho Zabaco Heritage Vines	24	$
Woodbridge	24	$
Rancho Zabaco Dancing Bull	24	$
St. Francis Old Vines	23	$$$

*Scores were rounded off. Wines are listed in order of actual ranking.

BEST OF THE BARGAIN-PRICED WINES

Top 20 Budget Whites

Name	Taste Score*
Nobilo Sauvignon Blanc	28
J. Lohr Bay Mist Riesling	27
Casa Lapostolle Sauvignon Blanc	26
Columbia Winery Cellarmaster's Reserve Riesling	26
Fetzer Valley Oaks Gewurztraminer	25
Babich Sauvignon Blanc	24
Bolla Soave	24
Casa Lapostolle Chardonnay Classic	24
Chateau Ste. Michelle Columbia Valley Chardonnay	24
Edna Valley Vineyards Paragon Chardonnay	24
Fetzer Valley Oaks Chardonnay	24
Fetzer Valley Oaks Riesling	24
Jekel Riesling	24
Gallo of Sonoma Chardonnay	24
Hogue Fume Blanc	23
Bonny Doon Pacific Rim Riesling	23
Chateau Ste. Michelle Johannisberg Riesling	23
Covey Run Fume Blanc	23
Kenwood Sauvignon Blanc	23
Rodney Strong Sonoma Chardonnay	23

Top 20 Budget Reds

Lindemans Bin 50 Shiraz	27
Montecillo Rioja Crianza	27
Navarro Correas Malbec	27
Santa Rita 120 Cabernet Sauvignon	26
Concannon Petite Sirah	26
Alice White Shiraz	25
Bogle Old Vines Zinfandel	24

Casa Lapostolle Merlot Classic	24
Gallo of Sonoma Merlot	24
Georges Duboeuf Moulin-a-Vent	24
Marques de Caceres Rioja Crianza	24
Monte Antico	24
Montevina Amador	24
Montevina Amador Zinfandel	24
Osborne Solaz	24
Rancho Zabaco Heritage Vines Zinfandel	24
Rosemount Cabernet Merlot	24
Woodbridge Zinfandel	24
Gallo of Sonoma Cabernet Sauvignon	24
Rancho Zabaco Dancing Bull Zinfandel	24
Los Vascos Cabernet Sauvignon	24

Best of the Big 6 Grapes

Name	Taste Score*
Top 5 Budget Rieslings	
Columbia Winery Cellarmaster's Reserve	26
J. Lohr Bay Mist	24
Fetzer Valley Oaks	24
Jekel	24
Bonny Doon Pacific Rim	23
Top 5 Budget Sauvignon/Fume Blancs	
Nobilo	28
Casa Lapostolle	26
Babich	24
Hogue Fume Blanc	23
Covey Run Fume Blanc	23
Top 10 Budget Chardonnays	
Chateau Ste. Michelle Columbia Valley	24
Edna Valley Vineyards Paragon	24
Fetzer Valley Oaks	24
Gallo of Sonoma	24
Rodney Strong Sonoma	23
R. H. Phillips Dunnigan Hills	23
St. Francis Sonoma	23
Hess Select	22
Penfolds Koonunga Hill	22
Lindemans Bin 65	21

*Scores were rounded off. Wines are listed in order of actual ranking.

Name	Taste Score*
Top 5 Budget Pinot Noirs	
Duck Pond	23
Echelon	23
Gallo of Sonoma	21
Lindemans Bin 99	20
Meridian	20
Top 5 Budget Merlots	
Casa Lapostolle Classic	24
Gallo of Sonoma	24
Beringer Founders' Estate	23
Fetzer Valley Oaks	23
Columbia Crest Two Vines	22
Top 10 Budget Cabernets and Blends	
Santa Rita 120	26
Rosemount Cabernet Merlot	24
Gallo of Sonoma	24
Los Vascos	24
Robert Mondavi Private Selection	23
Beringer Founders' Estate	23
Chateau Ste. Michelle	22
Jacob's Creek	22
Kenwood	22
Black Opal	22

Best of the Rest

Name	Taste Score*
Top 5 Budget Other Whites	
Fetzer Valley Oaks Gewurztraminer	25
Bolla Soave	24
Hogue Gewurztraminer	22
Columbia Crest Gewurztraminer	20
Pepperwood Grove Viognier	20
Top 5 Budget Italian and Spanish Reds	
Montecillo Rioja Crianza	27
Monte Antico Toscana	24
Osborne Solaz	24
Cecchi Chianti	23
Allegrini Valpolicella Classico	22
Top 5 Budget Shiraz/Syrahs and Rhone-Style Reds	
Lindemans Bin 50	27
Alice White	25

Jacob's Creek Shiraz Cabernet	23
Penfolds Koonunga Hill Shiraz-Cabernet	23
Rosemount Diamond Label	22

Top 5 Budget Red Zinfandels

Bogle Old Vines	24
Montevina Amador	24
Rancho Zabaco Heritage Vines	24
Robert Mondavi Private Selection	24
Woodbridge	24

*Scores were rounded off. Wines are listed in order of actual ranking.

TOP VALUES FOR THE MONEY (ACROSS ALL PRICES)

Top 20 White Wine Values

Wine Name	Value Score*	Price Category
Casa Lapostolle Sauvignon Blanc	29	$
Chateau Ste. Michelle Columbia Valley Chardonnay	29	$
Nobilo Sauvignon Blanc	28	$
Kenwood Sauvignon Blanc	28	$
Columbia Winery Cellarmaster's Reserve Riesling	27	$
J. Lohr Bay Mist Riesling	27	$
Mer Soleil Chardonnay	27	$$$$
Babich Sauvignon Blanc	26	$
Casa Lapostolle Chardonnay Classic	26	$
Fetzer Valley Oaks Riesling	26	$
J. Lohr Riverstone Chardonnay	26	$$
Kim Crawford Sauvignon Blanc	26	$$
Fetzer Valley Oaks Gewurztraminer	26	$
Kendall-Jackson Vintner's Reserve Riesling	26	$$
Bolla Soave	26	$
Hogue Fume Blanc	25	$
Frog's Leap Sauvignon Blanc	25	$$
St. Supery Sauvignon Blanc	25	$$
Gallo of Sonoma Chardonnay	25	$
Covey Run Fume Blanc	25	$

Top 20 Red Wine Values

Wine Name	Value Score*	Price Category
Columbia Crest Two Vines Merlot	28	$
Santa Rita 120 Cabernet Sauvignon	28	$

Dynamite Cabernet Sauvignon	27	$$
Estancia Alexander Valley Meritage	27	$$$
Monte Antico Toscana	27	$
Montecillo Rioja Crianza	27	$
Osborne Solaz	27	$
Ramsay Pinot Noir	27	$$
Selvapiana Chianti Rufina Riserva	27	$$$
Gallo of Sonoma Merlot	27	$
Black Opal Cabernet Sauvignon	26	$
Concannon Petite Sirah	26	$
Bogle Old Vines Zinfandel	26	$
Chandon Terrazas Alto Malbec	26	$$
Escudo Rojo Cabernet blend	26	$$
Ferrari-Carano Siena Sonoma County	26	$$$$
Jacob's Creek Shiraz Cabernet	26	$
Taurino Salice Salentino	26	$$
Columbia Crest Cabernet Sauvignon Grand Estates	26	$$
Casa Lapostolle Cuvee Alexandre Cabernet Sauvignon	26	$$

*Scores were rounded off. Wines are listed in order of actual ranking.

THE REVIEWS

WHITE WINES
Sparkling/Champagne

Style Profile: Although all the world's bubblies are modeled on Champagne, only the genuine article from the Champagne *region* of France is properly called *Champagne. Sparkling wine* is the proper term for the other bubblies, some of which can be just as good as the real thing. Limited supply and high demand—plus a labor-intensive production process—make Champagne expensive compared to other sparklers but still an affordable luxury in comparison to other world-class wine categories, like top French Burgundy or California Cabernet estates. The other sparklers, especially Cava from Spain and Italian Prosecco, are affordable for everyday drinking. *Brut* (rhymes with root) on the label means the wine is utterly dry, with no perceptible sweetness. But that *doesn't* mean they all taste the same. In fact, each French Champagne house is known for a signature style, which can range from delicate and elegant to rich, full, and toasty—meaning there's something for every taste and food partner.

Serve: Well chilled; young and fresh (only the rare luxury French Champagnes improve with age). Open with utmost care: flying corks can be dangerous.

When: Anytime! It's not just for special occasions, and it's great with meals.

With: Anything and anyone, but especially sushi and shellfish.

In: A narrow tulip- or flute-type glass; the narrow opening preserves the bubbles.

Kitchen Fridge Survivor™ Tip for bubbly wine: Kitchenware shops and wine stores often sell "clamshell" stoppers specially designed to close Champagnes and sparkling wines if you don't finish the bottle. I've found that if you open the bottle carefully in the first place (avoid "popping" the cork, which is also the safest technique), a stoppered sparkling wine will keep its fizz for at least three days in the fridge, often longer. Having a hard time thinking of something else to toast? How about, "Here's to [insert day of week]." That's usually good enough for me!

Argyle Brut Sparkling	PC	T	V
Oregon	**$$**	**21**	**24**

The Asian pear scent and flavor are delicious just for sipping, but this bubbly's also an elegant accompaniment to subtle foods like scallops or Dungeness crab.

Kitchen Fridge Survivor™ Grade: A

Your notes: _____

Ballatore Gran Spumante	PC	T	V
California	**$**	**24**	**24**

"Delightful with or without food, crisp and fun," say my tasters, who "feel we get more than we pay for." It's "a little sweet—great for mimosas."

Kitchen Fridge Survivor™ Grade: A

Your notes: _____

Bollinger RD Champagne	PC	T	V
France	**$$$$**	**29**	**24**

"Expensive, but *sooo* good," with baked apple and croissant flavors and scents, and an endless finish.

Kitchen Fridge Survivor™ Grade: A

Your notes: _____

Price Ranges: **$** = $12 or less; **$$** = $12.01–20; **$$$** = $20.01–35; **$$$$** = > $35

Kitchen Fridge/Countertop Survivor™ Grades: *Avg.* = a "one-day wine," tastes noticeably less fresh the next day; *B* = holds its freshness for 2–3 days after opening; *B+* = holds *and gets better* over 2–3 days after opening; *A* = a 3- to 4-day "freshness window"; *A+* = holds *and gets better* over 3–4 days

Bollinger (*BOLL-ehn-jur*) Special   **PC**   **T**   **V**
Cuvee (*coo-VAY*) Brut Champagne,   **$$$$**   **29**   **18**
France

My taster's "big, toasty, full bodied" comment is right on. The complexity "really captures your attention." No wonder it's 007's favorite.

Kitchen Fridge Survivor™ Grade: A

Your notes: _____

Bouvet Brut (*boo-VAY broot*)   **PC**   **T**   **V**
Loire Valley Sparkling, France   **$**   **24**   **28**

Bouvet is both classy and affordable, with a complex scent of wilted blossoms and sweet hay, a crisp apple-quince flavor, and creamy texture.

Kitchen Fridge Survivor™ Grade: B+

Your notes: _____

Charles Heidsieck (*HIDE-sick*) Brut   **PC**   **T**   **V**
Champagne, France   **$$$$**   **24**   **24**

This "well rounded and luxurious" bubbly, one of my favorites, is known for its creamy texture, full body, and toasted hazelnut scent.

Kitchen Fridge Survivor™ Grade: A

Your notes: _____

Charles Heidsieck (*HIDE-sick*) Brut   **PC**   **T**   **V**
Vintage Champagne, France   **$$$$**   **24**   **19**

This Champagne is one of my favorites for its nutty, croissant-bakery scent.

Kitchen Fridge Survivor™ Grade: A

Your notes: _____

Domaine Carneros Brut Sparkling   **PC**   **T**   **V**
California   **$$$**   **22**   **20**

This wine's definitely on my "short list" of favorite California sparklers. It has very ripe fruit, expertly balanced between generous juiciness and elegant restraint. Fabulous with food, too.

Kitchen Fridge Survivor™ Grade: B

Your notes: _____

Domaine Carneros Le Reve   **PC**   **T**   **V**
Sparkling, California   **$$$$**   **26**   **23**

This top bottling for Domaine Carneros is one of CA's best bubblies, with a firm core of fresh pear fruit, floral and fresh-bread scent, and endless finish.

Kitchen Fridge Survivor™ Grade: A+

Your notes: _____

Domaine Chandon (*shahn-DOHN*)   PC   T   V
Blanc de Noirs Sparkling, California $$ 22   24

It's pronounced blahnk-duh-NWAHR, and it means this golden bubbly is made from black (Noir) grapes, which give it extra body and concentration.

Kitchen Fridge Survivor™ Grade: B

Your notes: _____

Domaine Chandon Extra Brut   PC   T   V
Classic Sparkling, California $$ 23   23

This American sparkler sibling of France's famous Moët & Chandon is a huge hit with my tasters for its yeasty, creamy style that's "classy but affordable."

Kitchen Fridge Survivor™ Grade: B+

Your notes: _____

Domaine Chandon Riche Sparkling   PC   T   V
California $$ 24   26

✔ What makes it "riche" is a hint of sweetness—not at all cloying. In fact, that bit of sweetness makes it a great accompaniment to foods with a kick.

Kitchen Fridge Survivor™ Grade: A

Your notes: _____

Domaine Ste. Michelle Cuvee Brut   PC   T   V
Sparkling, Washington $ 20   24

My tasters note, "you can't beat the price" of this nicely balanced, crisp, and appley sparkler. So it's great for weddings and parties or just for sipping.

Kitchen Fridge Survivor™ Grade: B

Your notes: _____

Dom Perignon Champagne Brut   PC   T   V
France $$$$ 24   18

Though some say "you can do better for the price," you can't beat the pedigree "when you want to impress," and the "good fruit flavor" and "yeasty" scent are "always reliable."

Kitchen Fridge Survivor™ Grade: B

Your notes: _____

Price Ranges: **$** = $12 or less; **$$** = $12.01–20; **$$$** = $20.01–35; **$$$$** = > $35

Kitchen Fridge/Countertop Survivor™ Grades: ***Avg.*** = a "one-day wine," tastes noticeably less fresh the next day; ***B*** = holds its freshness for 2–3 days after opening; ***B+*** = holds *and gets better* over 2–3 days after opening; ***A*** = a 3- to 4-day "freshness window"; ***A+*** = holds *and gets better* over 3–4 days

Freixenet (*fresh-uh-NETT*) Brut   PC   T   V
de Noirs, Cava Rose, Spain $ 18   24

☺ "Yum's the word" for this wine. The mouthwatering taste of tangy strawberries is great with fried foods, spicy foods . . . any foods. And it held up for weeks in the fridge.

Kitchen Fridge Survivor™ Grade: A+

Your notes: _____

Freixenet Cordon Negro Brut   PC   T   V
Sparkling, Spain $ 20   22

"Nice for the price" sums up the consensus among tasters who call this wine "simple and refreshing," and better "than most low-end California sparklers."

Kitchen Fridge Survivor™ Grade: Avg

Your notes: _____

Gosset (*go-SAY*) Brut Rose   PC   T   V
Champagne, France $$$$ 26   24

◉ This is one of my favorite Champagnes, period. The scent and flavors of dried cherries, exotic spices, and toasted nuts would please any serious wine drinker. Forget toasting and serve it with salmon, tuna, duck, or pork.

Kitchen Fridge Survivor™ Grade: A

Your notes: _____

Gruet (*groo-AY*) Brut St. Vincent   PC   T   V
Sparkling, New Mexico $$ 23   23

New Mexico? Gruet's "great bubblies which are tasty and of good value" prove "all that prickles in the desert isn't cactus!"

Kitchen Fridge Survivor™ Grade: B+

Your notes: _____

Iron Horse Wedding Cuvee Brut   PC   T   V
Sparkling, California $$$ 27   24

Brides, of course, love the romantic name, and it is my choice for receptions, having inspired more "What was the name of that wine?" reactions than any other in the history of my wine career. It's got great acidity and crisp tangerine and green apple flavors.

Kitchen Fridge Survivor™ Grade: B

Your notes: _____

J Vintage Brut Sparkling   PC   T   V
California $$$ 24   21

"J produces wonderful sparkling wine … refreshing and fun," say my tasters. It seems to get better and better every year, and the package is gorgeous.

Kitchen Fridge Survivor™ Grade: A

Your notes: _____

Korbel Brut Sparkling   PC   T   V
California $$ 20   19

This is the top-selling bubbly in America. That said, it's a tasty *sparkling wine* for the money. Korbel's use of the name "Champagne" on the label furthers consumer confusion over the term: true Champagne must come from that *region* in France.

Kitchen Fridge Survivor™ Grade: Avg

Your notes: _____

Krug Grande Cuvee Multivintage   PC   T   V
Champagne, France $$$$ 27   22

☺ This is one of my favorite wines in the world, and one of the few I really feel are worth the splurge. Krug's full, nutty, baked brioche style is truly unique among Champagnes. Serve it not just for sipping, but with dinner—shellfish, roasted game birds, anything mushroomy.

Kitchen Fridge Survivor™ Grade: A

Your notes: _____

Laurent-Perrier Brut LP,   PC   T   V
Champagne, France $$$$ 27   20

This wine's known for its elegance and racy acidity, which makes it a great food partner *and* a great Fridge Survivor.

Kitchen Fridge Survivor™ Grade: A+

Your notes: _____

Price Ranges: **$** = $12 or less; **$$** = $12.01–20; **$$$** = $20.01–35; **$$$$** = > $35

Kitchen Fridge/Countertop Survivor™ Grades: ***Avg.*** = a "one-day wine," tastes noticeably less fresh the next day; ***B*** = holds its freshness for 2–3 days after opening; ***B+*** = holds *and gets better* over 2–3 days after opening; ***A*** = a 3- to 4-day "freshness window"; ***A+*** = holds *and gets better* over 3–4 days

Mionetto DOC Prosecco Brut	**PC**	**T**	**V**
(*me-oh-NETT-oh pro-SECK-oh*)	**$$**	**24**	**18**
Veneto, Italy			

This Prosecco is dry, refreshing, and sophisticated but also affordable. Prosecco is the grape name. If you want, add peach puree to make the Bellini, Venice's signature cocktail.

Kitchen Fridge Survivor™ Grade: B

Your notes: _____

Moet & Chandon (*MWETT eh***	**PC**	**T**	**V**
shahn-DOHN) Brut Imperial	**$$$$**	**25**	**20**
Champagne, France			

This is one of the best Brut NVs on the market at the moment, with "medium body and more fruit flavor and acidity" than its sister bottling, Moet & Chandon White Star. I love it.

Kitchen Fridge Survivor™ Grade: B

Your notes: _____

Moet & Chandon White Star	**PC**	**T**	**V**
Champagne, France	**$$$$**	**24**	**20**

With its famous pedigree, flower and biscuit scents, and a peachy finish, my trade and consumer tasters alike tout this as "fantastic Champagne," and I agree. Its "reliable, crowd-pleasing style" is great with spicy foods and sushi.

Kitchen Fridge Survivor™ Grade: A

Your notes: _____

Mumm Cuvee Napa Brut	**PC**	**T**	**V**
Prestige Sparkling, California	**$$**	**19**	**19**

It's more popular then ever with my tasters, who rave about the "French style, for a great price."

Kitchen Fridge Survivor™ Grade: B

Your notes: _____

Perrier-Jouet Flower Bottle,	**PC**	**T**	**V**
Champagne, France	**$$$$**	**24**	**24**

The wine is just as beautiful as the painted bottle, with scents of biscuits, flower, and baked apples, and beautiful elegance.

Kitchen Fridge Survivor™ Grade: A

Your notes: _____

Perrier-Jouet (*PEAR-ee-ay JHWETT*)	PC	T	V
Grand Brut Champagne, France	$$$$	28	20

"PJ" was historically one of my favorites in the lighter-bodied Champagne style. My tastings of late have revealed a decline—less flavor depth and a touch of bitterness. The tasting panel still gives it high marks, however.

Kitchen Fridge Survivor™ *Grade: NA*

Your notes: _____

Piper-Heidsieck (*HIDE-sick*) Brut	PC	T	V
Cuvee Champagne, France	$$$$	26	20

This "really dry brut style" has a tangy, snappy acidity that makes it great with salty and fatty flavors and "an absolute joy to drink."

Kitchen Fridge Survivor™ *Grade: A*

Your notes: _____

Piper-Sonoma Brut Sparkling	PC	T	V
California	$$	20	20

This California outpost of the French Champagne Piper-Heidsieck yields one of California's best bubblies. It's got a toasty quality that's wonderful on its own and with food.

Kitchen Fridge Survivor™ *Grade: A+*

Your notes: _____

Pol Roger Brut Reserve	PC	T	V
Champagne, France	$$$$	26	18

"Wonderful producer. Great product at this price point," noted my tasters. It is one of my favorite brut Champagnes in the delicate, elegant style.

Kitchen Fridge Survivor™ *Grade: A+*

Your notes: _____

Pommery (*POMM-er-ee*) Brut	PC	T	V
Royal Champagne, France	$$$$	23	20

Pommery became well-known in the U.S. thanks to

Price Ranges: **$** = $12 or less; **$$** = $12.01–20; **$$$** = $20.01–35; **$$$$** = > $35

Kitchen Fridge/Countertop Survivor™ Grades: *Avg.* = a "one-day wine," tastes noticeably less fresh the next day; *B* = holds its freshness for 2–3 days after opening; *B+* = holds *and gets better* over 2–3 days after opening; *A* = a 3- to 4-day "freshness window"; *A+* = holds *and gets better* over 3–4 days

the trendy "Pops" mini-bottles. It's an elegant style with a creamy scent and subtle pear flavor.

Kitchen Fridge Survivor™ Grade: A

Your notes: _____

Roederer Estate Brut Sparkling	PC	T	V
California	$$$	24	24

☺ Wine trade and consumers alike say this is about as close to Champagne as you can get without buying French, and I agree. The full, toasty style is right in keeping with the house style of its French parent (they make Cristal). It's the best of both worlds: "reasonably priced," with the taste of "a special occasion wine."

Kitchen Fridge Survivor™ Grade: A

Your notes: _____

Segura Viudas (*seh-GUHR-uh*	PC	T	V
vee-YOU-duss) Aria Estate Extra	$$	18	24
Dry Cava, Spain			

☺ For the money, this is one of the most delicious sparklers on the market, with ripe, vibrant pear fruit and a creamy texture. The beautiful bottle brings an elegant look to parties, at a great party price.

Kitchen Fridge Survivor™ Grade: A

Your notes: _____

Taittinger (*TAIT-in-jur*) Brut La	PC	T	V
Française Champagne, France	$$$$	26	22

This is one of my favorites among the subtle, elegant house-style Champagnes. The generous proportion of Chardonnay in its blend lends finesse and delicacy that "simply dance across the tongue."

Kitchen Fridge Survivor™ Grade: A

Your notes: _____

Veuve Clicquot La Grande Dame	PC	T	V
Champagne, France	$$$$	24	20

"Pricey but worth it" is the consensus for this powerful yet elegant, biscuity, nutty/pear/cream–scented wine.

Kitchen Fridge Survivor™ Grade: A

Your notes: _____

Veuve Clicquot (*voov klee-COH*)	PC	T	V
Yellow Label Champagne, France	$$$$	23	20

Again this year, pro and consumer tasters were wishy-washy, some saying "great, as always," and others saying "not what it used to be." I still like the full-bodied house style, but judge for yourself.

Kitchen Fridge Survivor™ Grade: B+

Your notes: _____

Pinot Gris/Pinot Grigio

Grape Profile: Pinot Gris (*pee-no GREE*) is the French and Grigio (*GREE-jee-oh*) the Italian spelling for this crisp, delicate white wine grape whose sales under the "Grigio" label continue to see scorching growth. The French and American versions tend toward the luscious style, versus the Italians which are more tangy and crisp. To many of my trade tasters it's "the quintessential quaffing wine" and "a real winner by the glass" in restaurants. Happily, many of the cheapest Pinot Grigios remain among the best. I couldn't put it better than the taster who wrote, "If it doesn't *taste* a lot better, why should I *pay* a lot more?" As the Italians would say, *Ecco!*

Serve: Well chilled; young and fresh (as one of my wine buying buddies says to the waiters *she* teaches: "The best vintage for Pinot Grigio? As close to yesterday as possible!").

When: Anytime, but ideal with cocktails, outdoor occasions, lunch, big gatherings (a crowd-pleaser).

With: Very versatile, but perfect with hors d'oeuvres, salads, salty foods, and fried foods.

In: An all-purpose wine stem is fine.

	PC	T	V
Alois Lageder (*la-GAY-der;* no one says the first part) Pinot Grigio, Italy	**$$**	24	24

☺ ✓ The pear fruit, floral scent, and smoky finish add up to complexity that few expect from Pinot Grigio.

Kitchen Fridge Survivor™ Grade: B

Your notes: _____

Price Ranges: **$** = $12 or less; **$$** = $12.01–20; **$$$** = $20.01–35; **$$$$** = > $35

Kitchen Fridge/Countertop Survivor™ Grades: *Avg.* = a "one-day wine," tastes noticeably less fresh the next day; *B* = holds its freshness for 2–3 days after opening; *B+* = holds *and gets better* over 2–3 days after opening; *A* = a 3- to 4-day "freshness window"; *A+* = holds *and gets better* over 3–4 days

Bella Sera Pinot Grigio   PC   T   V
Italy $ 16   19

Although historically it was crisp and pleasant, the scores dropped because "there are better PGs for the $."

Kitchen Fridge Survivor™ Grade: B

Your notes: _____

Bolla (BOWL-uh) Pinot Grigio   PC   T   V
Italy $ 21   21

I keep looking for a quality leap from the Bolla name, but it still offers less flavor for the money than other PGs at the same price.

Kitchen Fridge Survivor™ Grade: Avg

Your notes: _____

Cavit (*CAV-it;* rhymes with   PC   T   V
"have-it") Pinot Grigio, Italy $ 22   22

Fans say this wine's "a nice summertime sipper" or for cocktail parties. It's light, crisp, and bargain-priced.

Kitchen Fridge Survivor™ Grade: B

Your notes: _____

Ecco Domani (*ECK-oh dough-*   PC   T   V
***MAH-nee*) Pinot Grigio, Italy** $ 18   20

"Tastes clean and refreshing," say fans of Gallo's Italian offspring that tastes crisp and lemony. Pros point out that it's "a great value for the money."

Kitchen Countertop Survivor™ Grade: B

Your notes: _____

Folonari (*foe-luh-NAH-ree*)   PC   T   V
Pinot Grigio, Italy $ 22   24

Trade buyers say this "underrated overachiever" is ideal when you're seeking a crisp, sippable, value-priced white.

Kitchen Fridge Survivor™ Grade: Avg

Your notes: _____

Gallo of Sonoma Pinot Gris   PC   T   V
California $ X   X

✗ As winemaker Gina Gallo says, this wine is "all about the fruit: white peach, fig, and apricot." Yum!

Kitchen Fridge Survivor™ Grade: Avg

Your notes: _____

King Estate Pinot Gris	PC	T	V
Oregon	$$	22	22

After a few years of inflation, this wine's price has returned to good (in most markets) for the quality. Enjoy the "cornucopia of tropical fruit flavors" with sushi, spicy fare, or just for sipping.

Kitchen Fridge Survivor™ Grade: A

Your notes: _____

Livio Felluga (*LIV-ee-oh fuh-LOO-*	PC	T	V
guh) Pinot Grigio, Italy	$$$	24	24

✔ "Lean," "stylish," and "exciting" are words pros use to describe this standout Pinot Grigio. I like the pretty floral nose and ripe apricot flavor.

Kitchen Fridge Survivor™ Grade: B

Your notes: _____

MezzaCorona (*METT-suh*	PC	T	V
coh-ROH-nuh) Pinot Grigio, Italy	$	18	21

"A nice staple" and "great everyday wine," whose scores improved in this year's survey. Tasters say it's a "mouthwatering" and "refreshing" crowd pleaser.

Kitchen Fridge Survivor™ Grade: B

Your notes: _____

Montevina Pinot Grigio	PC	T	V
California	$	20	21

This wine bursts with ripe pear fruit, while the crisp acidity keeps it flexible with a wide array of food partners, from spicy to garlicky.

Kitchen Fridge Survivor™ Grade: B

Your notes: _____

Ponzi Pinot Gris	PC	T	V
Oregon	$$	21	18

The mineral and ripe pear scent and flavor are like Alsace Pinot Gris, but without the weight.

Kitchen Fridge Survivor™ Grade: A

Your notes: _____

Price Ranges: **$** = $12 or less; **$$** = $12.01–20; **$$$** = $20.01–35; **$$$$** = > $35

Kitchen Fridge/Countertop Survivor™ Grades: ***Avg.*** = a "one-day wine," tastes noticeably less fresh the next day; ***B*** = holds its freshness for 2–3 days after opening; ***B+*** = holds *and gets better* over 2–3 days after opening; ***A*** = a 3- to 4-day "freshness window"; ***A+*** = holds *and gets better* over 3–4 days

Rancho Zabaco Pinot Grigio | PC | T | V
California | $$ | 18 | 28

An exotic flavor of honeydew makes this lovely for sipping, and with spicy food, too.

Kitchen Fridge Survivor™ Grade: B
Your notes: _____

Robert Mondavi Private Selection | PC | T | V
Pinot Grigio, California | $ | X | X

✗ One of the best budget Pinot Grigios from California! Easy-drinking, but with lots of lively apricot, peach, and melon flavors.

Kitchen Fridge Survivor™ Grade: B
Your notes: _____

Santa Margherita Pinot Grigio | PC | T | V
Italy | $$$ | 24 | 21

While some consumers and most trade tasters appraise Santa Margherita as "way overpriced," many still say it's a "favorite" that will "impress your friends." In my book, the exploding PG category offers so many better and cheaper alternatives.

Kitchen Fridge Survivor™ Grade: Avg
Your notes: _____

Willamette Valley Vineyard Pinot | PC | T | V
Gris, Oregon | $$ | 26 | 24

"Great with food," note my tasters, due to thc "crip tartness" and "loads of flavor"—pears and dried pineapple.

Kitchen Fridge Survivor™ Grade: Avg
Your notes: _____

Woodbridge (Robert Mondavi) | PC | T | V
Pinot Grigio, California | $ | 24 | 18

☺ This is my favorite wine in the Woodbridge line, and tasters clearly love the "lively peach fruit" that's "lipsmacking on its own as a sipping wine."

Kitchen Fridge Survivor™ Grade: B
Your notes: _____

Zemmer Pinot Grigio | PC | T | V
Italy | $$ | 24 | 18

This Pinot Grigio has "more concentration than most" in its price range, and "a great nose, great food compatibility."

Kitchen Fridge Survivor™ Grade: B
Your notes: _____

Riesling

Grape Profile: I'm thrilled to see that nationwide sales of Riesling (REES-ling—my favorite white grape) are growing! Clearly consumers are appreciating its virtues. Among them are great prices. Also, check out all the high survivor grades. Thanks to their tangy, crisp acidity, Riesling wines really hold up in the fridge. That makes them ideal for lots of everyday dining situations—you want a glass of white with your takeout sushi, but your dinner mate wants red with the beef teriyaki. At home I sometimes want to start with a glass of white while I'm cooking and then switch to red with the meal. It's nice to know that I can go back to the wine over several days, and every glass will taste as good as the first one.

Germany, the traditional source of great Rieslings, continues to grow its presence in the Guide. And that's great, because no other region offers so many *world class* wines for under $25. Look for German Rieslings from the Mosel, Rheingau, Pfalz, and Nahe regions. Other go-to Riesling regions are Washington State, Australia, New Zealand, and Alsace, France.

Prepare to be impressed. Rieslings are light-bodied but loaded with stunning fruit flavor, balanced with tangy acidity.

Serve: Lightly chilled is fine (the aromas really shine when it's not ice-cold); it's good young and fresh, but the French and German versions can evolve nicely for up to five years.

When: Every day (OK, my personal taste there); classy enough for "important" meals and occasions.

With: Outstanding with shellfish and ethnic foods with a "kick" (think Asian, Thai, Indian, Mexican). There's also an awesome rule-breaker match: braised meats!

In: An all-purpose wineglass.

Price Ranges: **$** = $12 or less; **$$** = $12.01–20; **$$$** = $20.01–35; **$$$$** = > $35

Kitchen Fridge/Countertop Survivor™ Grades: *Avg.* = a "one-day wine," tastes noticeably less fresh the next day; *B* = holds its freshness for 2–3 days after opening; *B+* = holds *and gets better* over 2–3 days after opening; *A* = a 3- to 4-day "freshness window"; *A+* = holds *and gets better* over 3–4 days

Beringer Johannisberg Riesling   **PC**   **T**   **V**
California   **$**   **24**   **24**

The fruit-salad-in-a-glass flavor of this wine rocks.
I think it's one of the best values in the Beringer
lineup.

Kitchen Fridge Survivor™ Grade: B+

Your notes: _____

Bonny Doon Pacific Rim Riesling   **PC**   **T**   **V**
USA/Germany   **$**   **23**   **25**

☺ This endures as one of the most written-about
wines in the survey—with raves about the "yummy,
juicy-fruity yet dry" flavor. "Pacific Rim" is the
winery's shorthand for "Drink this with Asian
foods."

Kitchen Fridge Survivor™ Grade: A

Your notes: _____

Chateau Ste. Michelle Johannisberg   **PC**   **T**   **V**
Riesling, Washington   **$**   **23**   **24**

Peach and apricot flavor and crisp, lively acidity give
this wine the balance that is the hallmark of well-
made Riesling. Bravo!

Kitchen Fridge Survivor™ Grade: A

Your notes: _____

Columbia Crest Johannisberg   **PC**   **T**   **V**
Riesling, Washington   **$**   **23**   **26**

This honeysuckle-peachy wine is "lip-smacking with
spicy foods," and "a super value."

Kitchen Fridge Survivor™ Grade: A

Your notes: _____

Columbia Winery Cellarmaster's   **PC**   **T**   **V**
Reserve Riesling, Washington   **$**   **26**   **27**

☺ ✓ This wine is lush with ripe peach, apricot, and
honey flavors, spiked with crisp acidity, at a bargain
price.

Kitchen Fridge Survivor™ Grade: A+

Your notes: _____

Dr. Konstantin Frank Dry Riesling   **PC**   **T**   **V**
New York   **$**   **25**   **24**

What an impressive fan base for this wine, the
"best dry Riesling in the U.S." (I concur) that

"comes close to German quality," with incredible peachy fruit density and zingy acidity.

Kitchen Fridge Survivor™ Grade: A

Your notes: _____

Dr. Loosen Riesling Kabinett   **PC**   **T**   **V**
Estate, Germany   **$$**   **26**   **26**

This dry, classic German Riesling is "perfect with Asian meals," say my tasters, because the mineral/petrol scents and steely acidity set off spicy and pungent flavors beautifully.

Kitchen Fridge Survivor™ Grade: A

Your notes: _____

Eroica (*ee-ROY-cuh*) Riesling   **PC**   **T**   **V**
Washington   **$$$**   **26**   **23**

☺ "The best Riesling made in America . . ."? I have to agree. The dense core of apple and peach fruit and mineral complexity make it "as good as German Riesling."

Kitchen Fridge Survivor™ Grade: A+

Your notes: _____

Fetzer Valley Oaks Johannisberg   **PC**   **T**   **V**
Riesling, California   **$**   **24**   **26**

My tasters "love" this "bold" Riesling, with "huge pear fruit" and a hint of sweetness "with spicy foods."

Kitchen Fridge Survivor™ Grade: B+

Your notes: _____

"Fish Label" Riesling Selbach-Oster   **PC**   **T**   **V**
(*ZELL-bock OH-stir*), Germany   **$$**   **24**   **24**

This wine has neither a tongue-twister name nor a flabby-sweet taste. It *does* have a delicate peaches-and-cream scent, tangerine and apricot fruit, and long finish.

Kitchen Fridge Survivor™ Grade: A

Your notes: _____

Price Ranges: **$** = $12 or less; **$$** = $12.01–20; **$$$** = $20.01–35; **$$$$** = > $35

Kitchen Fridge/Countertop Survivor™ Grades: *Avg.* = a "one-day wine," tastes noticeably less fresh the next day; *B* = holds its freshness for 2–3 days after opening; *B+* = holds *and gets better* over 2–3 days after opening; *A* = a 3- to 4-day "freshness window"; *A+* = holds *and gets better* over 3–4 days

Gunderloch Riesling Kabinett   PC   T   V
Jean Baptiste, Germany $$ 22   22

This wine exemplifies great German Riesling—so approachable, yet with amazing complexity: flowers, chamomile tea, fresh cream, white peach.

Kitchen Fridge Survivor™ Grade: A

Your notes: _____

Hogue Johannisberg Riesling,   PC   T   V
Washington $ 22   22

Attention all white Zin fans: here's a great alternative that's a little on the sweet side, with ripe, peachy fruit flavor and a candied orange finish.

Kitchen Fridge Survivor™ Grade: B

Your notes: _____

Jekel Riesling   PC   T   V
California $ 24   18

I love this wine's floral nose and juicy peach flavor. The touch of sweetness makes it a perfect partner for spicy foods.

Kitchen Fridge Survivor™ Grade: B+

Your notes: _____

JJ Prum Riesling Kabinett Wehlener   PC   T   V
Sonnenuhr, Germany $$ 23   23

This is textbook Mosel Riesling—peaches-and-cream and petrol character, packed with concentration.

Kitchen Fridge Survivor™ Grade: A+

Your notes: _____

J. Lohr Bay Mist Riesling   PC   T   V
California $ 24   24

✗ This wine's enticing floral scent and apple fruit, balanced by crisp acidity, make it a perfect aperitif.

Kitchen Fridge Survivor™ Grade: B+

Your notes: _____

Kendall-Jackson Vintner's Reserve   PC   T   V
Riesling, California $ 26   26

For tasters new to Riesling, I often recommend this one: a blue chip winery pedigree, lush peach and tangerine fruit, great price.

Kitchen Fridge Survivor™ Grade: A+

Your notes: _____

Kurt Darting Riesling Kabinett   PC   T   V
Germany $$ 27   26

I'm always thrilled when I find this on wine lists. Its bewitching floral aromas and spicy-tangy core are just glorious—with food, or without.

Kitchen Fridge Survivor™ Grade: A+

Your notes: _____

Lingenfelder Bird Label Riesling   PC   T   V
Germany $$ 21   24

This "awsome value from a top producer" has amazing acidity and snappy apple flavor that make it "perfect to sip on," great with food.

Kitchen Fridge Survivor™ Grade: A+

Your notes: _____

Pierre Sparr Carte D'Or Riesling   PC   T   V
Alsace, France $ 24   21

"When you're sick of oak, take this for the cure," say my tasters of this sleek, tangy, mouthwatering Riesling with the scent of honey and Asian pears. Yum!

Kitchen Fridge Survivor™ Grade: A+

Your notes: _____

Reichsgraf von Kesselstat   PC   T   V
Piesporter Goldtropfchen $$$ 27   25
Riesling Kabinett, Germany

The light body, honeysuckle and petrol scent, delicate peach-apple flavors and creamy finish are textbook Mosel Riesling.

Kitchen Fridge Survivor™ Grade: A

Your notes: _____

Robert Mondavi Private Selection   PC   T   V
Riesling, California $ X   X

✗ How do they do it? The petrol and peach are classic Riesling, but the yum factor and great price are "house wine" material. Bravo!

Kitchen Fridge Survivor™ Grade: B+

Your notes: _____

Price Ranges: **$** – $12 or less; **$$** = $12.01–20; **$$$** = $20.01–35; **$$$$** = > $35

Kitchen Fridge/Countertop Survivor™ Grades: *Avg.* = a "one-day wine," tastes noticeably less fresh the next day; *B* = holds its freshness for 2–3 days after opening; *B+* = holds *and gets better* over 2–3 days after opening; *A* = a 3- to 4-day "freshness window"; *A+* = holds *and gets better* over 3–4 days

Robert Weil Kiedricher Grafenberg **PC** **T** **V**
Riesling Trocken, Germany **$$$** **24** **23**
Riesling lovers, you haven't lived until you've tried this
one: wet slate and white peach, laser acidity, endless
finish. Amazing.

Kitchen Fridge Survivor™ Grade: A+
Your notes: _____

Schmitt Sohne (*SHMITT ZOHN-uh*; **PC** **T** **V**
Sohne is German for "sons") **$** **22** **22**
Riesling Kabinett, Germany
This "huge seller" is appley, crisp, and light, making it
a good summertime/picnic quaff.

Kitchen Fridge Survivor™ Grade: A
Your notes: _____

Strub Niersteiner Paterberg **PC** **T** **V**
Riesling Spatlese, Germany **$$** **24** **22**
☺ "What a great QPR" (quality price ratio), say my
tasters. And I agree, it's "one of the best" Rieslings
under $20. The creaminess and lively acidity remind
me of lemon custard.

Kitchen Fridge Survivor™ Grade: A+
Your notes: _____

Trimbach Riesling **PC** **T** **V**
Alsace, France **$$** **24** **21**
The fan club grows and grows for this Alsace classic.
It's bone dry, with an amazing acidity and deep lemon--
green apple flavor. World-class.

Kitchen Fridge Survivor™ Grade: A+
Your notes: _____

Trimbach Riesling Cuvee **PC** **T** **V**
Frederic Emile, France **$$$** **29** **27**
I agree it's "one of the world's great Rieslings" and
"a great value considering the quality." The rich
buttermilk scent, steely acidity, and lemon-pear fruit
are subtle and layered. Ages great.

Kitchen Fridge Survivor™ Grade: A
Your notes: _____

Wente (*WEN-tee*) Riesling **PC** **T** **V**
California **$** **24** **18**
This is one of the few California Rieslings with
the "petrol" scent and vibrant lemon-peach fruit

we Riesling fanatics look for. It goes with anything edible.

Kitchen Fridge Survivor™ Grade: A

Your notes: _____

Sauvignon Blanc/Fume Blanc

Grape Profile: Sauvignon Blanc (*soh-veen-yoan BLAHNK*), one of my favorite white wine grapes, is on the rise, and for good reason: truly great ones are still available for under $15—something you can't say about many wine categories these days. Depending on where it's grown (cool, moderate, or warm zones), the exotically pungent scent and taste range from zesty and herbal to tangy lime-grapefruit to juicy peach and melon, with vibrant acidity. The grape's home base is France's Loire Valley and Bordeaux regions. California and Washington state make excellent versions, sometimes labeled Fume Blanc (*FOO-may BLAHNK*). In the Southern Hemisphere, New Zealand Sauvignon Blancs continue to earn pro and consumer raves. Another of Sauvignon Blanc's major virtues is its food versatility: it goes so well with the foods many people eat regularly (especially those following a less-red-meat regimen), like chicken and turkey, salads, sushi, Mexican, and vegetarian.

> **THANKS, KIWIS!** Many NZ SBs are now bottled in screw cap for your convenience, and to ensure you get fresh wine without "corkiness" (see the glossary for a definition). Hooray!

Serve: Chilled but not ice-cold.

When: An amazing food partner, but the tasting notes also spotlight styles that are good on their own, as an aperitif.

Price Ranges: **$** = $12 or less; **$$** = $12.01–20; **$$$** = $20.01–35; **$$$$** = > $35

Kitchen Fridge/Countertop Survivor™ Grades: *Avg.* = a "one-day wine," tastes noticeably less fresh the next day; *B* = holds its freshness for 2–3 days after opening; *B+* = holds *and gets better* over 2–3 days after opening; *A* = a 3- to 4-day "freshness window"; *A+* = holds *and gets better* over 3–4 days

With: As noted, great with most everyday eats, as well as popular ethnic tastes like Mexican food.

In: An all-purpose wineglass.

Babcock 7 Oaks Sauvignon Blanc	PC	T	V
California	$$$	20	18

Super-Sauv-me! This is the no-oak, zingy, lemon grass, and tropical fruit style at its mouthwatering best.

Kitchen Fridge Survivor™ Grade: A

Your notes: _____

Babich Marlborough Sauvignon	PC	T	V
Blanc, New Zealand	$$	24	26

This "zingy, appley" bottling "gets better every year." It's "a great value and a great food wine."

Kitchen Fridge Survivor™ Grade: B+

Your notes: _____

Benziger Fume Blanc	PC	T	V
California	$$	23	21

A "great wine list buy," say fans, citing the bright citrus, apple, and melon aromas and, crisp acidity that make it great with a wide range of foods.

Kitchen Fridge Survivor™ Grade: B+

Your notes: _____

Beringer Founders' Estate	PC	T	V
Sauvignon Blanc, California	$	19	19

This wine has melon and grapefruit in luscious profusion, but not at all heavy. The "can't go wrong price" is a gift, and the open bottle stays fresh for days.

Kitchen Fridge Survivor™ Grade: A+

Your notes: _____

Brancott Reserve Sauvignon Blanc	PC	T	V
New Zealand	$$	26	24

"One of New Zealand's best" SBs, with "lavish" herb and passion fruit flavors. Holds up great in the fridge or by the glass.

Kitchen Fridge Survivor™ Grade: A+

Your notes: _____

Brancott Sauvignon Blanc	PC	T	V
New Zealand	$	22	19

One of my panel's perennial favorites: "Like summertime on the front porch," said one taster—and I couldn't agree more. "Forget the lemonade and pass the Brancott!"

Kitchen Fridge Survivor™ Grade: B+
Your notes: _____

Cakebread Sauvignon Blanc	PC	T	V
California	$$$	26	21

Fans of Cakebread's Chardonnay should try this. The vibrant grapefruit aromas with a hint of fig and vanilla give a much better bang for the buck.

Kitchen Fridge Survivor™ Grade: A
Your notes: _____

Canyon Road Sauvignon Blanc	PC	T	V
California	$	21	21

A great SB that shows the true character of the grape: a hint of grassiness and grapefruit pungency, with lots of melon and peach fruit.

Kitchen Fridge Survivor™ Grade: A
Your notes: _____

Casa Lapostolle (*lah-poh-STOLE*)	PC	T	V
Sauvignon Blanc, Chile	$	26	26

This bottling has so much more than I expect at this price: vivid honeydew, kiwi flavors, and a long finish.

Kitchen Fridge Survivor™ Grade: A
Your notes: _____

Chat. Ste. Michelle Columbia Valley	PC	T	V
Sauvignon Blanc, Washington	$	23	24

Three cheers: tasty, affordable, consistent. Okay, four—exotic: grapefruit and lemongrass scent, ginger flavor, creamy texture.

Kitchen Fridge Survivor™ Grade: B
Your notes: _____

Chateau St. Jean Fume Blanc	PC	T	V
California	$	24	18

A touch of barrel aging gives this wine a creamy scent,

Price Ranges: **$** = $12 or less; **$$** = $12.01–20; **$$$** = $20.01–35; **$$$$** = > $35
Kitchen Fridge/Countertop Survivor™ Grades: **Avg.** = a "one-day wine," tastes noticeably less fresh the next day; **B** = holds its freshness for 2–3 days after opening; **B+** = holds *and gets better* over 2–3 days after opening; **A** = a 3- to 4-day "freshness window"; **A+** = holds *and gets better* over 3–4 days

balanced by fruit flavors of grapefruit, melon, and fig, plus tangy acidity. Yum!

Kitchen Fridge Survivor™ Grade: B+

Your notes: _____

Clos du Bois (*Cloh-dew-BWAH***)**	PC	T	V
Sauvignon Blanc, California	$	18	18

Scores are weak compared to other CdB wines, but it's still got a blue chip name and oaky richness, balanced with a crisp grapefruit character.

Kitchen Fridge Survivor™ Grade: B

Your notes: _____

Cloudy Bay Sauvignon Blanc	PC	T	V
New Zealand	$$$	25	22

This wine put the now-famous kiwi-lime, "grassy" character of NZ SB on the map in the 1980s. The consensus now is that it's "hard to find" and "expensive," but "still yummy."

Kitchen Fridge Survivor™ Grade: A

Your notes: _____

Covey Run Fume Blanc	PC	T	V
Washington	$	23	25

The crisp lemongrass and pink grapefruit character make this wine tasty and food versatile.

Kitchen Fridge Survivor™ Grade: Avg

Your notes: _____

Didier Dagueneau Silex Pouilly Fume	PC	T	V
(*DID-ee-yay DAG-uh-no poo-YEE***	$$$	29	15
foo-MAY), **France**			

☺ While lamenting the high price, buyers love this wine anyway. I, too, find the "bewitching" earthy, exotic, tropical, and herbal notes, all in one bottle, to be truly unique and delicious and, thus, worth the money.

Kitchen Fridge Survivor™ Grade: A+

Your notes: _____

Dry Creek Fume Blanc	PC	T	V
California	$$	24	24

☺ Although the price has nudged up a bit, there's still flavor bang for the buck. You get "jam-packed, tangy" tangerine and peach flavors that get better and better over several days in the fridge.

Kitchen Fridge Survivor™ Grade: A+

Your notes: _____

Duckhorn Sauvignon Blanc   PC   T   V
California $$$ 23   21

The "high price" reflects a premium for the famous Duckhorn name. I think the tangerine fruit, nice balance, and good length are worth it when you want to impress.

Kitchen Fridge Survivor™ Grade: A
Your notes: _____

Dyed in the Wool Sauvignon Blanc   PC   T   V
New Zealand $$ X   X

✗ The cheeky sense of humor and the grassy-lime-melon wine style are both classically kiwi, and the price is great.

Kitchen Fridge Survivor™ Grade: A
Your notes: _____

Ferrari-Carano Fume Blanc   PC   T   V
California $$ 26   25

This is one of California's benchmark Fumes, balancing crisp tanginess with melony fig fruit, and richness due to the oak barrel aging. Delish!

Kitchen Fridge Survivor™ Grade: B+
Your notes: _____

Frog's Leap Sauvignon Blanc   PC   T   V
California $$ 25   25

This is a fine dining wine list "regular" worth looking for. The 100 percent Sauvignon Blanc character of gooseberries and flinty, penetrating citrus is delicious.

Kitchen Fridge Survivor™ Grade: A
Your notes: _____

Geyser Peak Sauvignon Blanc   PC   T   V
California $ 22   24

This is a lovely, classic California Sauvignon Blanc, combining the crisp tang of citrus with the juicier taste of kiwi

Kitchen Fridge Survivor™ Grade: B+
Your notes: _____

Price Ranges: **$** = $12 or less; **$$** = $12.01–20; **$$$** = $20.01–35; **$$$$** = > $35
Kitchen Fridge/Countertop Survivor™ Grades: ***Avg.*** = a "one-day wine," tastes noticeably less fresh the next day; ***B*** = holds its fresh-ness for 2–3 days after opening; ***B+*** = holds *and gets better* over 2–3 days after opening; ***A*** = a 3- to 4-day "freshness window"; ***A+*** = holds *and gets better* over 3–4 days

Giesen Sauvignon Blanc   PC   T   V
New Zealand $$ 18   18

NZ SB in the fruit-forward (as opposed to grassy)
style: passion fruit, mango, and kiwi flavors.

Kitchen Fridge Survivor™ Grade: A

Your notes: _____

Grgich (*GER-gich;* both are hard   PC   T   V
"g" like "girl") Hills Fume Blanc $$$ 27   21
California

I'm happy that Grgich keeps true to its distinct style:
crisp, with scents of fresh herbs and citrus and
flavors of grapefruit and melon. Quality's high, but
the blue chip name commands a premium price.

Kitchen Fridge Survivor™ Grade: B

Your notes: _____

Henri Bourgeois (ahn-REE buh-   PC   T   V
***JHWAH*) Pouilly Fume, France** $$ 26   19

This wine offers classic French subtlety and complex-
ity, with floral and smoky scents, bracing acidity, and
an elegant tanginess.

Kitchen Fridge Survivor™ Grade: B+

Your notes: _____

Hogue Fume Blanc   PC   T   V
Washington $ 23   25

"A very good wine at a very good price," with fresh
ginger spice, crushed herbs, citrus peel, plus a juicy
mouthfeel.

Kitchen Fridge Survivor™ Grade: A+

Your notes: _____

Honig Sauvignon Blanc   PC   T   V
California $$ 24   23

"Excellent!" and one of the few California Sauvignon
Blancs in the flinty, grassy, Loire Valley style.

Kitchen Fridge Survivor™ Grade: B+

Your notes: _____

Joel Gott Sauvignon Blanc   PC   T   V
California $$ X   X

✗ For the price, a scrumptious SB dripping with
honeydew, kiwi, and lime flavors.

Kitchen Fridge Survivor™ Grade: A

Your notes: _____

Jolivet (Pascal) Sancerre	PC	T	V
(*jhoe-lee-VAY sahn-SAIR*), France	$$	21	21

☺ A perennial favorite with my tasters, this wine's well-balanced and utterly "alive" taste and scent (lemongrass, lime cream, and honey) are great for the price.

Kitchen Fridge Survivor™ Grade: A+
Your notes: _____

Joseph Phelps Sauvignon Blanc	PC	T	V
California	$$	24	24

"Lots of ZING and ZANG" for the money, including "grapefruit and citrus flavors" and "softer fruit flavors" like peach and melon.

Kitchen Fridge Survivor™ Grade: B+
Your notes: _____

Kenwood Sauvignon Blanc	PC	T	V
California	$	23	28

The taste of this gorgeous SB reminds me of a summer melon salad with lime, honey, and mint.

Kitchen Fridge Survivor™ Grade: A
Your notes: _____

Kim Crawford Sauvignon Blanc	PC	T	V
New Zealand	$$	28	26

A "major favorite" with my panel; taste this one for a dose of the purest SB fruit—key lime, kiwi, and honeydew. A great food wine.

Kitchen Fridge Survivor™ Grade: A
Your notes: _____

Lucien Crochet (*loo-SYEN crow-*	PC	T	V
SHAY) Sancerre, France	$$	27	18

"Definitive Sauvignon Blanc" is the consensus on this top-scoring wine. The floral-herbaceous nose,

Price Ranges: **$** = $12 or less; **$$** = $12.01–20; **$$$** = $20.01–35; **$$$$** = > $35
Kitchen Fridge/Countertop Survivor™ Grades: *Avg.* = a "one-day wine," tastes noticeably less fresh the next day; *B* = holds its freshness for 2–3 days after opening; *B+* = holds *and gets better* over 2–3 days after opening; *A* = a 3- to 4-day "freshness window"; *A+* = holds *and gets better* over 3–4 days

creamy-but-not-heavy texture, crisp citrus flavor, and finesse are "a huge relief for the oak-weary."

Kitchen Fridge Survivor™ Grade: B+

Your notes: _____

Mason Sauvignon Blanc	PC	T	V
California	$$	24	23

My wine students love this kiwi and passion fruit–scented wine that's "like New Zealand SB without the grassiness." Great for spicy food.

Kitchen Fridge Survivor™ Grade: B

Your notes: _____

Merryvale Sauvignon Blanc	PC	T	V
California	$$	X	X

✗ One of the best in Merryvale's lineup, especially for the price. The kiwi, honeydew, and lime flavors are both luscious and lively.

Kitchen Fridge Survivor™ Grade: B

Your notes: _____

Monkey Bay Sauvignon Blanc	PC	T	V
New Zealand	$	X	X

✗ Amazing—this wine bested benchmark Cloudy Bay *twice* in blind tastings with pro palates. Cut grass, lime, grapefruit, long finish—cool label, too!

Kitchen Fridge Survivor™ Grade: A

Your notes: _____

Montevina Sauvignon Blanc	PC	T	V
California	$	20	22

This Zin specialist is putting great Sauvignon Blanc in the bottle, too. It's redolent with honeydew and tangerine flavors, with a crisp acidity that makes it great with spicy fare.

Kitchen Fridge Survivor™ Grade: B

Your notes: _____

Mulderbosch Sauvignon Blanc	PC	T	V
South Africa	$$	29	29

☺ ✓ This is one of the most "amazing" SBs in the world. Its kiwi, crushed mint, and grapefruit character is "unforgettable."

Kitchen Fridge Survivor™ Grade: A

Your notes: _____

Murphy-Goode Fume Blanc   PC   T   V
California $ 21   22

While some call it "too Chardonnay-like," many tasters were thumbs-up on the less herbaceous, passion fruit, and tropical flavor profile.

Kitchen Fridge Survivor™ Grade: Avg

Your notes: _____

Nobilo Sauvignon Blanc   PC   T   V
New Zealand $ 28   28

This kiwi Sauvignon Blanc has taken the market by storm, offering the signature grapefruit/herbal style the region is known for, at a "great price."

Kitchen Fridge Survivor™ Grade: A+

Your notes: _____

Pavillon Blanc du Chateau Margaux   PC   T   V
Bordeaux, France $$$ 24   18

An atypical white Bordeaux (because it's 100% SB) and thus quite distinctive: grassy, with intense lime and Granny Smith apple flavors and a racy Vitamin C with rosehips mineral scent.

Kitchen Fridge Survivor™ Grade: B+

Your notes: _____

R.H. Phillips Sauvignon Blanc   PC   T   V
California $ 22   22

The taste of this wine is like ripe tropical fruits — think mango, guava, and papaya.

Kitchen Fridge Survivor™ Grade: B+

Your notes: _____

Robert Mondavi Napa Fume Blanc   PC   T   V
California $$ 25   23

☺ This is perennially one of Robert Mondavi's best offerings, as the stellar reviews show. It's got fruit, spice, and lemongrass; crisp, vivid citrus notes; and a rich texture.

Kitchen Fridge Survivor™ Grade: B

Your notes: _____

Price Ranges: **$** – $12 or less; **$$** = $12.01–20, **$$$** – $20.01–35; **$$$$** = > $35

Kitchen Fridge/Countertop Survivor™ Grades: *Avg.* = a "one-day wine," tastes noticeably less fresh the next day; *B* = holds its freshness for 2–3 days after opening; *B+* = holds *and gets better* over 2–3 days after opening; *A* = a 3- to 4-day "freshness window"; *A+* = holds *and gets better* over 3–4 days

Silverado Sauvignon Blanc   PC   T   V
California $$ 24   22

On California's oak-lavished landscape, Silverado's
stainless-steel style offers an alternative: clean, crisp
apple and grapefruit character and medium body.

Kitchen Fridge Survivor™ Grade: B

Your notes: _____

Simi Sauvignon Blanc   PC   T   V
California $$ 24   20

This is Sauvignon Blanc in the rich style, with creamy
roundness from integrated oak and a proportion of
Semillon grapes in the blend.

Kitchen Fridge Survivor™ Grade: B+

Your notes: _____

Spy Valley Sauvignon Blanc   PC   T   V
New Zealand $$ 24   22

"Tart apples with a nice grassy finish" make this "won-
derful" wine a NZ classic, and one of the best on the
market for the $.

Kitchen Fridge Survivor™ Grade: A

Your notes: _____

Sterling Vineyards Napa   PC   T   V
Sauvignon Blanc, California $ 18   18

The price has dropped slightly for this "go-to brand."
It's vibrant with grapefruit, nectarines, and key lime
flavors and scents.

Kitchen Fridge Survivor™ Grade: B

Your notes: _____

St. Supery Sauvignon Blanc,   PC   T   V
California $$ 26   25

"One of the best" California SBs, with "bright, crisp
and amazingly complex" flavor—"peach and lime."

Kitchen Fridge Survivor™ Grade: A+

Your notes: _____

Veramonte Sauvignon Blanc   PC   T   V
Chile $ 24   24

☺ SB is Chile's best foot forward in whites, and
here's a great one, with exotic kiwi, honeydew, and
passion fruit flavors.

Kitchen Fridge Survivor™ Grade: B+

Your notes: _____

Villa Maria Private Bin Sauvignon Blanc, New Zealand

	PC	T	V
	$$	25	24

This NZ SB offers a nice balance between the grassy/herbal scent and tangy passion fruit-melon taste.

Kitchen Fridge Survivor™ Grade: B+

Your notes: _____

Voss Sauvignon Blanc California

	PC	T	V
	$$	24	22

A super-lively SB—juicy with kiwi, white peach, and grapefruit flavors that are sippable on their own, and great with food.

Kitchen Fridge Survivor™ Grade: B+

Your notes: _____

Chardonnay

Grape Profile: Chardonnay is the top-selling white varietal wine in this country, and the fullest-bodied of the major white grapes. That rich body, along with Chardonnay's signature fruit intensity, could explain its extraordinary popularity with Americans, although in truth this grape's style is pretty chameleonlike. It can yield wines of legendary quality, ranging from crisp and austere to soft and juicy to utterly lush and exotic (and very often oaky), depending on whether it's grown in a cool, moderate, or warm climate. I am pleased to say that, as these notes indicate, buyers find all of these styles worthy, perhaps offering some hope to pros who bemoan a noticeable "sameness" to many of the brand names. All Chardonnays are modeled on white Burgundy wines from France. The world-class versions are known for complexity, and often oakiness, the very best are age-worthy. The rest, in the $ and $$ price categories, are pleasant styles meant for current drinking. California Chardonnays by far dominate store and restaurant sales, but the quality and value of both Washington State's and Aus-

Price Ranges: **$** = $12 or less; **$$** = $12.01–20; **$$$** = $20.01–35; **$$$$** = > $35

Kitchen Fridge/Countertop Survivor™ Grades: *Avg.* = a "one-day wine," tastes noticeably less fresh the next day; *B* = holds its freshness for 2–3 days after opening; *B+* = holds *and gets better* over 2–3 days after opening; *A* = a 3- to 4-day "freshness window"; *A+* = holds *and gets better* over 3–4 days

tralia's are just as good. Although no New Zealand or Oregon offerings made the survey due to limited production, they're worth sampling.

Serve: Chilled; however, extreme cold mutes the complexity of the top bottlings. Pull them off the ice if they get too cold.

When: There's no occasion where Chardonnay *isn't* welcomed by the majority of wine lovers; the grape's abundant fruit makes it great on its own, as an aperitif or a cocktail alternative.

With: Some sommeliers carp that Chardonnay "doesn't go well with food," but I don't think most consumers agree. Maybe they have a point that it "overpowers" some delicate culinary creations in luxury restaurants, but for those of us doing most of our eating and drinking in less-rarefied circumstances, it's a great partner for all kinds of food. The decadent, oaky/buttery styles that are California's calling card can even handle steak.

In: An all-purpose wineglass.

Acacia Chardonnay Carneros California	PC	T	V
	$$$	24	24

I've been serving this elegant Chardonnay to my restaurant guests for more than ten years because its apple-vanilla subtlety lets the food star.
Kitchen Fridge Survivor™ *Grade: B*
Your notes: _____

Alice White Chardonnay Australia	PC	T	V
	$	24	24

A lot of lipsmacking golden delicious apple fruit for not a lot of money. Holds up well over several days, too.
Kitchen Fridge Survivor™ *Grade: B+*
Your notes: _____

Au Bon Climat Santa Barbara Chardonnay, California	PC	T	V
	$$$	24	23

☺ The "wow complexity" and "elegant tropical fruit" make this wine a major wine-pro pick; and, as tasters noted, "it's twice the wine at half the price" compared to many big-name California Chardonnays.
Kitchen Fridge Survivor™ *Grade: A*
Your notes: _____

Beaulieu Vineyard (BV) Coastal **PC** **T** **V**
Chardonnay, California **$** **20** **22**

Like the entire BV Coastal line, this Chardonnay is a solid performer with my tasters. It's textbook apple-pear Chardonnay in the not-too-heavy style.

Kitchen Fridge Survivor™ Grade: Avg

Your notes: _____

Beringer Founders' Estate **PC** **T** **V**
Chardonnay, California **$** **21** **24**

Citrus/tropical fruit, a whiff of vanilla-scented oak, and a juicy mouthfeel make this a top budget Chardonnay with my tasters.

Kitchen Fridge Survivor™ Grade: A

Your notes: _____

Beringer Napa Chardonnay **PC** **T** **V**
California **$$** **22** **22**

☺ This wine is benchmark Napa Valley Chardonnay—rich baked-apple fruit, creamy texture, toasty oak. Great quality for the money, too.

Kitchen Fridge Survivor™ Grade: Avg

Your notes: _____

Black Box Monterey Chardonnay **PC** **T** **V**
California (3L Box) **$** **X** **X**

✗ Tasters "can't believe it comes in a box," but quality isn't about the package, which here holds peachy-apple Chard with a kiss of spicy oak.

Kitchen Fridge Survivor™ Grade: NA

Your notes: _____

Cakebread Napa Chardonnay **PC** **T** **V**
California **$$$$** **24** **19**

This is a Napa Chardonnay classic, though sadly I've noticed increasing oakiness overtaking the pear and green apple fruit. The blue-chip name keeps it a top seller in fine restaurants.

Kitchen Fridge Survivor™ Grade: B

Your notes: _____

Price Ranges: **$** = $12 or less; **$$** = $12.01–20; **$$$** = $20.01–35; **$$$$** = > $35

Kitchen Fridge/Countertop Survivor™ Grades: *Avg.* = a "one-day wine," tastes noticeably less fresh the next day; *B* = holds its freshness for 2–3 days after opening; *B+* = holds *and gets better* over 2–3 days after opening; *A* = a 3- to 4-day "freshness window"; *A+* = holds *and gets better* over 3–4 days

Cakebread Reserve Chardonnay   PC   T   V
California $$$$ 26   23

"What American Chard should be": "buttery,"
"viscous," but "not over-oaked" and "in good balance."
Kitchen Fridge Survivor™ Grade: Avg
Your notes: _____

Cambria Katherine's Vineyard   PC   T   V
Chardonnay, California $$ 24   22

This wine is a "big seller," offering the big oaky
California Chardonnay style—rich and plump with
tropical fruit—for under $20 retail in most markets.
Kitchen Fridge Survivor™ Grade: Avg
Your notes: _____

Camelot Chardonnay   PC   T   V
California $ 23   19

As pros note, this Chardonnay from the Kendall-
Jackson family is "just darn good for the price," with
crowd-pleaser buttery aromas and flavors, and a
creamy finish.
Kitchen Fridge Survivor™ Grade: Avg
Your notes: _____

Casa Lapostolle Cuvee Alexandre   PC   T   V
Chardonnay, Chile $$ 22   24

☺ I serve this to my wine students as a benchmark
"oaky" Chardonnay: it's toasty, cinnamon-spicy, and
vanilla-scented, with soft and rich tropical fruit.
Kitchen Fridge Survivor™ Grade: B
Your notes: _____

Catena Chardonnay   PC   T   V
Argentina $$ 22   19

This winery put Argentina on the world's wine radar
screen with its red Malbec, but also with this "rarity"
among new world Chardonnays that "strikes the ideal
balance" between ripe fruit and oak.
Kitchen Fridge Survivor™ Grade: B
Your notes: _____

Chalk Hill Chardonnay   PC   T   V
California $$$ 22   16

☺ This classy Chardonnay's rich oak and luscious
tropical fruit flavor are big enough body to pair even
with steak. Although it's "pricey," it's a quality star

whose price still is reasonable compared to the overall category of luxury California Chards.

Kitchen Fridge Survivor™ *Grade: B*

Your notes: _____

Chalone Chardonnay	PC	T	V
California	$$$	29	24

☺ For decades, this pioneering Central Coast Chard has been a favorite of wine lovers—a bit "pricey," but "worth it." Pros cite its "unique mineral quality," elegance, and "beautiful stone fruit" flavor. It gets even better with age, if you can wait.

Kitchen Fridge Survivor™ *Grade: B+*

Your notes: _____

Chateau Montelena Chardonnay	PC	T	V
California	$$$	24	22

"Worth every penny," say tasters of Montelena's understated elegance, featuring flinty-spicy aromas, crisp apple fruit, and a subtle, long finish. It gains extraordinary complexity with age.

Kitchen Fridge Survivor™ *Grade: A*

Your notes: _____

Chateau Ste. Michelle Cold Creek	PC	T	V
Chardonnay, Washington	$$	24	23

Buttery and big with super-ripe tropical fruit and lavish, cocunut-scented oak.

Kitchen Fridge Survivor™ *Grade: Avg*

Your notes: _____

Chateau Ste. Michelle Columbia	PC	T	V
Valley Chardonnay, Washington	$$	24	26

"A lot of yum for the money": tasty pear-citrus fruit and a buttery scent.

Kitchen Fridge Survivor™ *Grade: B*

Your notes: _____

Price Ranges: **$** = $12 or less; **$$** = $12.01–20; **$$$** = $20.01–35; **$$$$** = > $35

Kitchen Fridge/Countertop Survivor™ Grades: *Avg.* = a "one-day wine," tastes noticeably less fresh the next day; *B* = holds its freshness for 2–3 days after opening; *B+* = holds *and gets better* over 2–3 days after opening; *A* = a 3- to 4-day "freshness window"; *A+* = holds *and gets better* over 3–4 days

Chateau Ste. Michelle Indian Wells PC   T   V
Chardonnay, Washington $$ X   X
✗ This is Chardonnay in the big buttery style with lots of toasty oak and intensity.
Kitchen Fridge Survivor™ Grade: Avg
Your notes: _____

Chateau St. Jean Robert Young PC   T   V
Vineyard Chardonnay, California $$$ 27   21
A "California classic" with "amazing balance" of "subtle" oak framing the Asian pear fruit.
Kitchen Fridge Survivor™ Grade: Avg
Your notes: _____

Chateau St. Jean Sonoma PC   T   V
Chardonnay, California $$ 21   23
A classic, offering great "quality for the price," rich tropical and pear fruit, and restrained oak.
Kitchen Fridge Survivor™ Grade: B
Your notes: _____

Clos du Bois Sonoma Chardonnay PC   T   V
California $$ 24   21
A huge seller, for good reason: there's lots of citrus, peach, and melon fruit, subtly framed in oak, at a good price.
Kitchen Fridge Survivor™ Grade: A+
Your notes: _____

Columbia Crest Grand Estates PC   T   V
Chardonnay, Washington $ 22   23
"Great value" is this brand's calling card. This wine's got sweet spices, baked-apple fruit, and a hint of butter; all in balance and not too heavy.
Kitchen Fridge Survivor™ Grade: B+
Your notes: _____

Cuvaison (*KOO-veh-sahn*) Napa PC   T   V
Valley Chardonnay, California $$ 24   24
This is a "wow" for the price, with a luscious tropical richness and lavish-but-balanced oak.
Fridge Survivor Grade: B
Your notes: _____

Domaine Laroche Chablis Grand PC   T   V
Cru 'Les Clos,' Burgundy, France $$$$ 26   23
Mouth-tingling yet supremely elegant, this top-level,

squeeze-of-lemon wine with a chamomile finish is awesome with oysters on the half-shell.

Fridge Survivor Grade: A+

Your notes: _____

Edna Valley Vineyard Chardonnay
California

	PC	T	V
	$	24	24

☺ While "outstanding quality and taste" and "nice price" are accurate, they don't do the wine justice. It's got Burgundian complexity in the scent—cream, pear, toasted nuts, smoke—and vibrant fruit in the taste. It ages well, too.

Kitchen Countertop Survivor™ Grade: A

Your notes: _____

Estancia Pinnacles Chardonnay
California

	PC	T	V
	$$	22	23

Although the price is inching up, this Chardonnay remains nice for the money, balancing vibrant acidity and soft tropical fruit.

Kitchen Fridge Survivor™ Grade: A

Your notes: _____

Far Niente Chardonnay
California

	PC	T	V
	$$$$	26	17

CA ripeness along with French-style subtlety are this wine's hallmarks. The concentrated pineapple fruit and toasty mineral scent are delicious young, but the wine ages well for 7+ years.

Kitchen Fridge Survivor™ Grade: A

Your notes: _____

Ferrari-Carano Napa-Sonoma
Chardonnay, California

	PC	T	V
	$$$	27	22

"A value if you can afford it" sums up the fact that in the luxury category this Chard is among the most accessible. With its spicy fruit and oak scent and luscious tropical flavors, this splurge is worth it.

Kitchen Fridge Survivor™ Grade: B

Your notes: _____

Price Ranges: **$** = $12 or less; **$$** = $12.01–20; **$$$** = $20.01–35; **$$$$** = > $35

Kitchen Fridge/Countertop Survivor™ Grades: *Avg.* = a "one-day wine," tastes noticeably less fresh the next day; *B* = holds its freshness for 2–3 days after opening; *B+* = holds *and gets better* over 2–3 days after opening; *A* = a 3- to 4-day "freshness window"; *A+* = holds *and gets better* over 3–4 days

Fetzer Valley Oaks Chardonnay   PC   T   V
California $$ 22   21

The style remains consistent—fruity, and oaky—but "it's gotten more pricey."

Kitchen Fridge Survivor™ *Grade: B*

Your notes: _____

Fetzer Sundial Chardonnay   PC   T   V
California $ 21   21

The bargain price and juicy pear and apple fruit make this a fail-safe crowd pleaser.

Kitchen Fridge Survivor™ *Grade: B*

Your notes: _____

Franciscan Oakville Chardonnay   PC   T   V
California $$ 22   20

"The same characteristics" of the monster Chards— toasty oak and ripe pineapple/mango fruit, but "not overblown"—"let you (affordably) impress."

Kitchen Fridge Survivor™ *Grade: Avg*

Your notes: _____

Gallo of Sonoma Chardonnay   PC   T   V
California $ 24   25

☺ I keep waiting for this "outstanding for the price" Chard to get expensive, or over-oaked. It's neither, offering ripe, intense flavors of pineapples, pears, and apples, and nice balance. Impressive.

Kitchen Fridge Survivor™ *Grade: A*

Your notes: _____

Geyser Peak Chardonnay   PC   T   V
California $$ 22   20

The scores fell, but this wine still has pleasant balanced apple, pear, and melon fruit, and nuances of smoky oak.

Kitchen Fridge Survivor™ *Grade: B*

Your notes: _____

Grgich Hills Chardonnay   PC   T   V
California $$$$ 26   18

The name (pronounced "GER-gich") has for decades promised blue-chip Napa Chard that's packed with rich fruit, yet elegant.

Kitchen Fridge Survivor™ *Grade: A*

Your notes: _____

Hess Select Chardonnay   PC   T   V
California $$ 22   23

A "great value for the money" favorite with my panel thanks to the incredible fruit: pineapple, mango, pear, and lemon.

Kitchen Fridge Survivor™ *Grade: B*

Your notes: _____

Jacob's Creek Chardonnay   PC   T   V
Australia $ 21   22

Both trade and consumers rate this a value star. I give it extra credit for consistency and for the bright citrus and peach flavor.

Kitchen Fridge Survivor™ *Grade: Avg*

Your notes: _____

J. Lohr Riverstone Chardonnay   PC   T   V
California $ 26   26

This Chard in the big buttery style is a great value for the price, with flavors and scents of lime, peaches, minerals, and toasty oak.

Kitchen Fridge Survivor™ *Grade: B*

Your notes: _____

Jordan Chardonnay   PC   T   V
California $$$ 22   16

Although tasters aren't convinced, I think Jordan's Chardonnay has come of age. It's got crisp vibrancy and length, creamy citrus flavors, and gentle oak. A great food wine.

Kitchen Fridge Survivor™ *Grade: B*

Your notes: _____

Joseph Drouhin Pouilly-Fuisse   PC   T   V
(*poo-YEE fwee-SAY*), France $$ 22   22

This wine offers classic, understated Pouilly-Fuisse character, with creamy apple and fresh almond scents, plus steely dryness and a long finish.

Kitchen Fridge Survivor™ *Grade: A*

Your notes: _____

Price Ranges: **$** = $12 or less; **$$** = $12.01–20; **$$$** = $20.01–35; **$$$$** = > $35

Kitchen Fridge/Countertop Survivor™ Grades: *Avg.* = a "one-day wine," tastes noticeably less fresh the next day; *B* = holds its freshness for 2–3 days after opening; *B+* = holds *and gets better* over 2–3 days after opening; *A* = a 3- to 4-day "freshness window"; *A+* = holds *and gets better* over 3–4 days

Kendall-Jackson Vintner's Reserve   PC   T   V
Chardonnay, California $ 21   21

Thanks to competition from Yellow Tail, this top-selling Chard's price has come down a bit. It still shines for style consistency—juicy fruit and soft oak—and the quality remains high, so I think the fan club will endure.

Kitchen Fridge Survivor™ Grade: A

Your notes: _____

Kim Crawford Unoaked   PC   T   V
Chardonnay, New Zealand $$ 24   21

My tasters love the "pure fruit"—apple, pineapple, and peach—uncluttered by oak, and so will you. It's scrumptious.

Kitchen Fridge Survivor™ Grade: A+

Your notes: _____

Kistler Durell Chardonnay   PC   T   V
California $$$$ 28   18

A "beautiful," "very powerful" Chardonnay with incredible apples-and-mangoes fruit density and a bewitching hazelnut scent.

Kitchen Fridge Survivor™ Grade: B+

Your notes: _____

Kistler Sonoma Coast Chardonnay   PC   T   V
California $$$$ 28   18

☺ Yes, it's "expensive," but no other CA Chard achieves such French Burgundy-like elegance, nuttiness, and concentration. The Kistler Chardonnays age really well, too, picking up toasted nut and toffee scents atop the deep baked-apple fruit flavor.

Kitchen Fridge Survivor™ Grade: B

Your notes: _____

Laboure-Roi (lah-boo-ray WAH)   PC   T   V
Meursault, Burgundy, France $$$$ 22   19

It is hard to find relatively affordable Meursault (pronounced murr-SEW) with the character of the appellation, but this is it: nutty-toasty scent, baked-apple fruit, cinnamon-toast finish.

Kitchen Fridge Survivor™ Grade: B

Your notes: _____

Laboure-Roi Puligny-Montrachet   PC   T   V
(*poo-leen-YEE mohn-rah-SHAY*) $$$$ 21   19
France

The subtle apple and mineral complexity of this wine earn good marks for taste, but at that price most buyers want more. Since Burgundy is pretty vintage-sensitive, look for years with good harvest season weather to get this wine at its best.

Kitchen Fridge Survivor™ Grade: B

Your notes: _____

La Crema Chardonnay   PC   T   V
California $$ 24   23

"Balanced and yummy" and classically California: vividly ripe peach and tropical fruit, framed with toasty-sweet oak.

Kitchen Fridge Survivor™ Grade: Avg

Your notes: _____

Landmark Vineyards Overlook   PC   T   V
Chardonnay, California $$$ 24   22

This "California tropical" Chard has "huge body, heavy-duty oak, and smooooth" texture, and (yay!) the price has dropped!

Kitchen Fridge Survivor™ Grade: Avg

Your notes: _____

Leflaive (luh-FLEV) (Domaine)   PC   T   V
Puligny-Montrachet $$$$ 25   19
France

☺ Domaine Leflaive's "delicious," "finessed" white Burgundies sing with style, complexity, and layers of baked-apple and peach fruit. Such quality is pricey, but the consistency and ageability earn this wine points for value.

Kitchen Fridge Survivor™ Grade: B+

Your notes: _____

Price Ranges: **$** = $12 or less; **$$** = $12.01–20; **$$$** – $20.01–35; **$$$$** = > $35

Kitchen Fridge/Countertop Survivor™ Grades: *Avg.* = a "one-day wine," tastes noticeably less fresh the next day; *B* = holds its freshness for 2–3 days after opening; *B+* = holds *and gets better* over 2–3 days after opening; *A* = a 3- to 4-day "freshness window"; *A+* = holds *and gets better* over 3–4 days

Leflaive (Olivier) (*luh-FLEV, oh-LIV-ee-ay***) Puligny-Montrachet France**

PC	T	V
$$$$	24	22

Because Olivier Leflaive blends wines from many growers, this wine can be cheaper and easier to find than Domaine Leflaive (the families are related). Though not quite on a par with the Domaine's, this Puligny is a worthy example, with refined citrus and pear fruit, and hints of mineral and toasty oak.

Kitchen Fridge Survivor™ Grade: B

Your notes: _____

Lindemans Bin 65 Chardonnay Australia

PC	T	V
$	21	23

☺ This wine encores as one of the top Chardonnay values with my tasters. The fragrant tropical fruit is balanced with bright acidity, "for a great price."

Kitchen Fridge Survivor™ Grade: B+

Your notes: _____

Louis Jadot Macon-Villages (*LOO-ee jhah-DOUGH mah-COHN vill-AHJH***) Chardonnay, France**

PC	T	V
$$	21	21

The clean, refreshing green apple and citrus fruit, sparked with vivid acidity and free of oak heaviness, is wonderful by itself and with food.

Kitchen Fridge Survivor™ Grade: B+

Your notes: _____

Louis Jadot Pouilly-Fuisse France

PC	T	V
$$$	27	25

Scores climbed for this fresh, unoaked Chardonnay fruit with a touch of mineral, a long finish, and pure crisp fruit. Check it out!

Kitchen Fridge Survivor™ Grade: A

Your notes: _____

Matanzas Creek Chardonnay California

PC	T	V
$$$	24	21

A "wine list stalwart" that's dropped in price (yay!) and always delivers on intense fruit and toasty oak. Big enough even for steak, and a good choice when you want to impress the client.

Kitchen Fridge Survivor™ Grade: B

Your notes: _____

Meridian Chardonnay   PC   T   V
California $ 20   24

Meridian is ripe with pineapple fruit, inexpensive, and versatile with food.

Kitchen Fridge Survivor™ Grade: B

Your notes: _____

Merryvale Starmont Chardonnay   PC   T   V
California $$ 24   18

"A bit pricy," but the "ripe, tropical fruit flavors" and "toasty oak" are splurge-worthy.

Kitchen Fridge Survivor™ Grade: Avg

Your notes: _____

Mer Soleil (mare sew-LAY)   PC   T   V
Chardonnay, California $$$$ 27   27

✓ The Wagner family (owners of Caymus) keeps the oak subtle on this dripping-with-banana-mango fruit Chard. Luscious!

Kitchen Fridge Survivor™ Grade: B

Your notes: _____

Michel Laroche Chablis St. Martin   PC   T   V
Burgundy, France $$$ 23   19

☺ This is a rare find: true French white Burgundy that's relatively available and affordable. It's a textbook Chablis: piercingly pure apple and citrus fruit and a bit of mineral (like the smell of wet rocks). Awesome!

Kitchen Fridge Survivor™ Grade: A+

Your notes: _____

Mirassou Chardonnay   PC   T   V
California $ X   X

✗ The pineapple and lemon flavors make this Chardonnay both luscious and refreshing, and the quality for the price rocks.

Kitchen Fridge Survivor™ Grade: B+

Your notes: _____

Price Ranges: **$** = $12 or less; **$$** = $12.01–20; **$$$** = $20.01–35; **$$$$** = > $35

Kitchen Fridge/Countertop Survivor™ Grades: *Avg.* = a "one-day wine," tastes noticeably less fresh the next day; *B* = holds its freshness for 2–3 days after opening; *B+* = holds *and gets better* over 2–3 days after opening; *A* = a 3- to 4-day "freshness window"; *A+* = holds *and gets better* over 3–4 days

Morgan Metallico Chardonnay   PC   T   V
California $$ X   X

✗ What a delicious addition to the Morgan portfolio; the restrained oak, passion fruit, and peach practically sing out of the glass.

Kitchen Fridge Survivor™ Grade: A+

Your notes: _____

Papio Chardonnay   PC   T   V
California $ X   X

✗ The lively peach fruit and balance make this one of the nicest budget Chards I've had all year, and it held its own in a blind tasting with quite a few of CA's top Chards.

Kitchen Fridge Survivor™ Grade: A

Your notes: _____

Penfolds Koonunga Hill   PC   T   V
Chardonnay, Australia $ 22   22

This Chard's boatload of tropical fruit and creamy butterscotch character offer great bang for the buck.

Kitchen Countertop Survivor™ Grade: B

Your notes: _____

Penfolds Rawson's Retreat   PC   T   V
Chardonnay, Australia $ 26   27

The lipsmacking apple and tangerine flavor is clean, refreshing, not heavy—"so easy-drinking," as my tasters note.

Kitchen Fridge Survivor™ Grade: Avg

Your notes: _____

R.H. Phillips Chardonnay   PC   T   V
California $ 23   24

This wine's always a solid value, with vivid citrus and nectarine fruit and a nice kiss of oak that's not too heavy.

Kitchen Fridge Survivor™ Grade: A

Your notes: _____

R.H. Phillips Toasted Head   PC   T   V
Chardonnay, California $$ 24   23

"Toasted Head" refers to more oakiness—they toast not only the inside of the barrel staves for flavor but the "head" (end piece) of the barrel, too. The result is very oaky, toasty, rich, butterscotch-scented Chardonnay.

Kitchen Fridge Survivor™ Grade: Avg

Your notes: _____

Robert Mondavi Private Selection   PC   T   V
Chardonnay, California $ 22   22

Most of my tasters consider this citrus and oak–laced Chard to be "rock-solid" for the money.

Kitchen Fridge Survivor™ Grade: B

Your notes: _____

Robert Mondavi Napa Chardonnay   PC   T   V
California $$ 23   23

This blue-chip brand delivers the baked-apple and toasty-spice flavor of benchmark Napa Chardonnay.

Kitchen Fridge Survivor™ Grade: Avg

Your notes: _____

Rodney Strong Sonoma Chardonnay PC   T   V
California $$ 23   22

This huge seller is classic Sonoma: a coconut-sweet scent from oak and ripe apple fruit.

Kitchen Fridge Survivor™ Grade: Avg

Your notes: _____

Rombauer Chardonnay   PC   T   V
California $$$ 28   18

"Buttery and lightly toasty" is Napa's signature Chardonnay style, and it's perfectly rendered here. Tastes a lot more expensive than it is, too!

Kitchen Fridge Survivor™ Grade: B

Your notes: _____

Rosemount Diamond Label   PC   T   V
Chardonnay, Australia $ 20   22

Although competition's heated up in the Aussie

Price Ranges: **$** = $12 or less; **$$** = $12.01–20; **$$$** = $20.01–35; **$$$$** = > $35

Kitchen Fridge/Countertop Survivor™ Grades: *Avg.* = a "one-day wine," tastes noticeably less fresh the next day; *B* = holds its freshness for 2–3 days after opening; *B+* = holds *and gets better* over 2–3 days after opening; *A* = a 3- to 4-day "freshness window"; *A+* = holds *and gets better* over 3–4 days

Chard world, this one's "still solid," with peach and citrus fruit, a little bit of oak, and a clean finish.

Kitchen Fridge Survivor™ Grade: B+

Your notes: _____

Smoking Loon Chardonnay   PC   T   V

California $ X   X

✗ This Chard packs a lot of fruit flavor—pineapple and juicy citrus—for the price.

Kitchen Fridge Survivor™ Grade: Avg

Your notes: _____

Sonoma-Cutrer Russian River   PC   T   V

Ranches Chardonnay, California $$$ 27   24

This is "quintessential California Chardonnay." In contrast to the "monster Chardonnay genre," it holds out for elegance and complexity.

Kitchen Fridge Survivor™ Grade: B+

Your notes: _____

Staglin Family Chardonnay   PC   T   V

California $$$$ X   X

✗ I think this is one of CA's best and most Burgundian Chards—truly elegant with gorgeous apple-pear fruit and a subtle, toasted hazelnut oakiness. The wine ages well, too.

Kitchen Fridge Survivor™ Grade: A

Your notes: _____

Sterling Vineyards North Coast   PC   T   V

Chardonnay, California $$ 23   22

Although this wine has made a frustrating jump in price in the last few years, the style has stayed consistent, with a vanilla, brown sugar, and nutmeg scent, and vibrant peach fruit on the palate.

Kitchen Fridge Survivor™ Grade: A

Your notes: _____

St. Francis Sonoma Chardonnay   PC   T   V

California $ 23   22

I don't think you can find this much real Sonoma Chardonnay character at a better price. That means ripe pear and tropical fruit, soft vanilla oak, buttery scent, and a nice acid balance.

Kitchen Fridge Survivor™ Grade: A+

Your notes: _____

Sutter Home Chardonnay   PC   T   V
California $ 21   21

My consumer tasters give credit where it's due, saying this wine's "pretty good for the price," with nice tangerine fruit flavor that's food-versatile and pleasant.
Kitchen Fridge Survivor™ Grade: Avg
Your notes: _____

Talbott (Robert) Sleepy Hollow   PC   T   V
Vineyard Chardonnay, California $$$$ 26   23

Every guest I've ever served it adored the exotic marzipan, toasted nut, and tart pear flavors of this "restaurant wine" (rarely found in stores). Although it's "pricey," among California's big-ticket Chards it remains fairly reasonable for the quality.
Kitchen Fridge Survivor™ Grade: B
Your notes: _____

Trefethen Estate Chardonnay   PC   T   V
California $$$ 24   16

Trefethen's signature wine, this Chardonnay has extremely subtle oak, pear, and pineapple fruit, and tremendous concentration.
Kitchen Fridge Survivor™ Grade: B
Your notes: _____

Turning Leaf Chardonnay   PC   T   V
California $ 15   15

I have always found Chardonnay to be the Turning Leaf brand's best foot forward—soft, clean, and citrusy, not heavy.
Kitchen Fridge Survivor™ Grade: Avg
Your notes: _____

Veramonte Chardonnay   PC   T   V
Chile $ 21   21

This Chard gives you lovely tropical fruit flavor

Price Ranges: **$** = $12 or less; **$$** = $12.01–20; **$$$** = $20.01–35; **$$$$** = > $35
Kitchen Fridge/Countertop Survivor™ Grades: *Avg.* = a "one-day wine," tastes noticeably less fresh the next day; *B* = holds its freshness for 2–3 days after opening; *B+* = holds *and gets better* over 2–3 days after opening; *A* = a 3- to 4-day "freshness window"; *A+* = holds *and gets better* over 3–4 days

that's not too heavy. "Tastes more expensive than it is."

Kitchen Fridge Survivor™ Grade: Avg

Your notes: _____

Woodbridge (Robert Mondavi)	PC	T	V
Chardonnay, California	$	15	18

The quality's improved, and the scores have, too, for this popular soft and appley Chard.

Kitchen Fridge Survivor™ Grade: Avg

Your notes: _____

Yellow Tail Chardonnay	PC	T	V
Australia	$	20	24

This wine is still giving all the big brands a run for their money, and with its "delicious, easy-drinking" taste, it's giving buyers a value for theirs.

Kitchen Fridge Survivor™ Grade: Avg

Your notes: _____

Other Whites

Category Profile: A label of "other" for wines that don't fit neatly into a major category means some do not get the respect they deserve. The group includes a wildly diverse collection of wine types, from uncommon grapes and regions to unique blends and proprietary branded wines. Here is some background on each:

Uncommon Grapes and Regions—This category includes the grapes Albarino (from Spain), Pinot Blanc, Gewurztraminer, Gruner-Veltliner (from Austria), and Viognier, all meriting high marks from tasters and definitely worth your attention. The other–than–Pinot Grigio Italian whites are also here, along with Spanish regional whites. (See the Wine List Decoder for more on these.)

Unique Blends—Blends of the white grapes Semillon and Chardonnay, mainly from Australia and Washington state, are increasingly popular. This category also includes a growing crop of specialty multigrape blends well worth trying—a sign consumers are continuing to branch out—yay!

Proprietary Brands—These used to dominate the wine market in the seventies, and a few like Blue Nun have retained significant market presence.

Serve: Well chilled.

When: The uncommon grapes (like Gewurztraminer) and unique blends are wonderful when you want to surprise guests with a different flavor experience; see the notes that follow for ideas with the budget blends, but most tasters think of them when cost is a major consideration.

With: In my opinion, Gewurztraminer, Albarino, and the unusual grape blends are some of the most exciting food partners out there. My Best Bets indexes are full of specific food recommendations.

In: An all-purpose wineglass.

	PC	T	V
Alain Graillot Crozes-Hermitage Blanc, Rhone, France	$$$	24	24

Rare, but "worth the search," with an exotic lily-kiwi scent, subtle pineapple flavor, long finish.
Kitchen Fridge Survivor™ Grade: B
Your notes: _____

	PC	T	V
Alice White Semillon (sem-ee-YOHN)/Chardonnay Australia	$	19	20

"What a great value" for such juicy peach flavor streaked with a zingy lime tanginess.
Kitchen Fridge Survivor™ Grade: Avg
Your notes: _____

	PC	T	V
Aveleda Vinho Verde Portugal	$	21	24

Like biting into a crisp Granny Smith apple! The zingy acidity and light body make it a great summer refresher.
Kitchen Fridge Survivor™ Grade: A
Your notes: _____

Price Ranges: **$** = $12 or less; **$$** – $12.01–20; **$$$** = $20.01–35; **$$$$** = > $35
Kitchen Fridge/Countertop Survivor™ Grades: *Avg.* = a "one-day wine," tastes noticeably less fresh the next day; *B* = holds its freshness for 2–3 days after opening; *B+* = holds *and gets better* over 2–3 days after opening; *A* = a 3- to 4-day "freshness window"; *A+* = holds *and gets better* over 3–4 days

Becker Viognier   PC   T   V
Texas $$ X   X

✗ One of the best Viogniers made in America, so it's worth the search. Gorgeous white peach and floral scents and tangerine-mango flavors.

Kitchen Fridge Survivor™ Grade: B
Your notes: _____

Beringer Chenin Blanc   PC   T   V
California $ 23   24

My tasters "love" this "huge bargain" with huge fruit: juicy tangerine and peach.

Kitchen Fridge Survivor™ Grade: Avg
Your notes: _____

Beringer Gewurztraminer   PC   T   V
California $ 22   22

My tasters "adore the price" and the apricot fruit flavor that makes this wine a "great aperitif."

Kitchen Fridge Survivor™ Grade: Avg
Your notes: _____

Blue Nun Liebfraumilch   PC   T   V
(*LEEB-frow-milk*), Germany $ 12   12

If you liked it in its 1970s heyday, you'll like it now: light, fresh, soft like a fruit salad.

Kitchen Fridge Survivor™ Grade: B
Your notes: _____

Bodegas Godeval Godello   PC   T   V
(go-DAY-oh), Spain $$ 22   23

This wine comes from Valdeorras, one of Spain's unsung regions that's recently gained attention. The scents of pear, lime, and wet stone are complex, and the racy acidity "rocks with food."

Kitchen Fridge Survivor™ Grade: B
Your notes: _____

Burgans Albarino (*boor-GAHNS*   PC   T   V
***all-buh-REEN-yoh*), Bodegas** $$ 24   23
Vilarino-Cambados, Spain

☺ "A wonderful alternative to Chardonnay; great with shellfish," say my tasters, who note that this peachy, aromatic white specialty from Spain "won't stay a secret for long."

Kitchen Fridge Survivor™ Grade: B+
Your notes: _____

Ca' del Solo Big House White PC T V
California $ 24 24
☺ This "great blend of ABCs" (a who's who of **A**nything **B**ut **C**hardonnay white grapes) offers "totally refreshing" flavors of peach and kiwi.
Kitchen Fridge Survivor™ Grade: A+
Your notes: _____

Ceretto Arneis PC T V
Italy $$ 24 18
Check out the Arneis (ahr-NACE) grape's unique honeysuckle scent and delicate honey-pear fruit when you want something "deliciously different."
Kitchen Fridge Survivor™ Grade: Avg
Your notes: _____

Chateau Ste. Michelle PC T V
Gewurztraminer, Washington $ 24 24
Fragrant! Candied ginger and apricots, and delicious "with Chinese food."
Kitchen Fridge Survivor™ Grade: B
Your notes: _____

Columbia Crest Columbia Valley PC T V
Gewurztraminer, Washington $ 20 21
This wine's "hint of sweetness" makes it "great with spicy and ethnic foods." The "tutti-frutti" flavor, laced with honey and sweet spice, is classic Gewurz.
Kitchen Fridge Survivor™ Grade: B+
Your notes: _____

Columbia Crest Semillon/ PC T V
Chardonnay, Washington $ 18 24
Blending the Semillon grape into Chardonnay adds acidity, earthiness, honey, and lime to the ripe Chardonnay fruit.
Kitchen Fridge Survivor™ Grade: B
Your notes: _____

Price Ranges: **$** = $12 or less; **$$** = $12.01–20; **$$$** = $20.01–35; **$$$$** = > $35
Kitchen Fridge/Countertop Survivor™ Grades: *Avg.* = a "one-day wine," tastes noticeably less fresh the next day; *B* = holds its freshness for 2–3 days after opening; *B+* = holds *and gets better* over 2–3 days after opening; *A* = a 3- to 4-day "freshness window"; *A+* = holds *and gets better* over 3–4 days

Conundrum (formerly Caymus Conundrum), California

	PC	T	V
	$$$	27	24

Scores soared for this "interesting combination" of grapes (everything from Chard to Sauvignon Blanc to Chenin Blanc and more!) The oak's been lightened up, letting the exotic tropical style come through. The wine's devoted following will no doubt dig the new screw-cap package.

Kitchen Fridge Survivor™ Grade: B
Your notes: _____

Domaine Weinbach Gewurztraminer Cuvee Theo France

	PC	T	V
	$$$	27	24

"Immense" tropical, lychee, and apricot fruit layers, unctuous texture, yet not at all heavy. An Alsace classic.

Kitchen Fridge Survivor™ Grade: A
Your notes: _____

Dry Creek Vineyard Chenin Blanc California

	PC	T	V
	$	27	27

"Like biting a Golden Delicious apple"—juicy, with a pretty snap of acidity and a creamy finish. De-lish.

Kitchen Fridge Survivor™ Grade: B
Your notes: _____

Fetzer Valley Oaks Gewurztraminer California

	PC	T	V
	$	25	26

✓ If you haven't tried Gewurz, here's a "favorite" of my tasters, who praise its luscious floral and apricot aromas and flavors. De-lish!

Kitchen Fridge Survivor™ Grade: B
Your notes: _____

Folie a Deux Menage a Trois White blend, California

	PC	T	V
	$	X	X

✗ The *trois* (3) grapes are Chardonnay, Sauvignon Blanc, and Chenin Blanc, yielding a crisp-and-ripe palate and intoxicatingly floral scent that's irresistible.

Kitchen Fridge Survivor™ Grade: Avg
Your notes: _____

Herbauges Muscadet France

	PC	T	V
	$	24	24

This carafe quaff of Parisian bistros offers crisp

apple lemon flavors, mineral scents, and maximum refreshment.

Kitchen Fridge Survivor™ *Grade: B*

Your notes: _____

Hildago La Gitana (ee-DAHL-go la hee-TAH-nuh) Manzanilla Sherry, Spain	PC $$	T 24	V 24

This sherry's "nutty," "clean" flavor is super with salty fare and fried foods, too.

Kitchen Fridge Survivor™ *Grade: A*

Your notes: _____

Hogue Gewurztraminer Washington	PC $	T 22	V 24

Hogue "really puts it in the bottle for the money" with all their wines. This apricot-gingery Gewurz is no exception—"del-ish for sipping" and with "Chinese food."

Kitchen Fridge Survivor™ *Grade: B+*

Your notes: _____

Hugel (hew-GELL) Gewurztraminer France	PC $$	T 25	V 22

☺ A huge success with my tasters for the beautiful floral and sweet spice scent, and lychee-nut/apricot flavor. Scrumptious.

Kitchen Fridge Survivor™ *Grade: A*

Your notes: _____

Hugel Pinot Blanc France	PC $$	T 21	V 21

The apple-pear flavor, mineral complexity, and liveliness of this Pinot Blanc are great for the price.

Kitchen Fridge Survivor™ *Grade: B*

Your notes: _____

Price Ranges: **$** = $12 or less; **$$** = $12.01–20; **$$$** = $20.01–35; **$$$$** = > $35

Kitchen Fridge/Countertop Survivor™ Grades: *Avg.* = a "one-day wine," tastes noticeably less fresh the next day; *B* = holds its freshness for 2–3 days after opening; *B+* = holds *and gets better* over 2–3 days after opening; *A* = a 3- to 4-day "freshness window"; *A+* = holds *and gets better* over 3–4 days

Indaba Chenin Blanc   PC   T   V
South Africa $ 24   24

"Yum"'s the word from tasters for this wine's lively
Golden Delicious apple flavor. A portion of sales
funds winemaking scholarships for black South
Africans.

Kitchen Fridge Survivor™ Grade: B+
Your notes: _____

Knoll Gruner-Veltliner (*kuh-NOLL*   PC   T   V
***GROO-ner Velt-LEEN-er*) Smaragd** $$ 22   23
Trocken Wachau, Austria

Sommeliers (including me) "love this wine" because
the "zippy, grapefruit-spice character" is "magic with
food."

Kitchen Fridge Survivor™ Grade: A
Your notes: _____

La Scolca Black Label Gavi   PC   T   V
Italy $$$$ 19   19

As with many Italian whites, it's a perfectly "nice,
appley" food wine, but the prices for wines from the
Gavi region can be high. Pinot Grigio generally offers
the same quality and style, for less.

Kitchen Fridge Survivor™ Grade: B
Your notes: _____

Marques de Riscal Rueda (*mar-KESS* PC   T   V
***deh ree-SCAHL roo-AY-duh*), Spain** $ 22   18

This wine is fresh, sleek, and vibrant, tasting of Key
lime and kiwi, without oak flavor and yummy with
food.

Kitchen Fridge Survivor™ Grade: B+
Your notes: _____

Martin Codax Albarino   PC   T   V
(*all-buh-REEN-yo*), Spain $$ 24   21

This is "magic with food," say my tasters. It's got
gorgeous floral and citrus scents, passion fruit and
pear flavor, all on an ultralight, oak-free frame.

Kitchen Fridge Survivor™ Grade: B+
Your notes: _____

Miguel Torres Vina Sol   PC   T   V
Spain $ 18   18

I love this wine—the bargain price, fresh, crisp apple
flavor, and zingy finish.

Kitchen Fridge Survivor™ Grade: B+
Your notes: _____

Navarro Gewurztraminer	PC	T	V
California	$$	24	21

Apricot fruit and wilted rose-petal scents make this one of my panel's "favorite Gewurztraminers."
Kitchen Fridge Survivor™ Grade: B+
Your notes: _____

Paul Blanck Gewurztraminer	PC	T	V
Classique, France	$$	24	24

I think this is one of Alsace's best Gewurzes for the money—beautiful lychee, rose-petal, peach, and minerals, all in balance.
Kitchen Fridge Survivor™ Grade: B+
Your notes: _____

Penfolds Koonunga Hill	PC	T	V
Semillon/Chardonnay Australia	$	23	24

My tasters call this a "delicious sleeper of a wine," with provocative pear aromas and citrus flavors.
Kitchen Fridge Survivor™ Grade: B+
Your notes: _____

Pepperwood Grove Viognier	PC	T	V
California	$	20	21

The Viognier grape is often pricey because it's rare and tough to grow. This is an exception. It has real Viognier character—honeysuckle, lavender, and ripe pineapple scents and flavors—at a great price.
Kitchen Fridge Survivor™ Grade: Avg
Your notes: _____

Pierre Sparr Alsace-One	PC	T	V
France	$	18	29

☺ This mix of Riesling, Pinot Blanc, Muscat, Gewurztraminer and Pinot Gris is a classic trick in

---

Price Ranges: **$** = $12 or less; **$$** = $12.01–20; **$$$** = $20.01–35; **$$$$** = > $35
Kitchen Fridge/Countertop Survivor™ Grades: *Avg.* = a "one-day wine," tastes noticeably less fresh the next day; *B* = holds its freshness for 2–3 days after opening; *B+* = holds *and gets better* over 2–3 days after opening; *A* = a 3- to 4-day "freshness window"; *A+* = holds *and gets better* over 3–4 days

Alsace: blend all the local grapes to make a "yummy" wine with lots of peach and pear fruit that's "great with food, great price."

Kitchen Fridge Survivor™ Grade: B

Your notes: _____

Pierre Sparr Pinot Blanc	PC	T	V
France	$	24	24

There's no oak or high alcohol here to distract from the lip-smacking pear and quince fruit, with a whisper of mineral scent. Yum.

Kitchen Fridge Survivor™ Grade: B

Your notes: _____

Ruffino Orvieto	PC	T	V
Italy	$	19	21

This wine's crisp acidity, clean melon fruit, and nutty qualities are what everyday Italian white wine should be.

Kitchen Fridge Survivor™ Grade: B

Your notes: _____

Smoking Loon Viognier	PC	T	V
California	$	X	X

✗ It's hard to find a Viognier with this much character for the price—floral/apricot scents and flavors, and juicy acidity.

Kitchen Fridge Survivor™ Grade: B

Your notes: _____

Sokol Blosser Evolution	PC	T	V
Oregon	$$	23	20

The scent and juicy flavor of this nifty wine are like an aromatherapy treatment—honeysuckle, peach, apricot, pear, and more—but a lot cheaper!

Kitchen Fridge Survivor™ Grade: B

Your notes: _____

Sutter Home Gewurztraminer	PC	T	V
California	$	21	23

From one of the top-selling wine brands, a fruit salad in a glass, with a gingery scent.

Kitchen Fridge Survivor™ Grade: B

Your notes: _____

Walter Glatzer Gruner-Veltliner	PC	T	V
Kabinett, Austria	$$	23	21

Another sommelier favorite, this wine's "tangy, mouth-

watering lemongrass and spice" are an exotic, afford-
able treat.
Kitchen Fridge Survivor™ Grade: A
Your notes: _____

Weingartner (*WINE-gart-ner*)   **PC**   **T**   **V**
Gruner-Veltliner Federspiel, Austria   **$**   **24**   **18**
☺ The easy price of this wine makes it a good intro to
Austria's signature white grape, which Austrians call
Gru-V (as in groovy) for short. And that it is—ginger,
grapefruit, and cardamom scents; apple, peach, and
lemon zest flavors. Try it!
Kitchen Fridge Survivor™ Grade: A
Your notes: _____

Zind-Humbrecht Wintzenheim   **PC**   **T**   **V**
Gewurztraminer, France   **$$**   **27**   **21**
Z-H wines have an amazing viscous texture without
being heavy. And my tasters "love" the "apricot,"
"lychee," and tangerine fruit.
Kitchen Fridge Survivor™ Grade: Avg
Your notes: _____

BLUSH/PINK/ROSE WINES

Category Profile: Although many buyers are snobby
about the blush category, the truth is that for most of
us white Zinfandel was probably the first wine we
drank that had a cork. It's a juicy, uncomplicated style
that makes a lot of buyers, and their wallets, very
happy. Now for the gear switch—rose. The only thing
true roses have in common with the blush category is
appearance. Rose wines are classic to many world-
class European wine regions. They are absolutely dry,

Price Ranges: **$** = $12 or less; **$$** = $12.01–20; **$$$** = $20.01–35;
$$$$ = > $35
Kitchen Fridge/Countertop Survivor™ Grades: *Avg.* = a "one-day
wine," tastes noticeably less fresh the next day; *B* = holds its fresh-
ness for 2–3 days after opening; *B+* = holds *and gets better* over 2–3
days after opening; *A* = a 3- to 4-day "freshness window"; *A+* =
holds *and gets better* over 3–4 days

tangy, crisp, and amazingly interesting wines for the money. I often say that with their spice and complexity they have red wine flavor, but the lightness of body and chillability gives them white wine style. They are *great* food wines. Don't miss the chance to try my recommendations or those of your favorite shop or restaurant. You will love them.

Serve: The colder the better.

When: The refreshing touch of sweetness in blush styles makes them great as an aperitif. Roses are great for both sipping and meals.

With: A touch of sweetness in wine can tone down heat, so spicy foods are an especially good partner for blush wine. Dry roses go with everything.

In: An all-purpose wineglass.

	PC	T	V
Beringer White Zinfandel **California**	$	17	20

The standard-bearer in the WZ category, and for good reason. It's got lots of fresh strawberry and sweet raspberry flavors, and a juicy texture.
Kitchen Fridge Survivor™ Grade: B
Your notes: _____

	PC	T	V
Bodegas Ochoa (oh-*CHOH*-uh) **Garnacha Rosado, Spain**	$	22	26

This "wonderful summer rosé," completely dry with scents of "strawberry" and a "beautiful color," is "further proof that Spain is coming on strong."
Kitchen Fridge Survivor™ Grade: B+
Your notes: _____

	PC	T	V
Bonny Doon Vin Gris de Cigare **Pink Wine, California**	$$	24	29

Randall Grahm of Bonny Doon fearlessly launched this "pink wine," a bone-dry, tangy, spicy refresher, long before the style became cool. It's still a favorite.
Kitchen Fridge Survivor™ Grade: B
Your notes: _____

	PC	T	V
Domaine Ott Bandol Rose **France**	$$	27	24

"One of the best from Southern France," said one

taster; it's a classically styled rose: spicy, strawberry-fruity, thirst-quenching.

Kitchen Fridge Survivor™ Grade: B

Your notes: _____

Marques de Caceres Rioja Rosado	PC	T	V
Spain	$	18	18

This wine's tangy strawberry-watermelon-spice flavor is de-lish! You can invite *any* food to this party.

Kitchen Fridge Survivor™ Grade: Avg

Your notes: _____

Regaleali Rosato, Tasca D'Almerita	PC	T	V
Italy	$$	21	20

Proof that Italians put all their *passione* into reds (the hot-weather version of which are rosatos like this one). If you don't like white, you can have this spicy, summery, bone-dry rose to cool you down.

Kitchen Fridge Survivor™ Grade: B

Your notes: _____

Solorosa Rose	PC	T	V
California	$$	23	22

☺ This is real rose, not at all sweet, and with lots of spice and savor. It's also got some added richness from barrel fermentation, and has in just a few vintages gained a cult following. Fabulous with grill fare.

Kitchen Fridge Survivor™ Grade: B+

Your notes: _____

Sutter Home White Zinfandel	PC	T	V
California	$	14	16

Purportedly invented out of necessity in the 1980s (the winery had lots of red grapes planted, but taste trends had shifted to favor white wines), Sutter Home's trailblazing WZ is still one of the best. It's juicy and pleasing.

Kitchen Fridge Survivor™ Grade: B

Your notes: _____

Price Ranges: **$** = $12 or less; **$$** = $12.01–20; **$$$** = $20.01–35; **$$$$** = > $35

Kitchen Fridge/Countertop Survivor™ Grades: *Avg.* = a "one-day wine," tastes noticeably less fresh the next day; *B* = holds its freshness for 2–3 days after opening; *B+* = holds *and gets better* over 2–3 days after opening; *A* = a 3- to 4-day "freshness window"; *A+* = holds *and gets better* over 3–4 days

RED WINES
Beaujolais/Gamay

Category Profile: Beaujolais Nouveau (*bow-jhoe-LAY*), the new wine of the vintage that each year is shipped from France on the third Thursday in November (just in time for Thanksgiving), dominates sales in this category. (It also inspires scores of nouveau imitators riding its cash-cow coattails.) You can have fun with nouveau, but don't skip the real stuff—particularly Beaujolais-Villages (*vill-AHJH*) and Beaujolais Cru (named for the town where they're grown, e.g., Morgon, Brouilly, Moulin-à-Vent, etc.). These Beaujolais categories are a wine world rarity, in that they offer real character at a low price. The signature style of Beaujolais is a juicy, grapey fruit flavor and succulent texture with, in the crus, an added layer of earthy spiciness. All red Beaujolais is made from the Gamay grape.

Serve: Lightly chilled, to enhance the vibrant fruit.

When: Great as an aperitif and for alfresco occasions such as picnics and barbecues.

With: Many tasters said they swear by it for Thanksgiving. It's so soft, smooth, and juicy I think it goes with everything, from the simplest of sandwich meals to brunch, lunch, and beyond. It's often a great buy on restaurant wine lists and versatile for those really tough matching situations where you've ordered everything from oysters to osso bucco but you want one wine.

In: An all-purpose wineglass.

	PC	T	V
Barton & Guestier (B&G) Beaujolais			
France	$	20	20

Here's a good-value, food-friendly wine that's great for parties, because it won't break your bank. What more could you ask for?" (FYI: Insiders call it "B&G" for short.)
Kitchen Countertop Survivor™ Grade: Avg
Your notes: _____

	PC	T	V
Chateau de la Chaize Brouilly			
France	$	18	17

The village of Brouilly, pronounced Broo-YEE, is one

of the 10 "crus," or top villages, of the region. This is classic Beaujolais, with lots of soft berry fruit and a smoky, earthy scent that reminds me of autumn leaves.

Kitchen Countertop Survivor™ Grade: B

Your notes: _____

Duboeuf (*Duh-BUFF*) (Georges)	PC	T	V
Beaujolais Nouveau, France	$	19	22

Duboeuf's nouveau is always a fun, juicy crowd-pleaser that consumers find "drinkable with or without food," great with Thanksgiving dinner, and bargain-priced.

Kitchen Countertop Survivor™ Grade: Avg

Your notes: _____

Duboeuf (Georges) Beaujolais-	PC	T	V
Villages, France	$	19	21

I agree with trade colleagues that it's "hard not to love" this widely available bottling from the King of Beaujolais. Its plump berry flavor is great with a wide variety of foods, good for those who don't normally drink red.

Kitchen Countertop Survivor™ Grade: B

Your notes: _____

Duboeuf (Georges) Moulin-A-Vent	PC	T	V
France	$	24	21

"A great intro to the Beaujolais crus," this is "great for the money" with lots of "spice, smooth berry fruit" and "more complexity than you'd expect."

Kitchen Countertop Survivor™ Grade: B

Your notes: _____

Louis Jadot Beaujolais-Villages	PC	T	V
France	$	22	24

☺ I've tasted—and sold in restaurants—*every* vintage of this wine for the last ten years, and my guests' upbeat reaction is as consistent as the wine: de-lish!

Price Ranges: **$** = $12 or less; **$$** = $12.01–20; **$$$** = $20.01–35; **$$$$** = > $35

Kitchen Fridge/Countertop Survivor™ Grades: **Avg.** = a "one-day wine," tastes noticeably less fresh the next day; **B** = holds its freshness for 2–3 days after opening; **B+** = holds *and gets better* over 2–3 days after opening; **A** = a 3- to 4-day "freshness window"; **A+** = holds *and gets better* over 3–4 days

The light body and berry fruit make it "the perfect sipping wine."

Kitchen Countertop Survivor™ Grade: B

Your notes: _____

Pinot Noir

Category Profile: Pinot Noir is my favorite of the major classic red grape varieties, because I love its smoky-ripe scent, pure fruit flavor, and, most of all, silken texture. It also offers red wine intensity and complexity, without being heavy. Although Pinot Noir's home turf is the Burgundy region of France, few of those wines make the list of top sellers in the U.S., because production is tiny. The coolest parts of coastal California (especially the Russian River Valley, Carneros, Monterey, Sonoma Coast, and Santa Barbara County) specialize in Pinot Noir, as does Oregon's Willamette (*will-AM-ett*) Valley. New Zealand is also becoming an important Pinot source. Pinot Noir from all the major regions is typically oak aged, but as with other grapes the amount of oakiness is matched to the intensity of the fruit. Generally the budget bottlings are the least oaky.

Serve: *Cool* room temperature; don't hesitate to chill the bottle briefly if needed.

When: Although the silky texture makes Pinot Noir quite bewitching on its own, it is also the ultimate "food wine." It is my choice to take to dinner parties and to order in restaurants, because I know it will probably delight both white and red wine drinkers and will go with most any food.

With: Pinot's versatility is legendary, but it is *the* wine for mushroom dishes, salmon, rare tuna, and any bird (especially duck).

In: An all-purpose wineglass. Or try a larger balloon stem; the extra air space enhances the wine's aroma.

| **Acacia Carneros Pinot Noir** | PC | T | V |
| **California** | $$$ | 22 | 20 |

This "smooth as silk Pinot" has a "lovely berry flavor," "spice and earth" scent, and "ages nicely for a few years."

Kitchen Countertop Survivor™ Grade: B+

Your notes: _____

Adelsheim Pinot Noir	PC	T	V
Oregon	$$$	24	21

This wine's rep as one of Oregon's perennial greats is well deserved. The subtle dried cranberry fruit and dusty-herbal scent are quite distinctive.
Kitchen Countertop Survivor™ Grade: B

Your notes: _____

Archery Summit Arcus Estate	PC	T	V
Pinot Noir, Oregon	$$$$	26	19

The "intense and opulent" black cherry fruit and layers of flavor have lots of fans, but some pros find it "over-oaked for the amount of fruit." It needs aeration to soften up.
Kitchen Countertop Survivor™ Grade: B

Your notes: _____

Argyle Pinot Noir	PC	T	V
Oregon	$$	21	19

One of Oregon's most consistent and drop-dead-delicious Pinots is also one of its most affordable. The flavor reminds me of cherry Lifesavers, and the feeling on the palate is of bursting berry fruit. Yum!
Kitchen Fridge Survivor™ Grade: B

Your notes: _____

Artesa Pinot Noir Russian River	PC	T	V
Valley, California	$$	25	25

Classic Russian River Pinot style: a deep core of cherry-cola fruit and almost syrupy-smooth texture.
Kitchen Fridge Survivor™ Grade: B

Your notes: _____

Au Bon Climat Pinot Noir Rincon	PC	T	V
and Rosemary's, California	$$$$	24	24

Downright sexy, with a layer of bacony-smoky complexity enveloping the strawberry-rhubarb fruit. Ages well, too.
Kitchen Fridge Survivor™ Grade: A

Your notes: _____

Price Ranges: **$** = $12 or less; **$$** = $12.01–20; **$$$** = $20.01–35; **$$$$** = > $35
Kitchen Fridge/Countertop Survivor™ Grades: *Avg.* = a "one-day wine," tastes noticeably less fresh the next day; *B* = holds its freshness for 2–3 days after opening; *B+* = holds *and gets better* over 2–3 days after opening; *A* = a 3- to 4-day "freshness window"; *A+* = holds *and gets better* over 3–4 days

Au Bon Climat Pinot Noir Santa   PC   T   V
Barbara, California $$ 26   23

☺ *Oh-bohn-clee-MAHT* has a cult following and a nickname—"ABC." It's among the truly great American Pinots, with vivid black cherry fruit, oak, body, and tannin in perfect balance. Super stuff.

Kitchen Countertop Survivor™ Grade: B+

Your notes: _____

Au Bon Climat Pinot Noir Talley   PC   T   V
Vineyard, California $$$$ 24   21

One of the more elegant of the ABC PN bottlings, with pure cherry Jolly Rancher fruit on the palate, cinnamon spice on the scent.

Kitchen Countertop Survivor™ Grade: B

Your notes: _____

Beaulieu Vineyards (BV) Carneros   PC   T   V
Pinot Noir, California $$ 19   18

The "classic Carneros Pinot" style delivers silky cherry fruit, spice, and soft texture.

Kitchen Countertop Survivor™ Grade: Avg

Your notes: _____

Benton Lane Pinot Noir   PC   T   V
Oregon $$ 26   22

If you've not yet had an Oregon Pinot Noir, give this easy-priced wine—with a red postage-stamp label— a lick, and taste its "lovely" red berry and earthy tea-leaf flavors.

Kitchen Countertop Survivor™ Grade: Avg

Your notes: _____

Beringer Founders' Estate Pinot Noir PC   T   V
California $$ 19   22

The scores have slipped but it's still "solid as budget Pinots go," with soft berry fruit and smooth texture.

Kitchen Countertop Survivor™ Grade: Avg

Your notes: _____

Brancott Vineyards Marlborough   PC   T   V
Reserve Pinot Noir, New Zealand $$$ 22   22

This wine's cherry cola scent and cinnamon-black cherry flavors are lush, but structured. Good stuff.

Kitchen Countertop Survivor™ Grade: B

Your notes: _____

Buena Vista Carneros Pinot Noir

	PC	T	V
California	$$$	20	20

This wine is classic Carneros, with aromas of potpourri and tea leaves, and flavors of dried cherry and spice.

Kitchen Countertop Survivor™ Grade: B

Your notes: _____

Byron Central Coast Pinot Noir

	PC	T	V
California	$$	24	19

This Pinot's "spicy cranberry" fruit is classic Central Coast. Soft and supple.

Kitchen Countertop Survivor™ Grade: B

Your notes: _____

Calera Central Coast Pinot Noir

	PC	T	V
California	$$$	24	20

This Pinot delivers consistency year in and year out: a "supple, earthy" style, redolent of "dried cherry fruit."

Kitchen Countertop Survivor™ Grade: B+

Your notes: _____

Cambria (*CAME-bree-uh*) Julia's Vineyard Pinot Noir, California

	PC	T	V
	$$$	24	22

This wine's savory earth and spice, lush plum flavor, and tug of tannin make it "memorable."

Kitchen Countertop Survivor™ Grade: B

Your notes: _____

Cavit Pinot Noir

	PC	T	V
Italy	$	22	24

It truly is "amazing to find real Pinot Noir character at this price." This one's in the silky, earthy style with pomegranate and dried cherry flavor.

Kitchen Countertop Survivor™ Grade: Avg

Your notes: _____

Price Ranges: **$** = $12 or less; **$$** = $12.01 20; **$$$** = $20.01–35; **$$$$** = > $35

Kitchen Fridge/Countertop Survivor™ Grades: *Avg.* = a "one-day wine," tastes noticeably less fresh the next day; *B* = holds its freshness for 2–3 days after opening; *B+* = holds *and gets better* over 2–3 days after opening; *A* = a 3- to 4-day "freshness window"; *A+* = holds *and gets better* over 3–4 days

Chateau St. Jean Pinot Noir   PC   T   V
California $$ 24   23

"A great beginner's Pinot Noir," but even old hands can't resist the "yummy" "cherry jam" fruit and silky texture.

Kitchen Countertop Survivor™ Grade: Avg

Your notes: _____

Clos du Bois Sonoma County   PC   T   V
Pinot Noir, California $$$ 20   21

This Pinot is it: strawberry-rhubarb and smoky scent, "great Bing cherry flavors, and the perfect amount of acid" are just delicious.

Kitchen Countertop Survivor™ Grade: A

Your notes: _____

Coldstream Hills Pinot Noir,   PC   T   V
Australia $$ 23   23

☺ This Aussie offering has a knack for getting Burgundian smokiness and complexity in the bottle, as well as the ripe black cherry fruit you'd expect from sunny Australia. At this price, it's a gift to Pinot lovers.

Kitchen Countertop Survivor™ Grade: B

Your notes: _____

Cristom Jefferson Cuvee Pinot Noir   PC   T   V
Oregon $$$$ 27   23

This wine's signature smoky/cocoa scent, deep cherry fruit, and satiny texture are amazing.

Kitchen Countertop Survivor™ Grade: B+

Your notes: _____

David Bruce Santa Cruz Pinot   PC   T   V
Noir, California $$$ 24   21

Pinot lovers, check it out: this one's gamy, savory spice, earth, and raspberry fruit are truly distinctive.

Kitchen Countertop Survivor™ Grade: B

Your notes: _____

Dehlinger Pinot Noir   PC   T   V
California $$$ 24   21

This wine drips with cherry cola and rhubárb scent and flavor, and the satiny texture is downright sexy.

Kitchen Countertop Survivor™ Grade: B

Your notes: _____

Deloach Pinot Noir PC T V
California $$ 24 24

The winery's had a change of control, but so far the wines have held their quality and style—in this case a rich, cinnamon-spiced cherry flavor.

Kitchen Countertop Survivor™ Grade: B

Your notes: _____

Domaine Carneros Pinot Noir PC T V
California $$$ 26 21

☺ This wine, great since the first vintage, still gets better every year. It's got a "sophisticated" scent, subtle oakiness, and long finish "like GREAT red Burgundy," yet with the "bold fruit" of its California home base. A "wow" with me and my panel.

Kitchen Countertop Survivor™ Grade: A

Your notes: _____

Domaine Drouhin (*droo-AHN*) PC T V
Willamette Valley Pinot Noir $$$$ 26 23
Oregon

This wine has "exuberant raspberry and cherry fruit," and intense oak, which dominates when the wine is young. Pros point out that "it needs at least 2 years' bottle age to show its classy complexity."

Kitchen Countertop Survivor™ Grade: B

Your notes: _____

Duck Pond Pinot Noir PC T V
Oregon $ 23 24

A "light on the wallet" Pinot with strawberry aromas, ripe raspberry flavors, and great food compatibility, for a great price.

Kitchen Countertop Survivor™ Grade: B

Your notes: _____

Price Ranges: **$** = $12 or less; **$$** = $12.01–20; **$$$** = $20.01–35; **$$$$** = > $35

Kitchen Fridge/Countertop Survivor™ Grades: *Avg.* = a "one-day wine," tastes noticeably less fresh the next day; *B* = holds its freshness for 2–3 days after opening; *B+* = holds *and gets better* over 2–3 days after opening; *A* = a 3- to 4-day "freshness window"; *A+* = holds *and gets better* over 3–4 days

Echelon Central Coast Pinot Noir   PC   T   V
California $ 23   25

☺ "Burgundy meets California" is how my tasters put it. The smoky, wild raspberry scent and flavor and silky texture are a triumph at this price.

Kitchen Countertop Survivor™ Grade: B+

Your notes: _____

Elk Cove Pinot Noir   PC   T   V
Oregon $$ 26   23

Pinot in the lighter style, with savory spice and dried cherry character that make it versatile with food.

Kitchen Countertop Survivor™ Grade: Avg

Your notes: _____

Estancia Pinnacles Pinot Noir   PC   T   V
California $$ 22   22

With its distinct herbal, strawberry compote, and smoky character, this is great for the money.

Kitchen Countertop Survivor™ Grade: B+

Your notes: _____

Etude Carneros Pinot Noir   PC   T   V
California $$$$ 27   22

☺ My enthusiasm is just a drop in the bucket of tasters' raves for this wine's "great structure" and elegance. The fragrant, cherry-spice scent, juicy cherry-cranberry fruit, and long finish have been style signatures since the first vintage. Gorgeous.

Kitchen Countertop Survivor™ Grade: A

Your notes: _____

Firesteed Pinot Noir   PC   T   V
Oregon $ 19   21

Delicious cranberry and dried cherry fruit, a nice kick of acid, and a "great price" make it "easy to love."

Kitchen Countertop Survivor™ Grade: B

Your notes: _____

Five Rivers Ranch Pinot Noir   PC   T   V
California $ X   X

✗ A find, for its true PN character at a super price: a touch of wet-clay earthiness and soft raspberry-strawberry fruit.

Kitchen Countertop Survivor™ Grade: B

Your notes: _____

Flowers Pinot Noir   PC   T   V
California $$$$ 28   20

One of the more heralded CA Pinots; my Pinot-loving tasters are "obsessed" with its elegant cherry and intoxicating spice-tea notes.

Kitchen Countertop Survivor™ Grade: B

Your notes: _____

Frei Brothers Reserve Pinot Noir   PC   T   V
California $$ 22   21

A steal at this price, with cherry cola and cinnamon on the nose, and silky richness on the palate.

Kitchen Countertop Survivor™ Grade: B+

Your notes: _____

Gallo of Sonoma Pinot Noir   PC   T   V
California $$ 21   24

Both trade and consumer tasters lauded this Pinot's classic character—pure "raspberry and cherry" fruit, a soft vanilla-cream oakiness, and supple-but-lively texture—especially for the price.

Kitchen Countertop Survivor™ Grade: B+

Your notes: _____

Gary Farrell Pinot Noir   PC   T   V
California $$$$ 28   28

The extraordinary complexity—smoke, pomegranate, cinnamon, meaty cherry—emerged in the bottle over several days. Superb.

Kitchen Countertop Survivor™ Grade: B+

Your notes: _____

Iron Horse Estate Pinot Noir   PC   T   V
California $$$ 23   21

☺ This "wow" Pinot Noir's black cherry compote and cola accents and flavors are framed with vanilla-scented oak. Luscious yet balanced.

Kitchen Countertop Survivor™ Grade: B

Your notes: _____

Price Ranges: **$** = $12 or less; **$$** = $12.01–20; **$$$** = $20.01–35; **$$$$** = > $35

Kitchen Fridge/Countertop Survivor™ Grades: *Avg.* = a "one-day wine," tastes noticeably less fresh the next day; *B* = holds its freshness for 2–3 days after opening; *B+* = holds *and gets better* over 2–3 days after opening; *A* = a 3- to 4-day "freshness window"; *A+* = holds *and gets better* over 3–4 days

J Wine Company Russian River	PC	T	V
Pinot Noir, California	$$$	26	22

"So incredibly jammy and rich, yet it maintains the balance and silkiness Pinot lovers look for. The scent of sweet oak frames a lovely ripe, black cherry flavor. Open ahead because it really blossoms with aeration.

Kitchen Countertop Survivor™ Grade: B

Your notes: _____

Ken Wright Pinot Noir	PC	T	V
Oregon	$$$	26	22

The sleek texture, subtle earth and tea-leaf scent, and subtle cherry-jam fruit are elegance in a bottle.

Kitchen Countertop Survivor™ Grade: Avg

Your notes: _____

Kendall-Jackson Vintner's Reserve	PC	T	V
Pinot Noir, California	$$	21	21

This is a good intro Pinot, with classic silky cherry and spice character at an affordable price.

Kitchen Countertop Survivor™ Grade: A

Your notes: _____

King Estate Pinot Noir	PC	T	V
Oregon	$$$	23	18

There's still soft cherry fruit, but the price has gone up for essentially the same quality.

Kitchen Countertop Survivor™ Grade: B

Your notes: _____

La Crema Sonoma Pinot Noir	PC	T	V
California	$$	23	22

This fuller-bodied style is a "favorite Pinot" choice for many. It has deep cherry-cola flavor and a toasty scent.

Kitchen Countertop Survivor™ Grade: Avg

Your notes: _____

Lindemans Bin 99 Pinot Noir	PC	T	V
Australia	$	20	25

My tasters say you "can't beat the value" of this light, soft Pinot with supple cherry fruit and a silky texture.

Kitchen Countertop Survivor™ Grade: Avg

Your notes: _____

MacMurray Ranch Sonoma Coast   **PC**   **T**   **V**
Pinot Noir, California   **$$**   **29**   **24**

Fred's (as in *My Three Sons*) daughter Kate works with the Gallo family to produce this silky Pinot with deep, black cherry–raspberry fruit, and fragrant vanilla and cinnamon in the scent. De-lish.

Kitchen Countertop Survivor™ Grade: B+

Your notes: _____

Meridian Pinot Noir   **PC**   **T**   **V**
California   **$**   **20**   **20**

Perfect for every day, especially for the price. The mouthwatering flavor "tastes like biting into fresh cherries."

Kitchen Countertop Survivor™ Grade: B

Your notes: _____

Merry Edwards Russian River   **PC**   **T**   **V**
Valley Pinot Noir, California   **$$$$**   **28**   **23**

The texture of this elegant Pinot is silky but very rich and plump, with flavors of cola, dark cherry, and chocolate.

Kitchen Countertop Survivor™ Grade: B

Your notes: _____

Mirassou Pinot Noir   **PC**   **T**   **V**
California   **$**   **21**   **22**

A great value: soft cherry-and-spice Pinot. Perfect for every day.

Kitchen Countertop Survivor™ Grade: A

Your notes: _____

Morgan 12 Clones Pinot Noir   **PC**   **T**   **V**
California   **$$**   **21**   **24**

Morgan's Pinot Noirs are known for their ripe cherry fruit, exotic smoky character, and rock-solid quality, year after year. Bravo!

Kitchen Countertop Survivor™ Grade: B+

Your notes: _____

Price Ranges: **$** = $12 or less; **$$** = $12.01–20; **$$$** = $20.01–35; **$$$$** = > $35

Kitchen Fridge/Countertop Survivor™ Grades: *Avg.* = a "one-day wine," tastes noticeably less fresh the next day; *B* = holds its freshness for 2–3 days after opening; *B+* = holds *and gets better* over 2–3 days after opening; *A* = a 3- to 4-day "freshness window"; *A+* = holds *and gets better* over 3–4 days

Panther Creek Pinot Noir   **PC**   **T**   **V**
Oregon   **$$$**   23   27

The black cherry jam flavors and a juicy texture makes this one of Oregon's most luscious-style Pinots.

Kitchen Countertop Survivor™ Grade: Avg

Your notes: _____

Pedroncelli Pinot Noir   **PC**   **T**   **V**
California   **$$**   18   21

Worth the search, since value PNs with varietal character—silky strawberry-rhubarb fruit and a little earth—are so rare.

Kitchen Countertop Survivor™ Grade: Avg

Your notes: _____

Pepperwood Grove Pinot Noir   **PC**   **T**   **V**
California   **$**   18   22

Tasters laud the smoothness, "lively cherry fruit," and "great price."

Kitchen Countertop Survivor™ Grade: Avg

Your notes: _____

Perdrix Mercurey   **PC**   **T**   **V**
Burgundy, France   **$$$**   22   20

The Mercurey appellation in Burgundy offers great value because it's less well known. This wine's scent of wood smoke, red cherries, and tobacco is typical of the region. The palate is silky with just a tug of tannin.

Kitchen Countertop Survivor™ Grade: B

Your notes: _____

Ponzi Pinor Noir   **PC**   **T**   **V**
Oregon   **$$$**   25   21

One of OR's most complex and coveted PNs, for a reason—spicy cherry and wilted rose-petal scent, a touch of earth, great complexity and elegance.

Kitchen Countertop Survivor™ Grade: Avg.

Your notes: _____

Ramsay Pinot Noir   **PC**   **T**   **V**
California   **$$**   24   27

✓ So much character for the money! A smoky-meaty quality, strawberry-jam fruit, and that silky texture that's the joy of Pinot Noir lovers.

Kitchen Countertop Survivor™ Grade: B

Your notes: _____

| Rex Hill Willamette Valley | PC | T | V |
| Pinot Noir, Oregon | $$ | 26 | 23 |

The spicy "cherry and earthy flavors" are typical of the Willamette Pinot style. Check it out: the price dropped and the taste score is better than ever.
Kitchen Countertop Survivor™ Grade: Avg
Your notes: _____

| Robert Mondavi Carneros Pinot | PC | T | V |
| Noir, California | $$$ | 26 | 20 |

They've done a good job showcasing the Carneros character with herbal tea scents, dried cherry, earthiness, and elegance.
Kitchen Countertop Survivor™ Grade: B
Your notes: _____

| Robert Mondavi Napa Pinot Noir | PC | T | V |
| California | $$$ | 24 | 18 |

A bit of aeration is needed to unlock the "gorgeous cherry fruit," smoky spice, and complexity. Delicious.
Kitchen Countertop Survivor™ Grade: B
Your notes: _____

| Robert Mondavi Private Selection | PC | T | V |
| Pinot Noir, California | $$ | 24 | 21 |

One of the best varietals in the Mondavi Private Selection line, and true to the grape with its silky berry fruit. It's one of the better Pinots at this price point.
Kitchen Countertop Survivor™ Grade: B+
Your notes: _____

| Robert Sinskey Los Carneros | PC | T | V |
| Pinot Noir, California | $$$$ | 26 | 23 |

The beloved-by-my-tasters Sinskey style emphasizes oak, along with spicy, supple, dark berry fruit
Kitchen Countertop Survivor™ Grade: B
Your notes: _____

Price Ranges: **$** = $12 or less; **$$** = $12.01–20; **$$$** = $20.01–35; **$$$$** = > $35
Kitchen Fridge/Countertop Survivor™ Grades: *Avg.* = a "one-day wine," tastes noticeably less fresh the next day; *B* = holds its freshness for 2–3 days after opening; *B+* = holds *and gets better* over 2–3 days after opening; *A* = a 3- to 4-day "freshness window"; *A+* = holds *and gets better* over 3–4 days

Rochioli Pinot Noir   PC   T   V
California $$$$ 27   20

Simply one of the greatest CA PNs made, with a scent of vanilla, pure cherry fruit, mineral finish, and *very* subtle oak.

Kitchen Countertop Survivor™ Grade: A

Your notes: _____

Saintsbury Carneros Pinot Noir   PC   T   V
California $$$ 23   20

This "Carneros stalwart" is all about elegance: cranberry, rhubarb, spice scents and flavors, sleek texture, and an "endless finish."

Kitchen Countertop Survivor™ Grade: B+

Your notes: _____

Sanford Pinot Noir   PC   T   V
California $$$ 27   22

This Santa Barbara pioneer still makes one of the region's most characterful PNs, with exotic strawberry-rhubarb fruit touched with a meaty-smoky scent, and satin-smooth texture.

Kitchen Countertop Survivor™ Grade: B

Your notes: _____

Sea Smoke Botella Pinot Noir   PC   T   V
California $$$ 24   26

Watch this PN specialist—the rookie scores for this Guide newcomer are justified. The incredible fruit intensity—spiced cherry, strawberry-rhubarb—and earthy complexity are exactly what PN lovers are looking for.

Kitchen Countertop Survivor™ Grade: B

Your notes: _____

Sebastiani Sonoma County Pinot   PC   T   V
Noir, California $$ X   X

✗ Like Sebastiani's other wines in the *Guide,* a price/value star. This PN's got great varietal character, sleek minerally-pomegranate-strawberry compote flavors, spicy nose.

Kitchen Countertop Survivor™ Grade: B

Your notes: _____

Siduri Pinot Noir   PC   T   V
California $$$ 23   20

Among the "best made" PNs in CA but in a unique,

high-impact style with a heady meaty-gaminess and big plum fruit.

Kitchen Countertop Survivor™ Grade: B

Your notes: _____

Smoking Loon Pinot Noir	PC	T	V
California	$	18	24

Budget PN with character: a hint of herbal-spice in the scent, and lovely strawberry fruit flavor.

Kitchen Countertop Survivor™ Grade: Avg

Your notes: _____

Sokol-Blosser Reserve Pinot Noir	PC	T	V
Oregon	$$$$	28	26

I love this winery's distinctive PN style: pomegranate and sun-dried tomato notes, with a savory herbal smokiness.

Kitchen Countertop Survivor™ Grade: B

Your notes: _____

Solaris Pinot Noir	PC	T	V
California	$	24	27

Carneros PN at the $ pice level? With a "fruity" style that pairs "with almost anything," it's hard to go wrong with this one.

Kitchen Countertop Survivor™ Grade: B

Your notes: _____

Steele Mendocino Pinot Noir	PC	T	V
California	$$$	18	18

I'm a bigger fan than my tasting panel, because I love PN in this style: heady-gamy-savory-pomegranate. Very distinctive.

Kitchen Countertop Survivor™ Grade: B+

Your notes: _____

Truchard Pinot Noir	PC	T	V
California	$$$	X	X

✗ I love the raspberry tea and mineral scents, and

Price Ranges: **$** = $12 or less; **$$** = $12.01–20; **$$$** = $20.01–35; **$$$$** = > $35

Kitchen Fridge/Countertop Survivor™ Grades: *Avg.* = a "one-day wine," tastes noticeably less fresh the next day; *B* = holds its freshness for 2–3 days after opening; *B+* = holds *and gets better* over 2–3 days after opening; *A* = a 3- to 4-day "freshness window"; *A+* = holds *and gets better* over 3–4 days

especially the satiny texture, of this always-reliable Carneros Pinot.

Kitchen Countertop Survivor™ Grade: B

Your notes: _____

| Wild Horse Pinot Noir | PC | T | V |
| California | $$$ | 23 | 20 |

The cherry-cola aromas and plump berry fruit typical of Santa Barbara Pinot are in abundance, but the price has inched up.

Kitchen Countertop Survivor™ Grade: B

Your notes: _____

| Willakenzie Willamette Valley | PC | T | V |
| Pinot Noir, Oregon | $$$ | 24 | 21 |

☺ This wine is tasty, elegant, and a value for this quality, with "luscious black cherry fruit" and "lovely cedar and herbal nuances."

Kitchen Countertop Survivor™ Grade: B

Your notes: _____

| Willamette Valley Vineyards Pinot | PC | T | V |
| Noir, Oregon | $$ | 23 | 21 |

This winery delivers consistent quality every year in a cherry-and-spice-scented style that's subtle and doesn't hit you over the head with too much wood.

Kitchen Countertop Survivor™ Grade: Avg

Your notes: _____

| Willamette Valley Vineyards | PC | T | V |
| Reserve Pinot Noir, Oregon | $$$ | 23 | 21 |

My tasters "could drink it every day if it cost less," though the consensus is that for the price the "smooth, fruity" "soft tannins" character with "a little spice" offers a lot.

Kitchen Countertop Survivor™ Grade: B

Your notes: _____

| Williams-Selyem Hirsch Vineyard | PC | T | V |
| Pinot Noir, California | $$$$ | 29 | 24 |

"Expensive, but so worth it" is the consensus for this earthy cherry-vanilla-cinnamon PN that's "one of the best made."

Kitchen Countertop Survivor™ Grade: B

Your notes: _____

Williams-Selyem Pinot Noir	PC	T	V
Sonoma Coast, California	$$$$	26	20

"Pricey" but "great," though some tasters note it's "not legendary" as it once was. Still, I've found the wine's benchmark quality—with earthy tea leaf–dried spice scents and pure, ripe cherry fruit—continues to endure.
Kitchen Countertop Survivor™ Grade: B

Your notes: _____

Chianti and Sangiovese

Category Profile: Remember the days when "Chianti" meant those kitschy straw-covered bottles? Tuscany's signature red has come a long way in quality since then, pulling much of the Italian wine world with it. But let me clear up some understandable confusion about the labels and styles. As quality has improved, Chianti has "morphed" into three tiers of wine—varietal Sangiovese (*san-joe-VAY-zay*), labeled with the grape name; traditional Chianti in a range of styles; and the luxury tier, which includes top regional wines like Brunello, and the so-called "Super Tuscan" reds. Many of the major Tuscan wineries produce wines in all three categories. The basic Sangioveses largely populate the one-dollar-sign price tier, and some offer good value. (Most are, in my opinion, just "red wine" without a lot of character.) Chianti itself now spans the entire price and quality spectrum from budget quaff to boutique collectible, with the top-quality *classico* and *riserva* versions worthy of aging in the cellar. Finally, the Super Tuscans emerged because wineries wanted creative license to use international grapes outside the traditional Chianti "recipe" (and, I guess, with fantasy names like Summus, Sassicaia, and Luce, poetic license, too!). What they all have in common is that Italian "zest"—savory

Price Ranges: **$** = $12 or less; **$$** = $12.01–20; **$$$** = $20.01–35; **$$$$** = > $35

Kitchen Fridge/Countertop Survivor™ Grades: *Avg.* = a "one-day wine," tastes noticeably less fresh the next day; *B* = holds its freshness for 2–3 days after opening; *B+* = holds *and gets better* over 2–3 days after opening; *A* = a 3- to 4-day "freshness window"; *A+* = holds *and gets better* over 3–4 days

rustic spice in the scent, plus vibrant acidity—and international sophistication from the use of French oak barrels for aging and some French grapes (like Cab and Merlot) for blending. The wines are often cellar-worthy and nearly always pricey.

Serve: Room temperature (the varietal Sangioveses are also nice with a light chill); the "bigger" wines—classicos, riservas, and Super Tuscans—benefit from aeration (pour into the glass and swirl, or decant into a pitcher or carafe with plenty of air space).

When: Any food occasion, from snack to supper to celebration.

With: Especially great wherever tomato sauce, cheese, olive oil, or savory herbs (rosemary, basil, oregano) are present.

In: An all-purpose wineglass or larger-bowled red wine stem.

	PC	T	V
Antinori (Marchese) (*ahn-tee-NORE-ee mar-KAY-zee*) **Chianti Classico Riserva, Italy**	$$$	24	21

This wine's intensity, classic strawberry fruit, tannic grip, and peppery spice shine through now, but will also reward aging.
Kitchen Countertop Survivor™ Grade: B+
Your notes: _____

	PC	T	V
Atlas Peak Sangiovese California	$$	23	19

Although it doesn't taste like an Italian wine, this Sangiovese has "good varietal character" with "bright cherry fruit" and mouthwatering acidity.
Kitchen Countertop Survivor™ Grade: B+
Your notes: _____

	PC	T	V
Banfi Brunello di Montalcino Italy	$$$$	24	19

The scores slipped, I think because this wine needs some bottle age to show the potential. It's still got palate-coating tannin and dense fig and mocha flavors.
Kitchen Countertop Survivor™ Grade: A
Your notes: _____

Castello di Brolio Chianti Classico   PC   T   V
Italy $$ 22   22

Bring this if you're invited to dinner; it's got the spice, zing, and fruit to go with any food and please a lot of palates.

Kitchen Countertop Survivor™ Grade: B
Your notes: _____

Castello di Gabbiano Chianti   PC   T   V
Classico, Italy $ 21   20

A soft, light Chianti, with red cherry flavors and spicy nuances that "can't be beat for the price."

Kitchen Countertop Survivor™ Grade: B
Your notes: _____

Castello di Gabbiano Chianti   PC   T   V
Classico Riserva, Italy $$$ 24   19

☺ My tasters call it "textbook Chianti Classico Riserva," with a cornucopia of red fruit, lively acidity, and a nice tug of tannin. They point out "it's gotten pricey," too.

Kitchen Countertop Survivor™ Grade: B
Your notes: _____

Castello di Volpaia (*cass-TELL-oh*   PC   T   V
***dee vole-PYE-uh*) Chianti Classico** $$$ 23   18
Riserva, Italy

The spice, earth, leather, and fig fruit are "worth the price." Pour glasses ahead to open up the scent and flavors.

Kitchen Countertop Survivor™ Grade: A
Your notes: _____

Cecchi (*CHECK-ee*) Chianti   PC   T   V
Italy $ 23   21

A "basic Chianti," but at this price the "nice flavors" (dried cranberry and savory spice) are great for "pizza takeout."

Kitchen Countertop Survivor™ Grade: Avg
Your notes: _____

Price Ranges: **$** = $12 or less; **$$** = $12.01–20; **$$$** = $20.01–35; **$$$$** = > $35

Kitchen Fridge/Countertop Survivor™ Grades: *Avg.* = a "one-day wine," tastes noticeably less fresh the next day; *B* = holds its freshness for 2–3 days after opening; *B+* = holds *and gets better* over 2–3 days after opening; *A* = a 3- to 4-day "freshness window"; *A+* = holds *and gets better* over 3–4 days

Cecchi Chianti Classico   PC   T   V
Italy $$ 23   20

My tasters "love the quality for the price," and the soft berry fruit, tinged with a bit of spice and dried herbs.

Kitchen Countertop Survivor™ Grade: Avg

Your notes: _____

Felsina (*FELL-see-nuh*) Chianti   PC   T   V
Classico Riserva, Italy $$$ 24   22

This "worth the price," "ageable" Tuscan classic has subtle strawberry-raspberry fruit balanced with savory-earthy notes.

Kitchen Countertop Survivor™ Grade: B+

Your notes: _____

Frescobaldi Nippozano Chianti   PC   T   V
Rufina (*ROO-fin-uh*) Riserva, Italy $$$ 24   29

☺ Though fans say the riserva is hard to find, your search will be rewarded with plenty of ripe plum fruit, balsamic, and peppery nuances.

Kitchen Countertop Survivor™ Grade: B+

Your notes: _____

Monte Antico (*MOHN-tay ann-*   PC   T   V
***TEE-coh*) Toscana, Italy** $ 24   27

Served "by the glass at in-the-know Italian restaurants," because the "plum fruit" and lively spice are "a tasty package" that's "robust but not overpowering" for food.

Kitchen Countertop Survivor™ Grade: B+

Your notes: _____

Nozzole (*NOTES-oh-lay*) Chianti   PC   T   V
Classico Riserva, Italy $$ 24   24

The "rich red plum fruit," "great acidity," and "savory spice" make it "ready to drink" and "great with food."

Kitchen Countertop Survivor™ Grade: A

Your notes: _____

Ornellaia Super Tuscan   PC   T   V
Italy $$$$ 26   18

The "high price" hurts the value score of most Super Tuscans, but for distinctiveness and consistency this one's hard to beat. The sexy vanilla oak is cosmopolitan, while the licorice/balsamic/rosemary/dried-cherry complexity are quintessentially Italian.

Kitchen Countertop Survivor™ Grade: A+

Your notes: _____

Rocca della Macìe (*ROH-cuh dell-eh*) | PC | T | V
mah-CHEE-eh) **Chianti Classico, Italy** | $$ | 22 | 22

The "cherry and blackberry" flavor and "smooth" texture make this great for food, and "good value," too.

Kitchen Countertop Survivor™ Grade: B

Your notes: _____

Ruffino Chianti Classico Riserva | PC | T | V
Ducale (*ri-ZUR-vuh doo-CALL-eh*) | $$$$ | 26 | 22
Gold Label, Italy

One of the most-tasted wines by my panel! The "pricey" refrain endures, but in the same breath as "worth it," thanks to the "wow-level complexity and leathery-ness," and "roasted fig" fruit.

Kitchen Countertop Survivor™ Grade: A+

Your notes: _____

Ruffino Chianti Classico Riserva | PC | T | V
Ducale Tan Label, Italy | $$$ | 26 | 24

"Worth the extra $" over a bargain Chianti because its softness and spicy cranberry fruit "pairs beautifully" with so many foods.

Kitchen Countertop Survivor™ Grade: B

Your notes: _____

Santa Cristina Sangiovese, Antinori | PC | T | V
Italy | $ | 20 | 23

"What a deal" for this "easy to drink for everyday" wine with tangy cranberry fruit and good balance.

Kitchen Countertop Survivor™ Grade: B

Your notes: _____

Selvapiana (*SELL-vuh-pee-AH-nuh*) | PC | T | V
Chianti Rufina, Italy | $$ | 29 | 27

☺ ✓ Wow! My tasters "love" this wine's earthy mushroom and spice scents, bright cherry fruit, and velvety texture. Ages beautifully (5–7 years).

Kitchen Countertop Survivor™ Grade: A

Your notes: _____

Price Ranges: **$** = $12 or less; **$$** = $12.01–20; **$$$** = $20.01–35; **$$$$** = > $35

Kitchen Fridge/Countertop Survivor™ Grades: *Avg.* = a "one-day wine," tastes noticeably less fresh the next day; *B* = holds its freshness for 2–3 days after opening; *B+* = holds *and gets better* over 2–3 days after opening; *A* = a 3- to 4-day "freshness window"; *A+* = holds *and gets better* over 3–4 days

Straccali Chianti	PC	T	V
Italy	$	17	20

"I'd buy it again," say my tasters of this soft, juicy Chianti that's "a bargain for everyday drinking."

Kitchen Countertop Survivor™ Grade: Avg

Your notes: _____

Terrabianca Campaccio Super	PC	T	V
Tuscan, Italy	$$$$	24	22

It's rare to find "value" in the Super Tuscan category, but relative to others, this is—offering "dried fruit," "smoothness," and "a lot of complexity."

Kitchen Countertop Survivor™ Grade: Avg

Your notes: _____

Merlot

Grape Profile: When early nineties news reports linked heart health and moderate red wine drinking, Merlot joined the ranks of go-to wine grapes that inspire instant customer recognition. As with other market-leading varietals like Chardonnay and Cabernet Sauvignon, Merlot can range both in price, from budget to boutique, and in complexity, from soft and simple to "serious." Across the spectrum, Merlot is modeled on the wines from its home region of Bordeaux, France. At the basic level, that means medium

MERLOT'S KISSING COUSINS: If you are looking for something different but similar to Merlot, check out two South American specialties. First, there's Argentina's Malbec (*MAHL-beck*), a red grape originally from Bordeaux. It's similar in body and smoothness to Merlot, with lots of smoky aromatic complexity. Some wineries to look for: Altos Las Hormigas, Navarro Correas, Catena, and Chandon Terrazas. Second, from Chile, try Carmenere (*carmuh-NAIR-eh*), also a Bordeaux import that was originally misidentified as Merlot in many Chilean vineyards. Its smooth texture and plum fruit are complemented by an exotically meaty-smoky scent. Look for Carmeneres from Concha y Toro, Carmen, and Veramonte Primus. Check out the Other Reds for more on these.

body and soft texture, with nice plum and berry fruit flavor. The more ambitious versions have more body, tannin, and fruit concentration and usually a good bit of oakiness in the scent and taste. Washington state, California's Sonoma and Napa regions, and Chile are my favorite growing regions for varietal Merlot. Most Merlot producers follow the Bordeaux practice of blending in some Cabernet Sauvignon (or another of the classic Bordeaux red grapes) to complement and enhance the wines' taste and complexity.

Serve: *Cool* room temperature.

When: With meals, of course; and the basic bottlings are soft enough to enjoy on their own as a cocktail alternative.

With: Anything with which you enjoy red wine, especially cheeses, roasts, fuller-bodied fish, and grilled foods.

In: An all-purpose wineglass or larger-bowled red wine stem.

Barton & Guestier (B&G) Merlot	PC	T	V
France	$	19	20

France is the traditional HQ for Merlot, and my tasters like the style, "cherry cobbler" flavor, and "bargain price" of this one.
Kitchen Countertop Survivor™ Grade: Avg
Your notes: _____

Beringer Bancroft Ranch Merlot	PC	T	V
California	$$$$	27	15

I'm with the tasters who find this "well worth the price"; the incredible dusty-plum/chocolate scents and flavor evolve to velvety tobacco and cedar with age. World-class.
Kitchen Countertop Survivor™ Grade: B+
Your notes: _____

Price Ranges: **$** = $12 or less; **$$** = $12.01–20; **$$$** = $20.01–35; **$$$$** = > $35
Kitchen Fridge/Countertop Survivor™ Grades: *Avg.* = a "one-day wine," tastes noticeably less fresh the next day; *B* = holds its freshness for 2–3 days after opening; *B+* = holds *and gets better* over 2–3 days after opening; *A* = a 3- to 4-day "freshness window"; *A+* = holds *and gets better* over 3–4 days

Beringer Founders' Estate Merlot | PC | T | V
California | $ | 23 | 25

Higher scores reflect that "it's improved—more fruit," namely plum and berry, making for "smooth" everyday drinking.

Kitchen Countertop Survivor™ Grade: B

Your notes: _____

Blackstone Merlot | PC | T | V
California | $$ | 21 | 23

☺ Super scores for one of the most-tasted and "favorite value" wines in the survey. Folks "love the smooth-n-juicy plum" flavor.

Kitchen Countertop Survivor™ Grade: Avg

Your notes: _____

Bogle Merlot | PC | T | V
California | $ | 22 | 24

Another popular brand that's huge with my panel for the "soft cherry flavor" and "awesome value."

Kitchen Countertop Survivor™ Grade: Avg

Your notes: _____

Burgess Merlot | PC | T | V
California | $$$ | 24 | 23

☺ This sophisticated Merlot is deeply complex—chocolate, mint, cedar, and plum scents and flavors. It will cellar well, too.

Kitchen Countertop Survivor™ Grade: B+

Your notes: _____

Casa Lapostolle Classic Merlot | PC | T | V
California | $ | 24 | 25

Plum and cherry flavors and a gentle tug of tannin make this a "good everyday drinking wine for the price."

Kitchen Countertop Survivor™ Grade: Avg

Your notes: _____

Chateau Simard Bordeaux | PC | T | V
France | $$$$ | 28 | 18

My students always love the "incredibly subtle yet complex coffee scent" of this wine. The subtle earth, cedar, and plum fruit, and soft tannins, are textbook St. Emilion (the Bordeaux village where it's grown). It's a great way to try a red with some bottle age, since older vintages are available in the marketplace.

Kitchen Countertop Survivor™ Grade: B+

Your notes: _____

Chateau Souverain Alexander | PC | T | V
Valley Merlot, California | $$ | 24 | 23

Lots of tasters' plaudits for this wine's "exceptional quality for the price." It's got a deep, plummy scent touched with a "wet leaves" earthiness, concentrated, rich fruit on the palate, and a "very long finish."

Kitchen Countertop Survivor™ Grade: B

Your notes: _____

Chateau Ste. Michelle Cold Creek | PC | T | V
Merlot, Washington | $$ | 27 | 26

A chunky wine, loaded with dark plums and figs, coconutty oak, and a hint of herbal character.

Kitchen Countertop Survivor™ Grade: Avg

Your notes: _____

Chateau Ste. Michelle Columbia | PC | T | V
Valley Merlot, Washington | $$ | 20 | 21

This wine's "Bordeaux-style elegance" and smooth plum flavor are reliable year-in and year-out.

Kitchen Countertop Survivor™ Grade: B

Your notes: _____

Chateau Ste. Michelle Indian Wells | PC | T | V
Merlot, Washington | $$ | X | X

✗ A fuller-styled Merlot with mouth-coating dark-berry fruit, and a vanilla and cocoa scent.

Kitchen Countertop Survivor™ Grade: Avg

Your notes: _____

Christian Moueix (*Mwexx*) Merlot | PC | T | V
France | $ | 23 | 26

"Unmistakably Bordeaux," say my tasters—meaning elegant, soft, best when paired with food.

Kitchen Countertop Survivor™ Grade: Avg

Your notes: _____

Price Ranges: **$** = $12 or less; **$$** = $12.01–20; **$$$** = $20.01–35; **$$$$** = > $35

Kitchen Fridge/Countertop Survivor™ Grades: *Avg.* = a "one-day wine," tastes noticeably less fresh the next day; *B* = holds its freshness for 2–3 days after opening; *B+* = holds *and gets better* over 2–3 days after opening; *A* = a 3- to 4-day "freshness window"; *A+* = holds *and gets better* over 3–4 days

Clos du Bois Sonoma Merlot   PC   T   V
California $$ 22   23

Happily, the price has dropped for this very popular bottle that trade buyers call "a must on wine lists." I'm still underwhelmed by the fruit, but out-numbered by the many fans who say it's "yummy."

Kitchen Countertop Survivor™ Grade: Avg

Your notes: _____

Columbia Crest Grand Estates   PC   T   V
Merlot, Washington $ X   X

✗ Merlot is one of Washington's strong suits, and this one is a top choice for the money, with lots of plum fruit, and a vanilla-berry scent.

Kitchen Countertop Survivor™ Grade: B

Your notes: _____

Columbia Crest Two Vines Merlot   PC   T   V
Washington $ 22   28

Check out the value score for this Merlot with subtle plum-berry fruit and earth, in balance. Yum!

Kitchen Countertop Survivor™ Grade: B

Your notes: _____

Columbia Winery Merlot   PC   T   V
Washington $$ 21   22

"Amazing for the money," with succulent berry on the palate, "great structure," and a long finish.

Kitchen Countertop Survivor™ Grade: B+

Your notes: _____

Concha y Toro Frontera Merlot   PC   T   V
Chile $ 21   22

Tasters love the "wonderful blackberry" flavor at "a price that's easy to swallow."

Kitchen Countertop Survivor™ Grade: Avg

Your notes: _____

Dallas Conte Merlot   PC   T   V
Chile $ 26   26

The wood-smoke scent and chunky plum fruit give you a lot of yum for the money.

Kitchen Countertop Survivor™ Grade: Avg

Your notes: _____

Duckhorn Napa Merlot PC T V
California $$$$ 25 20

The full-throttle blackberry fruit, toasty oak, and lush texture are "for lovers of BIG Merlot," who are prepared for the fact that it's "pricey." It remains a CA Merlot benchmark.

Kitchen Countertop Survivor™ Grade: B+

Your notes: _____

Ecco Domani Merlot PC T V
Italy $ 20 20

Scores improved for this budget-priced Italian Merlot with soft plum fruit meant to complement and not overpower a wide range of foods.

Kitchen Countertop Survivor™ Grade: Avg

Your notes: _____

Fetzer Valley Oaks Merlot PC T V
California $ 23 25

Despite the label change from Eagle Peak, it's still among the best basic California Merlots on the market, with "juicy" cherry berry flavors and an impressive survivor grade.

Kitchen Countertop Survivor™ Grade: B

Your notes: _____

Franciscan Oakville Estate Merlot PC T V
California $$$ 28 24

✓ The raves continue to rack up for this quintessential Napa Merlot with lush cherry fruit, plush tannins, and just enough light, toasty oak to give it "layers and layers."

Kitchen Countertop Survivor™ Grade: B

Your notes: _____

Francis Coppola Diamond Series PC T V
Blue Label Merlot, California $$ 24 25

This is textbook California Merlot—plum flavors, soft earthiness, vanilla-scented oak, velvety tannins.

Price Ranges: **$** = $12 or less; **$$** = $12.01–20; **$$$** = $20.01–35; **$$$$** = > $35

Kitchen Fridge/Countertop Survivor™ Grades: *Avg.* = a "one-day wine," tastes noticeably less fresh the next day; *B* = holds its freshness for 2–3 days after opening; *B+* = holds *and gets better* over 2–3 days after opening; *A* = a 3- to 4-day "freshness window"; *A+* = holds *and gets better* over 3–4 days

Kitchen Countertop Survivor™ Grade: Avg
Your notes: _____

Frei Brothers Reserve Merlot   PC   T   V
California $$ 21   20
Plum-berry fruit, subtle oak, and tannins, "for a
decent price."
Kitchen Countertop Survivor™ Grade: B
Your notes: _____

Frog's Leap Merlot   PC   T   V
California $$$$ 23   18
Though it's expensive, devotees (me among them)
find the big fig and cassis fruit and complexity worth
the price.
Kitchen Countertop Survivor™ Grade: A
Your notes: _____

Gallo of Sonoma Merlot   PC   T   V
California $ 24   27
This top-selling Merlot has become increasingly oaky.
Still, the "very luscious" plum jam flavor pleases fans
of big reds, as does the price!
Kitchen Countertop Survivor™ Grade: A
Your notes: _____

Kendall-Jackson Vintner's Reserve   PC   T   V
Merlot, California $$ 20   20
This is Merlot in the luscious style—redolent with
black cherry flavor and smooth texture.
Kitchen Countertop Survivor™ Grade: B+
Your notes: _____

L'Ecole No. 41 Walla Walla Valley   PC   T   V
Merlot, Washington $$$ 24   22
Although it's "not cheap," there's "value for the
quality" in the form of deep berry flavor and exotic
coconutty oak that's not over the top. Yum!
Kitchen Countertop Survivor™ Grade: Avg
Your notes: _____

Lindemans Bin 40 Merlot   PC   T   V
Australia $ 21   22
At this price, it's no wonder there's a huge fan club for
this wine's "easy drinking" plump plum and berry fruit
flavor.

Kitchen Countertop Survivor™ Grade: Avg

Your notes: _____

The Little Penguin Merlot	PC	T	V
Australia	$	X	X

✗ Another soft and quaffable competitor to Yellow Tail (I think it beats it with the soft berry flavor).

Kitchen Countertop Survivor™ Grade: Avg

Your notes: _____

Markham Merlot	PC	T	V
California	$$$	24	21

Still a value compared to other high-end California Merlots, with rich plum fruit, smooth texture, and soft oak.

Kitchen Countertop Survivor™ Grade: B+

Your notes: _____

Meridian Merlot	PC	T	V
California	$$	19	19

An "easy-drinking" Merlot whose juicy flavor reminds me of black cherry Jell-O, balanced with a nice tang of acidity.

Kitchen Countertop Survivor™ Grade: B+

Your notes: _____

Montes Alpha "M"	PC	T	V
Chile	$$$$	25	22

With its huge chocolately-plum fruit, tasted blind we thought this mostly-Merlot "super Chilean" was a big-time Napa Meritage wine.

Kitchen Countertop Survivor™ Grade: B

Your notes: _____

Montes Merlot	PC	T	V
Chile	$	22	20

Montes remains a standard-bearer among Chilean Merlots: concentrated dark-berry flavors and cedar and earth scents—all on an elegant frame.

Price Ranges: **$** = $12 or less; **$$** = $12.01–20; **$$$** = $20.01–35; **$$$$** = > $35

Kitchen Fridge/Countertop Survivor™ Grades: **Avg.** = a "one-day wine," tastes noticeably less fresh the next day; *B* = holds its freshness for 2–3 days after opening; *B+* = holds *and gets better* over 2–3 days after opening; *A* = a 3- to 4-day "freshness window"; *A+* = holds *and gets better* over 3–4 days

Kitchen Countertop Survivor™ Grade: B
Your notes: _____

Penfolds Rawson's Retreat   PC   T   V
Merlot, Australia $ X   X
✗ This juicy berry jam–flavored Merlot is great for
everyday sipping and supping.

Kitchen Countertop Survivor™ Grade: Avg
Your notes: _____

Ravenswood Vintners Blend Merlot   PC   T   V
California $ 21   21
It's got "jammy, smooth" plum and cherry fruit, but
some say there are "better Merlots for the price."

Kitchen Countertop Survivor™ Grade: B+
Your notes: _____

R.H. Phillips Toasted Head Merlot   PC   T   V
California $$ 18   19
The extra toasting of the oak (toasting the "heads" or
ends of the barrel, as well as the sides) gives a spicy-
vanilla scent to this plummy Merlot.

Kitchen Countertop Survivor™ Grade: Avg
Your notes: _____

Rodney Strong Sonoma Merlot   PC   T   V
California $$ 25   24
"A big cut above other Merlots at this price" say my
tasters, who love the "cedar, spice, plum, berry, and
earth" qualities. Yum!

Kitchen Countertop Survivor™ Grade: Avg
Your notes: _____

Rutherford Hill Merlot   PC   T   V
California $$ 19   20
Scores dipped for this once-benchmark California
Merlot, likely because it now seems "overpriced"
given the light fruit and flavor.

Kitchen Countertop Survivor™ Grade: Avg
Your notes: _____

Sebastiani Sonoma County   PC   T   V
Merlot, California $$ 24   18
Where so many Merlots have become mundane, this
one has the deep and layered plum fruit and plump
texture of classic CA Merlot.

Kitchen Countertop Survivor™ Grade: Avg
Your notes: _____

Shafer Merlot   PC   T   V

Shafer Merlot	PC	T	V
California	$$$$	28	18

"Pricey but very tasty" sums it up for this rich, classy wine in the lush, powerful "cult" style (meaning huge dark-berry fruit and lavish vanilla-oak).
Kitchen Countertop Survivor™ Grade: B+
Your notes: _____

Stag's Leap Wine Cellars Napa	PC	T	V
Merlot, California	$$$$	26	24

"Dark and full of berry," earth, mocha, and mint, plus great balance.
Kitchen Countertop Survivor™ Grade: B
Your notes: _____

St. Francis Sonoma Merlot	PC	T	V
California	$$$	25	22

"Excellent," "consistent," "very blackberry," and "rich" are just some of the plaudits for this wine that saw a price drop in some markets. Yay!
Kitchen Countertop Survivor™ Grade: B
Your notes: _____

Sterling Vineyards Napa Merlot	PC	T	V
California	$$$	25	17

Mixed reviews! Some say "pricey" (hence the value score) and "too oaky," others say the "smooth, berry" style is worth it for a "special night."
Kitchen Countertop Survivor™ Grade: B+
Your notes: _____

Sutter Home Merlot	PC	T	V
California	$	19	23

The "always consistent" soft plum flavor is a "great surprise" at this price.
Kitchen Countertop Survivor™ Grade: Avg
Your notes: _____

Price Ranges: **$** = $12 or less; **$$** = $12.01–20; **$$$** = $20.01–35; **$$$$** = > $35

Kitchen Fridge/Countertop Survivor™ Grades: *Avg.* = a "one-day wine," tastes noticeably less fresh the next day; *B* = holds its freshness for 2–3 days after opening; *B+* = holds *and gets better* over 2–3 days after opening; *A* = a 3- to 4-day "freshness window"; *A+* = holds *and gets better* over 3–4 days

Swanson Vineyards Merlot	PC	T	V
California	$$$	27	18

This "big" and "luscious" Merlot with lavish vanilla-scented oak is "full of complexity" and "well worth the money."

Kitchen Countertop Survivor™ *Grade: Avg*

Your notes: _____

Two Tone Farm Merlot	PC	T	V
California	$$	X	X

✗ Napa Merlot—with real plum and cocoa character and plump tannis—is hard to come by at the price, so check this one out.

Kitchen Countertop Survivor™ *Grade: Avg*

Your notes: _____

Woodbridge (Robert Mondavi)	PC	T	V
Merlot, California	$	21	22

As pros noted, "the now-fruitier style is what soft, sippable red wine fans want."

Kitchen Countertop Survivor™ *Grade: Avg*

Your notes: _____

Yellow Tail Merlot	PC	T	V
Australia	$	18	21

A soft, easy-drinking Merlot that's priced right for everyday sipping.

Kitchen Countertop Survivor™ *Grade: Avg*

Your notes: _____

Cabernet Sauvignon and Blends

Grape Profile: Merlot may have been the *mucho*-trendy red of the late 1990s, but Cabernet Sauvignon remains a top-selling red varietal wine, I think for good reason. Specifically, Cabernet (for short) grows well virtually all over the wine world and gives excellent quality and flavor at every price level, from steal to splurge. Its flavor intensity and body can vary, based on the wine's quality level—from uncomplicated everyday styles to the superintense boutique and collector bottlings. Nearly every major wine-growing country produces Cabernets across that spectrum, but the most famous and plentiful sources are Bordeaux in France, California (especially Sonoma and Napa), Washington state, and Italy on the high end with its Super Tuscan versions. I think Chile shines in the mid-priced category, with some two-dollar-sign wines offering $$$ Cabernet character. Classically, that means a scent and taste of dark berries (blueberry, blackberry), plus notes of spice, earth, cocoa, cedar, and even mint that can be very layered and complex in the best wines. It also means medium to very full body and often more tannin—that bit of a tongue-gripping sensation that one of my waiters once described, perfectly I think, as "a slip-cover for the tongue, ranging from terry cloth to suede to velvet," depending on the wine in question. Oakiness, either a little or a lot, depending on the growing region and price category, is also a common Cabernet feature. Combined, these can make for a primo mouthful of a wine, which surely explains why Cabernet is king of collectible wines.

A note about "blends": As described previously for Merlot, Cabernet Sauvignon wines follow the Bordeaux blending model, with one or more of the traditional Bordeaux red grapes—Merlot, Cabernet Franc, Petit Verdot, and Malbec—blended in for balance and complexity. Australia pioneered blending Cabernet Sauvignon with Shiraz—a delicious combination that the wine buying market has embraced. Those blends are listed either here or in the Shiraz section, according to which of the two grapes is dominant in the blend (it will be listed first on the label, too).

Serve: Cool room temperature; the fuller-bodied styles benefit from aeration—pour into the glass a bit ahead of time or decant into a carafe (but if you forget, don't sweat it; if you care to, swirling the glass does help).

When: With your favorite red wine meals, but the everyday bottlings are soft enough for cocktail-hour sipping.

With: Anything you'd serve alongside a red; especially complements beef, lamb, goat cheese and hard

Price Ranges: **$** = $12 or less; **$$** = $12.01–20; **$$$** = $20.01–35; **$$$$** = > $35
Kitchen Fridge/Countertop Survivor™ Grades: ***Avg.*** = a "one-day wine," tastes noticeably less fresh the next day; ***B*** = holds its freshness for 2–3 days after opening; ***B+*** = holds *and gets better* over 2–3 days after opening; ***A*** = a 3- to 4-day "freshness window"; ***A+*** = holds *and gets better* over 3–4 days

cheeses, pesto sauce, and dishes scented with basil, rosemary, sage, or oregano.

In: An all-purpose wineglass or larger-bowled red wine stem.

Alice White Cabernet Shiraz	PC	T	V
Australia	$	23	23

My favorite of the Alice White reds, this "yummy budget choice" has "nice plum fruit" and a touch of cedar in the scent.

Kitchen Countertop Survivor™ *Grade: B*

Your notes: _____

Arrowood Cabernet Sauvignon	PC	T	V
Sonoma County, California	$$$$	26	23

A "favorite" that's always true to the classic Sonoma Cab style, with wild blackberry fruit, toasty-vanilla oak, and a long finish.

Kitchen Countertop Survivor™ *Grade: B*

Your notes: _____

Beaulieu Vineyard (BV) Coastal	PC	T	V
Cabernet Sauvignon, California	$	21	22

"Especially for the price," most tasters found it "pretty good," in the lighter, soft, everyday style.

Kitchen Countertop Survivor™ *Grade: Avg*

Your notes: _____

Beaulieu (BV) George de Latour	PC	T	V
Private Reserve Cabernet	$$$$	25	20
Sauvignon, California			

"Amazing" say my tasters who've enjoyed this wine's licorice, cedar, black cherry, and mineral aromas, all said to be typical of the region's "Rutherford Dust" soil. For tannin-phobes, it's smoother than other blue-chip Napa Cabs, too.

Kitchen Countertop Survivor™ *Grade: B*

Your notes: _____

Beaulieu Vineyard (BV) Rutherford	PC	T	V
Cabernet Sauvignon, California	$$$	24	22

This has the "typical Napa Cab" style of jammy Cabernet flavor, "big oak," and tannins: "complex and rich," but "used to be more affordable."

Kitchen Countertop Survivor™ *Grade: B*

Your notes: _____

Beringer Founders' Estate   PC   T   V
Cabernet Sauvignon, California $ 23   23

This is the best red in the Founders' line, offering "blackberries, currant . . . nice body, great value."

Kitchen Countertop Survivor™ Grade: B

Your notes: _____

Beringer Knights Valley Cabernet   PC   T   V
Sauvignon, California $$$ 24   23

The chewy cassis fruit with vanilla-scented oak are "as complex and balanced as a wine for twice the price." Many on my panel urge: pour or "decant and let it sit" for a few minutes to open up. It "gets better" with age, too.

Kitchen Countertop Survivor™ Grade: A

Your notes: _____

Beringer Private Reserve Cabernet   PC   T   V
Sauvignon, California $$$$ 27   18

This wine's amazing aromas of cedar, olives, tobacco, and black currants, plus beautiful balance and ageability (5–10 years depending on the vintage), make it one of Napa's blue-chip Cabs.

Kitchen Countertop Survivor™ Grade: B

Your notes: _____

Black Opal Cabernet Sauvignon   PC   T   V
Australia $ 22   26

"You couldn't possibly find more for the money," as the T/V scores affirm. It's "juicy, yummy," and "everywhere."

Kitchen Countertop Survivor™ Grade: B

Your notes: _____

Black Opal Cabernet/Merlot   PC   T   V
Australia $ 21   21

This Cab/Merlot blend from Australia "goes with any-thing" and has "pretty berry" flavors.

Kitchen Countertop Survivor™ Grade: B

Your notes: _____

Price Ranges: **$** = $12 or less; **$$** = $12.01–20; **$$$** = $20.01–35; **$$$$** = > $35

Kitchen Fridge/Countertop Survivor™ Grades: *Avg.* = a "one-day wine," tastes noticeably less fresh the next day; *B* = holds its fresh-ness for 2–3 days after opening; *B+* = holds *and gets better* over 2–3 days after opening; *A* = a 3- to 4-day "freshness window"; *A+* = holds *and gets better* over 3–4 days

Blackstone Cabernet	PC	T	V
Sauvignon, California	$$	21	24

"Inexpensive for what you get"—namely, "delicious" blackberry and cocoa scents and flavors.

Kitchen Countertop Survivor™ Grade: B

Your notes: _____

Cain Cuvee Bordeaux Style Red	PC	T	V
California	$$$	26	21

A "wow" that "wins hands down" versus more expensive CA Bordeaux style blends. Beautiful cassis fruit and cedar-oak aromas that "command your attention."

Kitchen Countertop Survivor™ Grade: A

Your notes: _____

Cakebread Napa Cabernet	PC	T	V
Sauvignon, California	$$$$	24	21

The "cedar, blackberry, and anise" complexity drew raves for this "great name from Napa." Compared to "other big CA Cabs," the value score rose, too.

Kitchen Countertop Survivor™ Grade: B+

Your notes: _____

Casa Lapostolle Cuvee Alexandre	PC	T	V
Cabernet Sauvignon, Chile	$$	26	26

The cedar, vanilla, cinnamon, dark dusky fruit, and earth give you "depth at an unbeatable price."

Kitchen Countertop Survivor™ Grade: Avg

Your notes: _____

Caymus Napa Cabernet	PC	T	V
Sauvignon, California	$$$$	27	21

One of the most sought-after Napa Cabs: jam-packed with huge dark fruit and strapping tannins that make it extremely cellar-worthy. Due to the price, my tasters peg it as a "special occasion wine."

Kitchen Countertop Survivor™ Grade: B

Your notes: _____

Chateau Clerc-Milon Bordeaux	PC	T	V
France	$$$$	27	18

A fairly priced, classic Bordeaux with a purebred Rothschild lineage? *Yes!* Needs age, but the delicious vanilla, cedar, wild/sour berry, and baking spice scents are worth the wait.

Kitchen Countertop Survivor™ Grade: B

Your notes: _____

Chateau Cos d'Estournel (coss   PC   T   V
dess-tur-NELL) Bordeaux, France $$$$ 26   24

Dusty cedar, cassis, sweet tobacco, anise, and coffee bean just begin to describe this wine's complexity. Ages 25+ years in great vintages (2000, for example).

Kitchen Countertop Survivor™ Grade: B

Your notes: _____

Chateau Duhart-Milon Rothschild   PC   T   V
Bordeaux, France $$$ 26   21

A favorite of my wine-and-food-pairing students, who love the wine's rhubarb, cedar, leather, and roasted coffee bean character, particularly with braised short ribs or other hearty meats.

Kitchen Countertop Survivor™ Grade: B

Your notes: _____

Chateau Greysac Bordeaux   PC   T   V
France $$ 23   23

The cedar and earth scent and smooth plum fruit add up to "excellent value Bordeaux" that's great "with cheese."

Kitchen Countertop Survivor™ Grade: B

Your notes: _____

Chateau Gruaud-Larose (*GROO-oh*   PC   T   V
***lah-ROSE*) Bordeaux, France** $$$$ 26   21

☺ It's "pricey," but still more affordable than many Bordeaux of comparable quality, with palate-coating tannins, dark fruit, cedar-coffee scents, and a long finish.

Kitchen Countertop Survivor™ Grade: A

Your notes: _____

Chateau Lagrange Bordeaux   PC   T   V
France $$$ 24   18

One of my favorites of the classified Bordeaux, for its textbook dusty, blackcurrant, and roasted coffee character at a doable price.

Kitchen Countertop Survivor™ Grade: B+

Your notes: _____

Price Ranges: **$** = $12 or less; **$$** = $12.01–20; **$$$** = $20.01–35; **$$$$** = > $35

Kitchen Fridge/Countertop Survivor™ Grades: *Avg.* = a "one-day wine," tastes noticeably less fresh the next day; *B* = holds its freshness for 2–3 days after opening; *B+* = holds *and gets better* over 2–3 days after opening; *A* = a 3- to 4-day "freshness window"; *A+* = holds *and gets better* over 3–4 days

Chateau Larose-Trintaudon   PC   T   V
(*la-ROSE TRENT-oh-DOAN*) $$ 21   22
Bordeaux, France

This wine has rich, round tannins, deep plum fruit, and a drink-it-young suppleness.

Kitchen Countertop Survivor™ Grade: A+

Your notes: _____

Chateau Les Ormes de Pez (lays   PC   T   V
ORM duh PEZZ) Bordeaux, France $$$ 27   24

The "cassis and earthy" (autumn leaves and wet gravel) character gives you classic Bordeaux at a manageable price.

Kitchen Countertop Survivor™ Grade: B

Your notes: _____

Chateau Lynch-Bages Bordeaux   PC   T   V
France $$$$ 27   20

A "deal and ready to drink" in so-so vintages, and always true to its style: cedar and lead-pencil scent, tightly packed but luscious cassis fruit, velvety-powerful texture.

Kitchen Countertop Survivor™ Grade: B+

Your notes: _____

Chateau Meyney Bordeaux   PC   T   V
France $$$ 18   18

You can't get more bang for your Bordeaux buck than this. The wine's smoky, dark cherry cedar aromas will intensify with age; or decant to enjoy it now.

Kitchen Countertop Survivor™ Grade: B

Your notes: _____

Chateau Montelena Cabernet   PC   T   V
Sauvignon, California $$$$ 25   22

One of the great Napa Cabs! Dense with blackberry fruit, licorice, and vanilla scents in youth, evolving amazingly to cigar box and dried fig with age.

Kitchen Countertop Survivor™ Grade: Avg

Your notes: _____

Chateau Prieure-Lichine   PC   T   V
Bordeaux, France $$$ 24   21

Priced like "a poor man's Bordeaux" because quality suffered for a while, but now it's back on form, with "round and approachable" cassis and plum fruit even in youth.

Kitchen Countertop Survivor™ Grade: Avg

Your notes: _____

Chateau Souverain Alexander Valley	**PC**	**T**	**V**
Cabernet Sauvignon, California	**$$$**	**24**	**18**

"Cellar-worthy Cab" at this price is a rarity. It's got powerful fig fruit and balanced tannins and oak.

Kitchen Countertop Survivor™ Grade: B

Your notes: _____

Chat. Ste. Michelle Columbia Valley	**PC**	**T**	**V**
Cabernet Sauvignon, Washington	**$$**	**22**	**22**

This Cabernet is one of Washington's best—especially for the price—with intense black cherry aromas, concentrated blackberry flavors, and a toasty-oak finish.

Kitchen Countertop Survivor™ Grade: A

Your notes: _____

Chateau St. Jean Cinq Cepages	**PC**	**T**	**V**
(*sank seh-PAHJH*) Cabernet	**$$$$**	**28**	**24**
Blend, California			

☺ The full-throttle blackberry fruit, earthy-smoky-spice scent, and power-with-elegance make this one of my favorite CA wines, period.

Kitchen Countertop Survivor™ Grade: B+

Your notes: _____

Clos du Bois Marlstone	**PC**	**T**	**V**
California	**$$$$**	**24**	**24**

Lots of complexity, with a mineral, briary scent and layers of intensity—black olive, black cherry, tobacco, vanilla.

Kitchen Countertop Survivor™ Grade: B

Your notes: _____

Price Ranges: **$** = $12 or less; **$$** = $12.01–20; **$$$** = $20.01–35; **$$$$** = > $35

Kitchen Fridge/Countertop Survivor™ Grades: *Avg.* = a "one-day wine," tastes noticeably less fresh the next day; *B* = holds its freshness for 2–3 days after opening; *B+* = holds *and gets better* over 2–3 days after opening; *A* = a 3- to 4-day "freshness window"; *A+* = holds *and gets better* over 3–4 days

Clos du Bois Sonoma Cabernet Sauvignon, California PC $$ T 23 V 21

A few tasters called it "light" and "pricey," and the scores of this typically solid Cabernet dropped, perhaps because its wild berry, anise, and eucalyptus character are increasingly overpowered by oak.

Kitchen Countertop Survivor™ Grade: Avg

Your notes: _____

Columbia Crest Grand Estates Cabernet Sauvignon, Washington PC $ T 23 V 26

☺ "Delicious" and "a 'wow' at this price" sums up the raves for this plush blackberry-and-earth Cab.

Kitchen Countertop Survivor™ Grade: B+

Your notes: _____

Concha y Toro Casillero del Diablo Cabernet Sauvignon, Chile PC $ T 22 V 24

A lot of Cab character for the money, with dusty-blackberry, cocoa, and cedar, plus a meaty gaminess typical of Chile.

Kitchen Countertop Survivor™ Grade: Avg

Your notes: _____

Concha y Toro Don Melchor Cabernet Sauvignon Reserva, Chile PC $$$$ T 23 V 23

☺ This is one of my favorite wines in the world and is surely one of the best wines coming out of the entire Southern Hemisphere. The velvety texture, mocha-coffee and cedar scent, and the incredibly dense but elegant blackberry fruit have fooled great palates into thinking it was top Bordeaux. 'Nuff said.

Kitchen Countertop Survivor™ Grade: A

Your notes: _____

Dry Creek Vineyard Cabernet Sauvignon, California PC $$ T 20 V 21

Tasters call this wild berry and spice Cab a "value" and "tasty," though some find the finish a little short.

Kitchen Countertop Survivor™ Grade: Avg

Your notes: _____

Dynamite Cabernet Sauvignon, California PC $$ T 24 V 23

This wine offers classic California Cabernet character—cassis fruit, vanilla scent—at a good price.

Your notes: _____

Escudo Rojo Cabernet Blend,   PC   T   V
Baron Philippe de Rothschild, Chile $$ 24   26
☺ My students love the complexity of this wine—
meaty-smokiness, dried spices, leather, coffee, figs,
mint—on an elegant, balanced frame.
Kitchen Countertop Survivor™ Grade: B+
Your notes: _____

Estancia Alexander Valley Red   PC   T   V
Meritage, California $$$ 27   27
☺ ✓ This wine's elegance and cedar/mint/mocha
scent and blackberry fruit are amazingly complex. A
"wow" for the price.
Kitchen Countertop Survivor™ Grade: B
Your notes: _____

Estancia Cabernet Sauvignon   PC   T   V
California $$ 23   24
"Real-deal California Cabernet" flavor—mint and
cassis—at a "good price" makes this a winner.
Kitchen Countertop Survivor™ Grade: B+
Your notes: _____

Far Niente Cabernet Sauvignon   PC   T   V
California $$$$ 25   19
This is Cab in the classic, classy Napa style—
big fruit and body minus the over-the-top oak
and alcohol that was trendy in the 1990s. The
layers of earth, leaves, smoke, and cedar enrich
with age.
Kitchen Countertop Survivor™ Grade: A
Your notes: _____

Price Ranges: **$** – $12 or less; **$$** = $12.01–20; **$$$** = $20.01–35;
$$$$ = > $35
Kitchen Fridge/Countertop Survivor™ Grades: *Avg.* = a "one-day
wine," tastes noticeably less fresh the next day; *B* = holds its fresh-
ness for 2–3 days after opening; *B+* = holds *and gets better* over 2–3
days after opening; *A* = a 3- to 4-day "freshness window"; *A+* =
holds *and gets better* over 3–4 days

Ferrari-Carano Siena Sonoma	PC	T	V
County, California	$$$	28	26

This is Cabernet blended with Sangiovese like a Super Tuscan wine, so you get the leathery-spiciness of the Italian grape, with "huge berry ripeness" from the Sonoma sun.

Kitchen Countertop Survivor™ Grade: A

Your notes: _____

Fetzer Valley Oaks Cabernet	PC	T	V
Sauvignon, California	$	20	24

Fetzer offers just what a "bargain"-priced Cab should: "generous fruit" (plum, berry) and "mild, food-friendly tannins."

Kitchen Countertop Survivor™ Grade: B

Your notes: _____

Francis Coppola Diamond Series	PC	T	V
Claret (*CLARE-ett*), California	$$	26	25

Claret—the Brits' term for Bordeaux—is sometimes used by CA wineries for their blends of Bordeaux's Cabernet and Merlot grapes. This one's got cedary, mocha scents and firm blackberry fruit and tannins. Excellent for the price.

Kitchen Countertop Survivor™ Grade: B

Your notes: _____

Francis Coppola Rubicon	PC	T	V
California	$$$$	X	X

✗ This wine's kaleidoscope of flavors—roasted coffee, dense black cherries, cedar, mint, and earth—evolve beautifully with bottle age if you've got the patience to wait.

Kitchen Countertop Survivor™ Grade: B+

Your notes: _____

Franciscan Magnificat Meritage	PC	T	V
California	$$$$	25	23

Given that it's one of the great CA Bordeaux blends, this wine's "a steal." The "packed-in blackberry," cedar-vanilla, tobacco, and autumn leaves character are "Bordeaux-complex, but California-ripe."

Kitchen Countertop Survivor™ Grade: A

Your notes: _____

Franciscan Napa Cabernet   PC   T   V
Sauvignon, California $$$ 25   23

☺ The real Napa Cabernet character—a whiff of cedar-mint, dark cassis fruit, sweet vanilla and spice from oak, and velvety tannins—distinguish this wine year-in and year-out. One of the best for the money.

Kitchen Countertop Survivor™ Grade: B

Your notes: _____

Frei Brothers Reserve Cabernet   PC   T   V
Sauvignon, California $$ 24   18

The dusty-cassis-mint-spice character of this wine is textbook Alexander Valley Cab.

Kitchen Countertop Survivor™ Grade: Avg

Your notes: _____

Frog's Leap Cabernet Sauvignon   PC   T   V
California $$$ 23   19

A Sauv Blanc specialist that also makes one of Napa's most distinctive Cabs, jam-packed with blackberry flavor, kissed with vanilla, licorice, and briary scents, elegant, impeccably balanced.

Kitchen Countertop Survivor™ Grade: B

Your notes: _____

Gallo of Sonoma Cabernet   PC   T   V
Sauvignon, California $$ 24   25

The price is edging up, and "it's gotten more oaky," but there's still lots of big, dark berry and fig fruit intensity.

Kitchen Countertop Survivor™ Grade: Avg

Your notes: _____

Geyser Peak Cabernet Sauvignon   PC   T   V
California $$ 23   22

This "textbook Sonoma Cab" "hits all the right notes"—cedar, berry fruit, fine tannins, for the price.

Kitchen Countertop Survivor™ Grade: B

Your notes: _____

Price Ranges: **$** = $12 or less; **$$** = $12.01–20; **$$$** = $20.01–35; **$$$$** = > $35

Kitchen Fridge/Countertop Survivor™ Grades: *Avg.* = a "one-day wine," tastes noticeably less fresh the next day; *B* = holds its freshness for 2–3 days after opening; *B+* = holds *and gets better* over 2–3 days after opening; *A* = a 3- to 4-day "freshness window"; *A+* = holds *and gets better* over 3–4 days

Greg Norman Cabernet/Merlot   PC   T   V
Australia $$ 26   24

The dark berry and chocolate flavors are "nice,"
but some tasters note they've "had other Aussie
Cab/Merlots that are just as good, for less
money."

Kitchen Countertop Survivor™ Grade: Avg
Your notes: _____

Groth Napa Cabernet Sauvignon   PC   T   V
California $$$$ 26   20

Although "pricey," I think this wine remains fairly
reasonable for a luxury Cabernet. And with its plush
tannins and deep cassis fruit, elegantly framed with
vanilla oak, it's a Napa benchmark.

Kitchen Countertop Survivor™ Grade: B+
Your notes: _____

Guenoc Cabernet Sauvignon   PC   T   V
California $$ 23   22

This is real California Cabernet flavor—berry and
cedar—with silky smooth texture and high quality for
the money.

Kitchen Countertop Survivor™ Grade: B
Your notes: _____

Heitz Napa Cabernet Sauvignon   PC   T   V
California $$$$ 28   18

The "fabulous earthy-minty qualities," and powerful
dark fruit are Heitz signatures. Although it scores
weak for value, I think it's priced fairly compared to
other luxury Napa Cabs.

Kitchen Countertop Survivor™ Grade: B+
Your notes: _____

Hess Estate Cabernet Sauvignon   PC   T   V
California $$$ X   X

✗ A great example of the Cab style from Napa's Mt.
Veeder subdistrict: dusky black fruits, a tarry-earthy
note, chewy tannins.

Kitchen Countertop Survivor™ Grade: B
Your notes: _____

Hess Select Cabernet Sauvignon   PC   T   V
California $$ 21   19

My tasters "love" this "always-reliable" Cabernet's

plum and blackberry flavors and touch of earthy spiciness, and you will, too.

Kitchen Countertop Survivor™ Grade: B

Your notes: _____

| **Jacob's Creek Cabernet Sauvignon** | PC | T | V |
| **Australia** | $ | 22 | 24 |

The nice minty-berry varietal character, soft tannin, and great price make it an "amazing value for the money."

Kitchen Countertop Survivor™ Grade: B

Your notes: _____

| **J. Lohr Hilltop Cabernet Sauvignon** | PC | T | V |
| **California** | $$$ | 22 | 22 |

I couldn't have said it better than this taster: "layers of spice and fruit and earth that just keep opening up and revealing themselves."

Kitchen Countertop Survivor™ Grade: B

Your notes: _____

| **J. Lohr 7 Oaks Cabernet Sauvignon** | PC | T | V |
| **California** | $$ | 24 | 24 |

This is one of my favorite CA Cabs at this price, offering powerful, exotic berry fruit and luxurious coconut cream scent from American oak.

Kitchen Countertop Survivor™ Grade: B |

Your notes: _____

| **Jordan Cabernet Sauvignon** | PC | T | V |
| **California** | $$$ | 25 | 21 |

Although the quality does vary by vintage, the elegant, silky style of this Cab distinguishes it from the huge "fruit and oak bomb" Cabs that critics love. Ages well in the best years.

Kitchen Countertop Survivor™ Grade: B+

Your notes: _____

Price Ranges: **$** = $12 or less; **$$** = $12.01–20; **$$$** = $20.01–35; **$$$$** = > $35

Kitchen Fridge/Countertop Survivor™ Grades: *Avg.* = a "one-day wine," tastes noticeably less fresh the next day; *B* = holds its freshness for 2–3 days after opening; *B+* = holds *and gets better* over 2–3 days after opening; *A* = a 3- to 4-day "freshness window"; *A+* = holds *and gets better* over 3–4 days

Joseph Phelps Insignia Cabernet Blend, California   PC   T   V $$$$ 24   18

A Napa blockbuster, with potent black fruit, licorice, toasted-coconutty oak, and thick tannins.

Kitchen Countertop Survivor™ Grade: B

Your notes: _____

Joseph Phelps Napa Cabernet Sauvignon, California   PC   T   V $$$$ 27   21

This is real Napa Cab that, while not cheap, is priced fairly for what you get: great structure, mint, cedar, coffee-spice scents, and blackberry fruit.

Kitchen Countertop Survivor™ Grade: B

Your notes: _____

Justin Isosceles Cabernet Blend California   PC   T   V $$$$ 26   22

This bottling put Paso Robles on the serious wine map. Its dark berry, minty, and oaky aromas grow more refined with age.

Kitchen Countertop Survivor™ Grade: Avg

Your notes: _____

Kendall-Jackson Vintner's Reserve Cabernet Sauvignon, California   PC   T   V $$ 21   22

The varietal character—blackberry flavor, a touch of earth, and a tug of tannin—is exemplary for the price.

Kitchen Countertop Survivor™ Grade: B

Your notes: _____

Kenwood Cabernet Sauvignon California   PC   T   V $ 22   22

Mixed reviews, with some tasters saying it "never lets you down," and others saying it's "light" and "should deliver more."

Kitchen Countertop Survivor™ Grade: Avg

Your notes: _____

Liberty School Cabernet Sauvignon, California   PC   T   V $$ 20   24

As it has for years, this bottling from the makers of Caymus delivers good Cab character—dark plum fruit and some spice—at a value price.

Kitchen Countertop Survivor™ Grade: Avg

Your notes: _____

| **The Little Penguin Cabernet** | PC | T | V |
| **Sauvignon, Australia** | $ | X | X |

✗ It's rare to find a Cabernet at this price that really tastes like Cabernet—blackberry fruit and a touch of cedary spice. Bravo!

Kitchen Countertop Survivor™ Grade: Avg

Your notes: _____

| **The Little Penguin Cabernet** | PC | T | V |
| **Sauvignon Shiraz, Australia** | $ | 24 | 24 |

"A little sweet" say some, but that makes this newcomer—which is giving Yellow Tail a run for its money—"yummy-fruity" to others.

Kitchen Countertop Survivor™ Grade: Avg

Your notes: _____

| **Los Vascos Cabernet Sauvignon** | PC | T | V |
| **Chile** | $ | 24 | 26 |

One of Chile's best budget Cabernets, with dark cherry fruit, a cedary scent, and smooth tannins.

Kitchen Countertop Survivor™ Grade: B

Your notes: _____

| **Louis Martini Cabernet Sauvignon** | PC | T | V |
| **Reserve, California** | $$$ | X | X |

✗ Tasted blind against Cabs at thrice the price, this bottling blew us away—coconutty spicy oak, huge but balanced blackberry fruit, mint, and eucalyptus. A real "wow" for the money.

Kitchen Countertop Survivor™ Grade: A

Your notes: _____

| **Meridian Cabernet Sauvignon** | PC | T | V |
| **California** | $ | 23 | 20 |

This juicy wine is "always a great value," say my tasters, with scents of black cherry and fruitcake and a soft texture.

Kitchen Countertop Survivor™ Grade: B

Your notes: _____

Price Ranges: **$** = $12 or less; **$$** = $12.01–20; **$$$** = $20.01–35; **$$$$** = > $35

Kitchen Fridge/Countertop Survivor™ Grades: *Avg.* = a "one-day wine," tastes noticeably less fresh the next day; *B* = holds its freshness for 2–3 days after opening; *B+* = holds *and gets better* over 2–3 days after opening; *A* = a 3- to 4-day "freshness window"; *A+* = holds *and gets better* over 3–4 days

Merryvale Profile Cabernet Blend PC T V
California $$$$ 27 18

Although it's "pricey"-ness dinged the value score,
tasters "love the jammy cassis" fruit and "lavish
vanilla" oak of this "blockbuster" style.

Kitchen Countertop Survivor™ Grade: B
Your notes: _____

Mt. Veeder Napa Cabernet PC T V
Sauvignon, California $$$$ 21 24

☺ One of my favorite Cabs, period. The gripping tannins, dense figlike fruit, and complexity for the price
are impressive.

Kitchen Countertop Survivor™ Grade: A
Your notes: _____

Opus One (Cabernet blend) PC T V
California $$$$ 27 18

A "powerful wine" with classy, toasty-vanilla oak
and blackcurrant-cedar flavors that are "so
Napa," plus a coffee scent that is, to me, Bordeaux-
like.

Kitchen Fridge Survivor™ Grade: B
Your notes: _____

Pahlmeyer Meritage Napa Valley PC T V
California $$$$ 26 18

This boutique Cabernet has "great fruit flavors of wild
dark berries," "massive oak," and a "great finish."
Collector-types find the "very high price" "worth it."

Kitchen Countertop Survivor™ Grade: B
Your notes: _____

Paraduxx Cabernet-Zinfandel PC T V
Blend, California $$$$ X X

✗ Somehow they've managed to get "balanced" and
"fruit bomb" together in the same bottle, so it's like a
black cherry tart with toasted nuts and cream, but not
at all cloying.

Kitchen Countertop Survivor™ Grade: B
Your notes: _____

Penfolds Bin 389 Cabernet PC T V
Sauvignon/Shiraz, Australia $$$ 27 23

☺ This "awesome" wine delivers on all counts: complexity, density of flavor, the "yum" factor, and value.

The vivid raspberry fruit and pepper/cedar/spice/ coconut scent are delicious young, but the wine also develops breathtaking complexity with age.

Kitchen Countertop Survivor™ Grade: A

Your notes: _____

Penfolds Koonunga Hill Cabernet/	PC	T	V
Merlot, Australia	**$$**	**21**	**23**

This blend gives you the cedar scent and structure of Cabernet, the plummy softness of Merlot, and thus lots of pleasure at a good price.

Kitchen Countertop Survivor™ Grade: B

Your notes: _____

Pine Ridge Cabernet Sauvignon	PC	T	V
Stag's Leap District, California	**$$$$**	**27**	**23**

A great example of the Stag's Leap district Cab style, with earthy-blackberry fruit, and a soft scent of cocoa and damp earth.

Kitchen Countertop Survivor™ Grade: B

Your notes: _____

Pride Mountain Vineyards	PC	T	V
Cabernet Sauvignon, California	**$$$$**	**26**	**19**

Major fans (me included) for this wine's "gorgeous aromas," "dense, incredible dark fruit," and "great quality price ratio when you compare it against some of the hard-to-find CA cult wines."

Kitchen Countertop Survivor™ Grade: B

Your notes: _____

Quintessa (Cabernet blend)	PC	T	V
California	**$$$$**	**26**	**18**

The price has jumped a lot since the wine's launch a few years ago, but its distinctiveness and elegance

---

Price Ranges: **$** = $12 or less; **$$** = $12.01–20; **$$$** = $20.01–35; **$$$$** = > $35

Kitchen Fridge/Countertop Survivor™ Grades: *Avg.* = a "one-day wine," tastes noticeably less fresh the next day; *B* = holds its freshness for 2–3 days after opening; *B+* = holds *and gets better* over 2–3 days after opening; *A* = a 3- to 4-day "freshness window"; *A+* = holds *and gets better* over 3–4 days

cannot be denied. It's very classically "Rutherford" (a
Napa sub-district), with deep cassis fruit flavor and
very layered scents of toasted coffee, autumn leaf pile,
and soft vanilla. Gorgeous.

Kitchen Countertop Survivor™ Grade: A

Your notes: _____

	PC	T	V
Raymond Napa Cabernet Sauvignon California	**$$**	**24**	**25**

The Raymonds put quality in the bottle for a good
price. It's "minty and elegant," balanced and not
heavy.

Kitchen Countertop Survivor™ Grade: B

Your notes: _____

	PC	T	V
R. H. Phillips Toasted Head Cabernet Sauvignon, California	**$$**	**27**	**27**

Tasters like the "big Cab flavor for a good price."

Kitchen Countertop Survivor™ Grade: Avg

Your notes: _____

	PC	T	V
Robert Mondavi Cabernet Sauvignon Reserve, California	**$$$**	**25**	**21**

A Napa blue chip for a reason; it's redolent of eucalyptus and bittersweet chocolate and delicious young,
but ages well, too.

Kitchen Countertop Survivor™ Grade: B

Your notes: _____

	PC	T	V
Robert Mondavi Private Selection Cabernet Sauvignon, California	**$**	**19**	**22**

Not among the best in this price point. It's "drinkable,"
but other brands beat it for flavor and quality.

Kitchen Countertop Survivor™ Grade: Avg

Your notes: _____

	PC	T	V
Robert Mondavi Napa Cabernet Sauvignon, California	**$$$**	**24**	**26**

I've found the quality uneven year to year, but at
its best this Cab's deeply concentrated cassis and
licorice flavor and cedary, spicy, minty scent are
consistent style signatures and a benchmark for the
category.

Kitchen Countertop Survivor™ Grade: Avg

Your notes: _____

Rodney Strong Sonoma Cabernet   **PC**   **T**   **V**
Sauvignon, California   **$$**   21   21

My tasters "love" the coconutty oak scent and "huge fruit" that "tastes more expensive than it is."

Kitchen Countertop Survivor™ Grade: Avg

Your notes: _____

Rosemount Diamond Label   **PC**   **T**   **V**
Cabernet Sauvignon Australia   **$**   24   24

My tasters rave that this "jammy," "very-well-made" Aussie Cab is "simply one of the best buys in wine."

Kitchen Countertop Survivor™ Grade: Avg

Your notes: _____

Santa Rita 120 Cabernet Sauvignon   **PC**   **T**   **V**
Chile   **$**   26   28

It is indeed "a price that's hard to believe" for the quality and flavor punch it delivers. The nice tannic grip and meaty-spicy scent and flavor show the rustic Chilean Cabernet character that I love.

Kitchen Countertop Survivor™ Grade: B

Your notes: _____

Sebastiani Sonoma Cabernet   **PC**   **T**   **V**
Sauvignon, California   **$$**   24   21

I agree with this taster's comment that "this winery is doing things so well at such affordable prices that it blows my mind." You just don't expect such complexity of "blackberry," "cassis," and spice at this price.

Kitchen Countertop Survivor™ Grade: B

Your notes: _____

Shafer Hillside Select Cabernet   **PC**   **T**   **V**
Sauvignon, California   **$$$$**   29   18

"Napa wine at its finest," "big and bold, yet balanced and refined." The cedar-autumn leaves and vanilla

Price Ranges: **$** = $12 or less; **$$** = $12.01–20; **$$$** = $20.01–35; **$$$$** = > $35

Kitchen Fridge/Countertop Survivor™ Grades: *Avg.* = a "one-day wine," tastes noticeably less fresh the next day; *B* = holds its freshness for 2–3 days after opening; *B+* = holds *and gets better* over 2–3 days after opening; *A* = a 3- to 4-day "freshness window"; *A+* = holds *and gets better* over 3–4 days

scent frames lush blackberry and cassis fruit layered with cocoa and licorice.

Kitchen Countertop Survivor™ *Grade: A*

Your notes: _____

Silverado Napa Cabernet Sauvignon, California	PC $$$$	T 24	V 20

Silverado's elegant but firm style is classy, with cassis flavor scented with sweet-vanilla oak and earthiness.

Kitchen Countertop Survivor™ *Grade: B*

Your notes: _____

Silver Oak Alexander Valley Cabernet Sauvignon, California	PC $$$$	T 27	V 19

Whether in auction rooms, on wine lists, or in boutique wine shops, this wine's die-hard devotees find its consistency and uniqueness "worth the price." But more than just "yummy" to drink, it is known for intense wild berry fruit, velvety-thick tannins, a coconut-dill scent coming from American oak barrels, and ageability.

Kitchen Countertop Survivor™ *Grade: B*

Your notes: _____

Simi Sonoma Cabernet Sauvignon California	PC $$$	T 24	V 25

Simi offers excellent value for the money and classy, true California Cabernet flavors: blackberry, earth, spice.

Kitchen Countertop Survivor™ *Grade: B*

Your notes: _____

Smoking Loon Cabernet Sauvignon, California	PC $	T 20	V 26

"Excellent for the money" is this brand's signature, making this Cab "good for everyday," yet unique for its "earthy" taste.

Kitchen Countertop Survivor™ *Grade: Avg*

Your notes: _____

Staglin Family Cabernet Sauvignon, California	PC $$$$	T 24	V 15

"Just delicious" and, like their Chard, so perfectly pitched between elegance (the texture) and intensity

(the dense black fruit and heady vanilla-coffee scent).
Bravo!

Kitchen Countertop Survivor™ Grade: B

Your notes: _____

Stag's Leap Wine Cellars Napa   PC   T   V
Cabernet Sauvignon, California $$$$ 26   20

Although it's "pricey," this wine's "incredible complexity"—with dark spices, mint, and berry character,
make it "worth the splurge." It "ages great," too.

Kitchen Countertop Survivor™ Grade: B

Your notes: _____

Sterling Vineyards Napa Cabernet   PC   T   V
Sauvignon, California $$$ 24   22

Tasters praise this blue-chip Cabernet's "concentrated"
"jammy fruits." I think it is good but outperformed of
late by many old Napa neighbors, as well as new
names from Sonoma, Paso Robles, and beyond.

Kitchen Countertop Survivor™ Grade: B

Your notes: _____

Stonestreet Alexander Valley   PC   T   V
Cabernet Sauvignon, California $$$ 24   18

This is classy California Cabernet, unencumbered by
excessive oak and alcohol, but with plenty of power.
The scents of vanilla, damp earth, crushed mint, and
blackberry are classic Alexander Valley.

Kitchen Countertop Survivor™ Grade: Avg

Your notes: _____

Terra Rosa Cabernet Sauvignon   PC   T   V
Chile/Argentina $ 24   29

This "Best Buy-plus" Cabernet is made by Laurel
Glen Winery's Patrick Campbell. Year in and year out
it offers "great fruit flavor" at a great price.

Kitchen Countertop Survivor™ Grade: B

Your notes: _____

Price Ranges: **$** = $12 or less; **$$** = $12.01–20; **$$$** = $20.01–35;
$$$$ = > $35
Kitchen Fridge/Countertop Survivor™ Grades: *Avg.* = a "one-day
wine," tastes noticeably less fresh the next day; *B* = holds its freshness for 2–3 days after opening; *B+* = holds *and gets better* over 2–3
days after opening; *A* = a 3- to 4-day "freshness window"; *A+* =
holds *and gets better* over 3–4 days

Veramonte Cabernet Sauvignon PC   T   V
Chile $ 17   19

The entire brand is a "real value find for consumers."
The licorice-berry fruit, chewy tannin, and a savory
spice note taste like twice the price.
Kitchen Countertop Survivor™ Grade: Avg

Your notes: _____

Viader Napa Valley Cabernet PC   T   V
blend, California $$$$ 28   18

This "wonderfully smooth" Napa Cab blend feels like
cashmere for the tongue. Its "glorious fruit," soft
vanilla-coffee scent of oak and awesome complexity
are "as good as any of the cult Cabs" but with a sense
of proportion and elegance that's rare in the category.
Kitchen Countertop Survivor™ Grade: A

Your notes: _____

Walnut Crest Cabernet Sauvignon PC   T   V
Chile $ 18   22

"Tastes more expensive than it is," say tasters, who
rank it accordingly for both taste and value. The
peppery, fruity, and crowd-pleasing style is at once
smooth and savory.
Kitchen Countertop Survivor™ Grade: Avg

Your notes: _____

Wynn's Coonawarra Estate PC   T   V
Cabernet Sauvignon, Australia $$ 20   25

I serve this to my students because the "smooth
blackcurrant fruit" and cedary, "minty" scent are
classic characteristics of Coonawarra Cab.
Kitchen Countertop Survivor™ Grade: A

Your notes: _____

Yellow Tail Cabernet/Merlot PC   T   V
Australia $ X   X

✗ A soft and fruity red to keep around for weeknight
dinners from stews to stuffed peppers.
Kitchen Countertop Survivor™ Grade: Avg

Your notes: _____

Yellow Tail Cabernet/Shiraz PC   T   V
Australia $ X   X

✗ Tasters call it "plummy and soft" and "a value."
Kitchen Countertop Survivor™ Grade: Avg

Your notes: _____

Rioja, Ribera del Duero, and Other Spanish Reds

Category Profile: Spain is smokin'! Seriously—it's hard to say whether the bigger story is the new life in her classic reions (Rioja (*ree-OH-huh*) and Ribera del Duero (*ree-BEAR-uh dell DWAIR-oh*) or the slew of new, quality-oriented appellations that have emerged. Like other classic Euro wines, it's the place—called a Denominación de Origen, or DO—rather than the grape on a Spanish wine label. Spain's signature red grape, used in both Rioja and Ribera del Duero, is called Tempranillo (*temp-rah-NEE-oh*). Depending on quality level, the style of Rioja ranges from easy-drinking and spicy to seriously rich, leathery/toffee in character—never ho-hum. Ribera del Duero is generally big and tannic. The other Spanish reds here are from Priorat (*pre-oh-RAHT*), known for strong, inky-dark cellar candidates (usually made from Tempranillo, Cabernet, and/or Grenache). Though not represented in the top red wine sellers, Penedes (*pen-eh-DESS*), which is better known for Cava sparkling wines, is also an outstanding source of values in every style and color. While the emerging regions—such as Jumilla, Toro, and Bierzo—are not yet sufficiently available to have made the *Guide*, they are exciting, so look for them and try them!

Serve: Cool room temperature; as a rule Spanish reds are exemplary food wines, but basic reds from Penedes and Rioja (with the word Crianza on the label), and emerging regions like Navarra, Toro, and Somontano, are good "anytime" wines and tasty on their own.

When: Rioja Crianza is my personal "house" red wine. Also, if you dine out often in wine-focused restaurants, Spanish reds are *the* red wine category for world-class drinking that's also affordable.

Price Ranges: **$** = $12 or less; **$$** = $12.01–20; **$$$** = $20.01–35; **$$$$** = > $35

Kitchen Fridge/Countertop Survivor™ Grades: *Avg.* = a "one-day wine," tastes noticeably less fresh the next day; *B* = holds its freshness for 2–3 days after opening; *B+* = holds *and gets better* over 2–3 days after opening; *A* = a 3- to 4-day "freshness window"; *A+* = holds *and gets better* over 3–4 days

With: Your next pig roast (!) . . . Seriously, the classic matches are pork and lamb, either roasted or grilled; also amazing with slow-roasted chicken or turkey and hams, sausages, and other cured meats. Finally, if you enjoy a cheese course in lieu of dessert, or are interested in trying one of the world's great pairings that's also easy to pull off, try a Spanish Ribera del Duero, Priorat, or Rioja Reserva or Gran Reserva with good-quality cheese. (Spanish Manchego is wonderful and available in supermarkets.)

In: An all-purpose wineglass or larger-bowled red wine stem.

	PC	T	V
Alvaro Palacios Les Terrasses (**ALL-vahr-oh puh-LAH-see-os lay tear-AHSS**) **Priorat, Spain**	$$$	27	24

For sheer drama it's hard to top this dark, brooding beauty from Priorat. This one is lush, intense, and inky, with beautiful black cherry flavors, toasty oak, and a finish that seems hours long.
Kitchen Countertop Survivor™ *Grade: B*
Your notes: _____

	PC	T	V
Arzuaga (*ahr-ZWAH-guh*) **Crianza** **Ribera del Duero, Spain**	$$$	22	22

My tasters gave this high taste and value marks for its power, blackberry-plum, ripeness, and complexity.
Kitchen Countertop Survivor™ *Grade: Avg*
Your notes: _____

	PC	T	V
Campo Viejo Rioja Reserva **Spain**	$$	X	X

✗ "Old style" Rioja with cedar, tobacco, and dried herb scents and a balsamic-dried fig flavor that's great with Manchego cheese.
Kitchen Countertop Survivor™ *Grade: B*
Your notes: _____

	PC	T	V
Marques de Arienzo Rioja Reserva **Spain**	$$	22	23

I love Arienzo's reservas, which adhere to a more traditional, subtle style of Rioja—tobacco, toffee, and dried spice scent, dark berry and raisin fruit flavor.
Kitchen Countertop Survivor™ *Grade: B*
Your notes: _____

Marques de Caceres (*mahr-KESS***   PC   T   V**
deh CAH-sair-ess) **Rioja Crianza** $$ 24   22**
Spain

With "lots of cherry fruit" and "typical toffee-spice,"
this Rioja Crianza is among my favorite basic Riojas.

Kitchen Countertop Survivor™ *Grade: B+*
Your notes: _____

Marques de Riscal (*mahr-KESS***   PC   T   V**
deh ree-SKALL) **Rioja Crianza, Spain** $ 20   18**

This wine earns praise for its lovely spicy nose, silken
texture, and savory-strawberry flavor.

Kitchen Countertop Survivor™ *Grade: B+*
Your notes: _____

Marques de Riscal Rioja Reserva   **PC   T   V**
Spain   **$$ 22   19**

The reserva is a "nice upgrade from the Crianza" (the
base level Riscal), with more oak aging. The oak gives
toffee/coconut scents, and the fruit tastes raisiny and
chocolatey. Yum!

Kitchen Countertop Survivor™ *Grade: B*
Your notes: _____

Montecillo (*mohn-teh-SEE-yoh***)   PC   T   V**
Rioja Crianza, Spain   **$ 27   27**

Another favorite of wine aficionados, for its Old World
savory spiciness and long finish. Very nice indeed.

Kitchen Countertop Survivor™ *Grade: Avg*
Your notes: _____

Montecillo Rioja Reserva   **PC   T   V**
Spain   **$$ 21   24**

It's such a joy to find a wine with such character for this
price. Extra oak aging creates layers of tobacco, toffee,
and sweet spice alongside the fig and raisin fruit.

Kitchen Countertop Survivor™ *Grade: B+*
Your notes: _____

Price Ranges: **$** = $12 or less; **$$** = $12.01–20; **$$$** = $20.01–35;
$$$$ = > $35
Kitchen Fridge/Countertop Survivor™ Grades: *Avg.* = a "one-day
wine," tastes noticeably less fresh the next day; *B* = holds its fresh-
ness for 2–3 days after opening; *B+* = holds *and gets better* over 2–3
days after opening; *A* = a 3- to 4-day "freshness window"; *A+* =
holds *and gets better* over 3–4 days

Muga (_MOO-guh_) Rioja Reserva   PC   T   V
Spain $$$ 25   22

This Rioja is a world class wine, and a relative value in that realm. The stunning fig, prune, and dried cherry fruit and dense but suede-smooth tannins make it "a brooding red" that's "cellerable."

Kitchen Countertop Survivor™ _Grade:_ A+
Your notes: _____

Osborne Solaz Tempranillo   PC   T   V
Spain $ 24   27

What a yummy wine and a great way to get to know Spain's signature Tempranillo grape (here blended with Cab). It's got a smoky scent, lots of pretty plum fruit, and a tug of tannin.

Kitchen Countertop Survivor™ _Grade:_ Avg
Your notes: _____

Pesquera (_pess-CARE-uh_) Ribera   PC   T   V
del Duero, Spain $$$ 24   24

This wine is back on form, with a balance of deep cherry fruit, oak, and structure that's "smooth" yet built for aging.

Kitchen Countertop Survivor™ _Grade:_ B
Your notes: _____

Vinicola del Priorat Onix   PC   T   V
(_veen-EE-co-lah dell PREE-oh-raht_ $$ 20   22
OH-nix), Spain

A great entrée to Spain's big, inky Priorat wines, because this one's "more affordable than most." It's not as teeth-staining as some, but still has the deep berry fruit, tarry scent, and chewy tannins of the region. Decant, and serve it "with cheese or big meat."

Kitchen Countertop Survivor™ _Grade:_ A
Your notes: _____

Other Reds

Category Profile: As with the whites, this isn't a co-hesive category but rather a spot to put big-selling reds that don't neatly fit a grape or region category—namely, proprietary blends, and uncommon varietals.

Proprietary blends—These may be tasty, inexpensive blends, or ambitious signature blends at luxury prices.

Uncommon varietals—These are quite exciting. I introduced Malbec and Carmenere in the Merlot section, because I think they are distinctive and delicious alternatives for Merlot lovers. Although the names and even the style (bold and a little peppery) are similar, Petite Sirah and Syrah (Shiraz) are not the same grape.

Serve: Cool room temperature, or even slightly chilled.

When: Anytime you need an interesting, value-priced red.

With: Snacks and everyday meals.

In: An all-purpose wineglass.

Bogle Petite Sirah	PC	T	V
California	$	27	26

The exec chef for P.F. Chang's turned me on to this black pepper and berries-a-go-go mouthful (with orange-flavor beef—wow) that my tasters call an "awesome value."
Kitchen Countertop Survivor™ Grade: B
Your notes: _____

Ca'del Solo Big House Red	PC	T	V
California	$$	22	19

This "spicy," juicy red offers "great value" and easy drinkability—a "fun for everyday" wine.
Kitchen Countertop Survivor™ Grade: A
Your notes: _____

Catena Alamos Malbec	PC	T	V
Argentina	$$$	24	20

This is the wine that caused the wine world to notice Argentina and its signature Malbec grape. The intense blackberry fruit, velvety texture, and vanilla-scented oak are at once sleek and powerful.
Kitchen Fridge Survivor™ Grade: Avg
Your notes: _____

Price Ranges: **$** = $12 or less; **$$** = $12.01–20; **$$$** = $20.01–35; **$$$$** = > $35
Kitchen Fridge/Countertop Survivor™ Grades: *Avg.* = a "one-day wine," tastes noticeably less fresh the next day; *B* = holds its freshness for 2–3 days after opening; *B+* = holds *and gets better* over 2–3 days after opening; *A* = a 3- to 4-day "freshness window"; *A+* = holds *and gets better* over 3–4 days

Concannon Petite Sirah   PC   T   V
California $$ 26   26

Concannon Petite Sirah	PC	T	V
California	$$	26	26

Take a black pepper and berry scent, add explode-in-your-mouth fruit-pie flavor, chewy tannins, and a long licorice finish, and you've got this unique, fun wine.

Kitchen Countertop Survivor™ Grade: B+

Your notes: _____

Concha y Toro Casillero del Diablo	PC	T	V
Carmenere, Chile	$$	24	24

The wine is spicy, raisiny, and oozing with character, and has a heady scent like molasses-cured bacon. Just try it!

Kitchen Fridge Survivor™ Grade: B

Your notes: _____

Concha y Toro Terrunyo Carmenere	PC	T	V
Chile	$$$	18	20

You'll have to search a bit for this, but it's worth the trouble. The flavor is like the concentrated essence of wild berries (huckleberries, raspberries), with a velvety-plush texture and sweet spice-cola scents.

Kitchen Countertop Survivor™ Grade: B

Your notes: _____

Coppola (Francis) Presents Rosso	PC	T	V
California	$	21	22

"Just what an everyday wine should be," said tasters of this juicy, fruity, and simple Coppola wine (yes, *that* Coppola). It's delicious and "fun."

Kitchen Countertop Survivor™ Grade: B+

Your notes: _____

Foppiano Petite Sirah	PC	T	V
California	$$	23	21

A "manly wine"—that's certainly an apt description of Petite Sirah, which has sturdy tannin and spice to support the dark berry fruit.

Kitchen Fridge Survivor™ Grade: B

Your notes: _____

Navarro Correas Malbec	PC	T	V
Argentina	$	25	25

This is rustic but really inviting, with an earthy, leathery, savory spice scent, silky, subtle plum fruit, and a smoky, earthy finish.

Kitchen Countertop Survivor™ Grade: B

Your notes: _____

Red Truck by Cline Cellars   PC   T   V
California $ 24   28

Mostly Rhone grapes in this fun blend, so there's lots of savory spice and juicy, "bowl-of-berries" fruit.

Kitchen Countertop Survivor™ Grade: Avg

Your notes: _____

Terrazas Alto Malbec   PC   T   V
Argentina $$ 22   26

This "juicy, plummy, spicy" Malbec gets "great value" marks from my tasters.

Kitchen Countertop Survivor™ Grade: Avg

Your notes: _____

Veramonte Primus   PC   T   V
Chile $$ 21   18

This, one of the first Chilean Carmenere blends on the market, is still one of the best, with a lot of exotic berry fruit, both savory and sweet spices, and a smoky-meaty note.

Kitchen Countertop Survivor™ Grade: B

Your notes: _____

Italian Regional Reds

Category Profile: This group includes small Italian regions like Valpolicella and Lambrusco, whose market presence is dominated by a few big-selling, well-known brands.

Serve: Cool room temperature or slightly chilled.

When: As the Italians would, for everyday drinking.

With: Snacks and everyday meals.

In: An all-purpose wineglass.

Price Ranges: **$** = $12 or less; **$$** = $12.01–20; **$$$** = $20.01–35; **$$$$** = > $35

Kitchen Fridge/Countertop Survivor™ Grades: *Avg.* = a "one-day wine," tastes noticeably less fresh the next day; *B* = holds its freshness for 2–3 days after opening; *B+* = holds *and gets better* over 2–3 days after opening; *A* = a 3- to 4-day "freshness window"; *A+* = holds *and gets better* over 3–4 days

Allegrini Valpolicella (*al-uh-GREE-nee val-pole-uh-CHELL-uh*), Italy

PC	T	V
$$	22	22

The winery patriarch's recent death saddened wine pros, who hail this bottling as "THE classic Valpolicella, with dried cherry flavor, spicy scent, vibrant acidity.

Kitchen Countertop Survivor™ Grade: B
Your notes: _____

Bolla Valpolicella Italy

PC	T	V
$	16	18

This Valpolicella is fruity and soft, but scores poorly compared to others at the price.

Kitchen Countertop Survivor™ Grade: Avg
Your notes: _____

Ceretto Barbarasco Asij Italy

PC	T	V
$$$$	24	18

New to the Nebbiolo grape? This bottle proudly shows off the grape's characteristic aromas of dark berries, tar, and smoke. Try it with an aged cheese to soften its tannic grip.

Kitchen Countertop Survivor™ Grade: A+
Your notes: _____

Citra Montepulciano d'Abruzzo (*CHEE-truh mon-teh-pool-CHAH-no dah-BROOT-so*), Italy

PC	T	V
$	18	22

This is just a yummy little wine for the money, whose fruity taste and touch of earthy spiciness make almost any dish taste better.

Kitchen Countertop Survivor™ Grade: B
Your notes: _____

Falesco Vitiano (*fuh-LESS-co vee-tee-AH-no*), Italy

PC	T	V
$	20	21

"There's probably no better wine for the money," say my tasters. It's "spicy," "fruity," "smooth," "just delicious!"

Kitchen Countertop Survivor™ Grade: B
Your notes: _____

Michele Chiarlo Le Orme Barbera d'Asti, Italy

PC	T	V
$	24	26

This Barbera is low in tannin, with lively acidity and a flavor of dried cherries, sweet spice, and balsamic.

Kitchen Countertop Survivor™ Grade: B
Your notes: _____

Morgante Nero d'Avola   PC   T   V
Italy   \$ 21   24

Nero d'Avola (NAIR-oh DAH-vo-luh) is one of Sicily's signature red grapes. The scent is of ink, licorice, and savory spices, and the spicy-berry palate is a mouth-watering compliment to food.

Kitchen Fridge Survivor™ Grade: Avg

Your notes: _____

Pio Cesare Barolo   PC   T   V
Italy   \$\$\$\$ 26   26

Here is a classy, real-deal Barolo with good availability, and a good price for the quality. The deep plum, cedar, and tar scent is textbook Barolo. The tannins are gripping but balanced, and the dusty berry-rhubarb flavor is mouthwatering.

Kitchen Countertop Survivor™ Grade: A

Your notes: _____

Taurino Salice Salentino   PC   T   V
Italy   \$ 26   26

The region name is pronounced suh-LEE-chay sah-len-TEE-no, and the tasters' raves are no surprise to me. They love the "rustic, mouth-watering bright berries" and the "great character for the price." The grape used is Montepulciano (not to be confused with the village of Montepulciano in Tuscany).

Kitchen Countertop Survivor™ Grade: B+

Your notes: _____

Zenato Amarone della Valpolicella   PC   T   V
Classico, Italy   \$\$\$\$ 24   21

This "delicious & decadent," deeply rich wine drips with ripe fig fruit, sweet spices and thick, mouth-coating tannins—a "worthy splurge."

Kitchen Countertop Survivor™ Grade: A

Your notes: _____

Price Ranges: **\$** = \$12 or less; **\$\$** = \$12.01–20; **\$\$\$** = \$20.01–35; **\$\$\$\$** = > \$35

Kitchen Fridge/Countertop Survivor™ Grades: *Avg.* = a "one-day wine," tastes noticeably less fresh the next day; *B* = holds its freshness for 2–3 days after opening; *B+* = holds *and gets better* over 2–3 days after opening; *A* = a 3- to 4-day "freshness window"; *A+* = holds *and gets better* over 3–4 days

Syrah/Shiraz and
Other Rhone-Style Reds

Category Profile: This category of reds continues as a sizzling seller—especially the varietal Shiraz, Australia's signature red, which is so hot that most pros say it has unseated Merlot as consumers' go-to grape. Popularity has its price for Shiraz lovers, though. While at the one-dollar-sign level you can still get real varietal character (a scent of sweet spice and jammy, succulent fruit), many of the biggest brands have begun to taste simple—like generic red wine rather than the spunky Shiraz with which we fell in love. The reviews reflect which brands have stayed true to the Shiraz taste. The same grape, under the French spelling *Syrah,* also forms the backbone for France's revered Rhone Valley reds with centuries-old reputations. These include Cotes-du-Rhone (*coat-duh-ROAN*), Cote-Rotie (*ro-TEE*), Hermitage (*uhr-muh-TAHJ*), and Chateauneuf-du-Pape (*shah-toe-NUFF-duh-POP*). Like Shiraz, Cotes-du-Rhone, with its lovely spicy fruit character, is a one-dollar-sign wonder. The latter three are true French classics and in my view currently lead that elite group in quality for the money. They are full-bodied, powerful, peppery, earthy, concentrated, and oak-aged. Finally, most major American wineries, and many smaller players, are bottling California or Washington state versions, often labeled with the Aussie spelling *Shiraz* rather than the French *Syrah.* Washington's Columbia Valley in particular is being lauded by pros as a potential star Syrah region.

Serve: Room temperature; aeration enhances the aroma and flavor.

When: Basic Syrah/Shiraz and Cotes-du-Rhone are great everyday drinking wines; in restaurants, these are great go-to categories for relative value.

With: Grilled, barbecued, or roasted anything (including fish and vegetables); outstanding with steaks, fine cheeses, and other dishes that call for a full red wine; I also love these styles with traditional Thanksgiving fare.

In: An all-purpose wineglass or a larger-bowled red wine stem.

Alain Graillot Crozes-Hermitage   **PC**   **T**   **V**
France   **$$$**   **24**   **24**

☺ This wine embodies the classic French Rhone style: leather and cracked black pepper scent, "chewy" tannins, and deep fig fruit with sweet spices on the palate.

Kitchen Countertop Survivor™ Grade: A+

Your notes: _____

Alice White Shiraz   **PC**   **T**   **V**
Australia   **$**   **25**   **25**

This Shiraz delivers "a lot of bang for the buck" and "stands out in the sea of Shiraz" thanks to its "spicy scent and wild raspberry fruit."

Kitchen Countertop Survivor™ Grade: B

Your notes: _____

Andrew Murray Syrah Tous Les   **PC**   **T**   **V**
Jours, California   **$$**   **26**   **24**

Tous les jours means every day, as in the affordability of this tasty, spicy-pomegranate-strawberry "gulper."

Kitchen Countertop Survivor™ Grade: B+

Your notes: _____

Black Opal Shiraz   **PC**   **T**   **V**
Australia   **$**   **18**   **19**

"Always a great value," with juicy fruit and a soft texture that makes it a great "house red."

Kitchen Countertop Survivor™ Grade: Avg

Your notes: _____

Bonny Doon Cigare Volant   **PC**   **T**   **V**
California   **$$$**   **26**   **24**

This powerful Grenache, Syrah, and Mouvedre blend makes a great party wine: the name inspires conversation (check out the Boony Doon Web site for its

Price Ranges: **$** = $12 or less; **$$** = $12.01–20; **$$$** = $20.01–35; **$$$$** = > $35

Kitchen Fridge/Countertop Survivor™ Grades: *Avg.* = a "one-day wine," tastes noticeably less fresh the next day; *B* = holds its freshness for 2–3 days after opening; *B+* = holds *and gets better* over 2–3 days after opening; *A* = a 3- to 4-day "freshness window"; *A+* = holds *and gets better* over 3–4 days

meaning), and the thick licorice and raspberry-liqueur flavors are quite beguiling. Make sure it's a *dinner* party—this big wine begs for food.

Kitchen Countertop Survivor™ Grade: Avg

Your notes: _____

| **Chapoutier Chateauneuf-du-Pape** | PC | T | V |
| **Le Bernardine, France** | $$$$ | 24 | 24 |

This wine is accessible young, but is also cellar worthy. The scent of sun-warmed figs, leather, pepper, and touch of rosemary transports you to the south of France.

Kitchen Countertop Survivor™ Grade: B

Your notes: _____

| **Chapoutier Cotes du Rhone Rouge** | PC | T | V |
| **France** | $ | 24 | 18 |

Rustically pepper-cumin scent, surprisingly silky strawberry-rhubarb flavor, awesome with herbed anything (chicken, lamb, goat cheese).

Kitchen Countertop Survivor™ Grade: A

Your notes: _____

| **Chateau de Beaucastel** | PC | T | V |
| **Chateauneuf-du-Pape, France** | $$$$ | 24 | 21 |

Although it's "expensive" and "hard to get," among the peer group of truly collectible, ageable, world-class wines, Beaucastel is a relative value, and the scores reflect that. The Asian spice and leather scent and powerful fig and dark berry fruit are fabulous young, but it cellars beautifully, too.

Kitchen Countertop Survivor™ Grade: A+

Your notes: _____

Chateau La Nerthe (*shah-TOE lah*	PC	T	V
***NAIRT*) Chateauneuf-du-Pape,**	$$$$	24	23
France			

Trade buyers and serious wine devotees rave about this "lovely," "smooth" Rhone wine, praising its "value relative to other classics" from regions like Burgundy and Bordeaux. The pepper/spicy/leathery scents, gripping tannins, and dried cranberry-anise flavors are textbook Chateauneuf, built for rich meats and stews.

Kitchen Countertop Survivor™ Grade: A

Your notes: _____

Cline Syrah

California

	PC	T	V
	$	22	23

Cline puts vibrant berry fruit flavor and spicy-zingy scent in the bottle for a great price.

Kitchen Countertop Survivor™ *Grade: B+*

Your notes: _____

D'Arenberg The Footbolt Shiraz

Australia

	PC	T	V
	$$	28	24

☺ I love this "intense and well balanced" wine whose flavors are so distinctive—meaty-smoky, tangy berries, savory and sweet spices, all at a "nice price."

Kitchen Countertop Survivor™ *Grade: B*

Your notes: _____

Domaine Andre Brunel Cotes-
du-Rhone Sommelonge, France

	PC	T	V
	$$	24	24

"Practically a meal in a glass," with a gamy-spicy scent and "mouthwatering" berries, pepper-spice, and dried herbs on the palate.

Kitchen Countertop Survivor™ *Grade: B+*

Your notes: _____

Domaine Santa Duc Gigondas
(*doh-MAIN santa duke*
***JHEE-gohn-dahss*), France**

	PC	T	V
	$$$$	24	18

The "gorgeous berry and cherry fruit" are spiked with the peppery spice typical of Gigondas wines from the Rhone. The gripping tannins and rustic earthiness make it great with smoked fare, bean dishes, and mushroom dishes.

Kitchen Countertop Survivor™ *Grade: B+*

Your notes: _____

Duboeuf (Georges) Cotes-du-Rhone
(*du-BUFF coat-duh-ROAN*), France

	PC	T	V
	$	24	24

This wine delivers character for cheap: it is juicy and

Price Ranges: **$** = $12 or less; **$$** = $12.01–20; **$$$** = $20.01–35; **$$$$** = > $35

Kitchen Fridge/Countertop Survivor™ Grades: *Avg.* = a "one-day wine," tastes noticeably less fresh the next day; *B* = holds its fresh-ness for 2–3 days after opening; *B+* = holds *and gets better* over 2–3 days after opening; *A* = a 3- to 4-day "freshness window"; *A+* = holds *and gets better* over 3–4 days

fresh tasting, with red cherry and a spicy pomegranate
note. Yum!

Kitchen Countertop Survivor™ Grade: B

Your notes: _____

E & M Guigal (*ghee-GALL*)	PC	T	V
Cotes-du-Rhone, France	$$	23	23

So many tasters, obviously enticed by the famous
Guigal name, have discovered and enjoyed the cherry
fruit and pepper-spice notes of this classic Cotes-du-
Rhone. For the money, it's a solid bet.

Kitchen Countertop Survivor™ Grade: A

Your notes: _____

E & M Guigal Cote-Rotie Brune et	PC	T	V
Blonde, France	$$$$	26	25

Is it the texture ("liquid velvet"), the scent ("pepper
and lavender"), or flavor ("blackberry") that's most
compelling? Any one or all of them will get your
attention if you drink it now, but my tasters are right:
it "will age 20 years."

Kitchen Countertop Survivor™ Grade: B+

Your notes: _____

Goats Do Roam	PC	T	V
South Africa	$	18	18

A tongue-in-cheek take on French Cotes du Rhone,
with a South African flair from Pinotage in the blend.
The result is meaty-peppery, dried cranberry flavors,
fun!

Kitchen Countertop Survivor™ Grade: Avg

Your notes: _____

Greg Norman Shiraz	PC	T	V
Australia	$$	20	20

It wasn't for everyone on my panel, but most tasters
loved the "smooth," "spicy" character at a "good price."

Kitchen Countertop Survivor™ Grade: Avg

Your notes: _____

Hill of Content Grenache/Shiraz	PC	T	V
Australia	$$	27	25

☺ The raspberry scent, the ripe, jammy berry fruit
taste, and juicy texture are de-lish!

Kitchen Countertop Survivor™ Grade: A

Your notes: _____

Jaboulet (*jhah-boo-LAY*)	PC	T	V
Parallele 45, Cotes-du-Rhone France	$	24	25

While Jaboulet stakes its reputation on its
luxurious Hermitage, this bottling is also
an impressive calling card in the budget price
category with succulent red-berry fruit and smoky
black pepper scents.

Kitchen Countertop Survivor™ Grade: B

Your notes: _____

Jacob's Creek Shiraz/Cabernet	PC	T	V
Sauvignon, Australia	$	23	26

"This wine is tough to beat in the 'great taste and great
value' category." The exotic raspberry and eucalyptus
notes and plump texture show the virtues of blending
Shiraz with Cabernet.

Kitchen Countertop Survivor™ Grade: B+

Your notes: _____

Jade Mountain Syrah	PC	T	V
California	$$$	24	24

☺ This is one of the best Syrahs coming from
California, and one of the few with real varietal
character—raspberry fruit, pepper-cumin-rosemary
scent, plump tannins. It ages well, too.

Kitchen Countertop Survivor™ Grade: B+

Your notes: _____

Jean-Luc Colombo Cotes-du-Rhone	PC	T	V
Les Abeilles, France	$	23	24

This is one of my favorite Cotes-du-Rhones. There's a
wonderful rustic tobacco character, plus spices both
savory (pepper, cumin) and sweet (nutmeg), layered
over the cherry fruit.

Kitchen Countertop Survivor™ Grade: B

Your notes: _____

Price Ranges: **$** = $12 or less; **$$** = $12.01–20; **$$$** = $20.01–35;
$$$$ => $35

Kitchen Fridge/Countertop Survivor™ Grades: *Avg.* = a "one-day
wine," tastes noticeably less fresh the next day; *B* = holds its freshness for 2–3 days after opening; *B+* = holds *and gets better* over 2–3
days after opening; *A* = a 3- to 4-day "freshness window"; *A+* =
holds *and gets better* over 3–4 days

Joseph Phelps Le Mistral   PC   T   V
California $$$ 26   20

This mainly Grenache-Syrah blend is "excellent," with a beautiful balance between strawberry-rhubarb fruit and zippy spice.

Kitchen Countertop Survivor™ Grade: B+

Your notes: _____

Joseph Phelps Pastiche (pah-STEESH) PC   T   V
Rouge, California $ 27   24

Pastiche is French for "a random mixture," as in the berry basket of grapes in this wine, similar to French Cotes du Rhone: peppery spice, and juicy strawberry-pomegranate fruit.

Kitchen Countertop Survivor™ Grade: B

Your notes: _____

La Vieille Ferme (*lah vee-yay*   PC   T   V
***FAIRM;* means "the old farm")** $ 21   26
Cotes-du-Ventoux, France

This raspberry-ripe, lively red is a tasting panel favorite, with "great character" for the price.

Kitchen Countertop Survivor™ Grade: B+

Your notes: _____

Lindemans Bin 50 Shiraz   PC   T   V
Australia $ 27   26

✓ The ripe raspberry fruit and a top note of black pepper scent, plus a plump and round mouthfeel, make this wine an all-around great drink and great buy.

Kitchen Countertop Survivor™ Grade: B+

Your notes: _____

Marquis Phillips Sarah's Blend   PC   T   V
Australia $$ 26   26

Take three favorites (Shiraz, Cab, and Merlot), and put Dan Phillips of the Grateful Palate behind them. The result is "explosive fruit and spiciness" and "velvety" tannins.

Kitchen Countertop Survivor™ Grade: B

Your notes: _____

Penfolds Coonawarra Shiraz   PC   T   V
Bin 128, Australia $$$ 22   21

"Smooth and polished" Shiraz with "rich but elegant" berry fruit, soft oak, and "chewy tannins."

Kitchen Countertop Survivor™ Grade: Avg
Your notes: _____

Penfolds Grange   **PC**   **T**   **V**
Australia   **$$$$**   **29**   **22**

For most of us, one for the "once in a lifetime" wine list, and here's what you'll behold: coconut-dill-clove-eucalyptus scent, the deepest raspberry fruit you can imagine, endless finish.

Kitchen Countertop Survivor™ Grade: B+
Your notes: _____

Penfolds Kalimna Shiraz Bin 28,   **PC**   **T**   **V**
Australia   **$$$**   **26**   **23**

☺ I serve this to my students as an example of real-deal Aussie Shiraz—it's full of black pepper, plum compote flavors, and thick velvety tannins.

Kitchen Countertop Survivor™ Grade: B
Your notes: _____

Penfolds Koonunga Hill Shiraz   **PC**   **T**   **V**
Cabernet, Australia   **$**   **23**   **23**

You can't beat this plummy, slightly spicy red for easy drinkability, yet with some nice tannic grip.

Kitchen Countertop Survivor™ Grade: Avg
Your notes: _____

Rosemount Diamond Label Shiraz   **PC**   **T**   **V**
Australia   **$**   **22**   **25**

Although "the price has gone up," this wine is still a "best buy" that counts legions of devotees. After having lost a bit of its Shiraz "oomph," I think the raspberry taste and spice scent are back.

Kitchen Countertop Survivor™ Grade: B+
Your notes: _____

Rosemount Diamond Label Shiraz/   **PC**   **T**   **V**
Cabernet Sauvignon, Australia   **$**   **21**   **21**

This bottling shows the virtues of blending Cabernet and Shiraz, with juicy, mouthwatering berry

Price Ranges: **$** = $12 or less; **$$** = $12.01–20; **$$$** = $20.01–35, **$$$$** = > $35
Kitchen Fridge/Countertop Survivor™ Grades: *Avg.* = a "one-day wine," tastes noticeably less fresh the next day; *B* = holds its freshness for 2–3 days after opening; *B+* = holds *and gets better* over 2–3 days after opening; *A* = a 3- to 4-day "freshness window"; *A+* = holds *and gets better* over 3–4 days

fruit, a touch of mint in the scent, and a gentle tug of tannin.

Kitchen Countertop Survivor™ Grade: A

Your notes: _____

Rosemount GSM (Grenache-Shiraz-Mourvedre), Australia

	PC	T	V
	$$$	27	23

☺ This "wow" wine shows all the hallmarks of blends from these three Rhone red grapes—both savory and sweet spices, polished tannins, an irresistible smoky/meaty character in the scent, and rich, jammy black cherry and blueberry flavors.

Kitchen Countertop Survivor™ Grade: A

Your notes: _____

Wolf Blass President's Selection Shiraz, Australia

	PC	T	V
	$$	26	20

The "intense blueberry and black pepper aromas" are surprising for the accessible price.

Kitchen Countertop Survivor™ Grade: Avg

Your notes: _____

Wyndham Bin 555 Shiraz Australia

	PC	T	V
	$	22	24

This "always reliable" Aussie Shiraz is rich but balanced and smooth, with "spicy plum" fruit.

Kitchen Countertop Survivor™ Grade: Avg

Your notes: _____

Yellow Tail Shiraz Australia

	PC	T	V
	$	19	23

Although the consensus is that it's "not as good as their Chardonnay" (I agree), most of my tasters call it a "good quaff" at an "unbeatable price."

Kitchen Countertop Survivor™ Grade: Avg

Your notes: _____

Yellow Tail Shiraz Cabernet Australia

	PC	T	V
	$	X	X

✗ Shiraz adds a spiciness to this lip-smacking, affordable-for-everyday red.

Kitchen Countertop Survivor™ Grade: Avg

Your notes: _____

Red Zinfandel

Category Profile: I'd say *groupie* is the apt moniker for devotees of this lovely red grape, a California specialty that ranges in style from medium-bodied, with bright and juicy raspberry flavors, to lush, full-bodied, and high in alcohol with intense blueberry, licorice, and even chocolate scents and flavors. Many of the best vineyards are pre-Prohibition plantings, whose gnarled old vines, often interplanted with other grapes (formerly a common European practice, brought to California by Italian immigrants), produce some amazingly intense, complex wines. Along with their big, bold red wine fruit and body, the wines usually are oaky—a little or a lot depending on the intensity of the grapes used. The grape intensity is a function of the vineyard—its age and its location. California's most famous red Zinfandel areas are Sonoma (especially the Dry Creek Valley subdistrict), Napa, Amador, and the Sierra foothills, whose most ambitious bottlings can be worthy of aging in the cellar. Lodi, in California's Central Valley, is also a good source. The value bottlings are usually regionally labeled as California or Lodi.

Serve: Room temperature; aeration enhances the aroma and flavor.

When: Value Zinfandels are excellent for everyday drinking; good restaurant lists (not necessarily the "big" ones) usually have a selection worth exploring across the price spectrum.

With: Burgers, pizza, lamb (especially with Indian or Moroccan spices), and quality cheeses are favorite matches. I have even enjoyed very rich, juicy Zinfandels with dark chocolate!

In: An all-purpose wineglass or a larger-bowled red wine stem.

Price Ranges: **$** = $12 or less; **$$** = $12.01–20; **$$$** = $20.01–35; **$$$$** = > $35

Kitchen Fridge/Countertop Survivor™ Grades: *Avg.* = a "one-day wine," tastes noticeably less fresh the next day; *B* = holds its freshness for 2–3 days after opening; *B+* = holds *and gets better* over 2–3 days after opening; *A* = a 3- to 4-day "freshness window"; *A+* = holds *and gets better* over 3–4 days

Beaulieu Vineyard Napa Valley   PC   T   V
Zinfandel, California $$ 20   20

I agree with tasters who recommend this wine's "jammy" fruit flavors (meaning the fruit tastes like jam—rich and juicy) "with grilled steaks."

Kitchen Countertop Survivor™ Grade: Avg

Your notes: _____

Beringer North Coast Zinfandel   PC   T   V
California $$ 22   20

This fruity Zin has cherry-berry flavors and soft tannins, making it a great sipper and food partner.

Kitchen Countertop Survivor™ Grade: A

Your notes: _____

Bogle Old Vines Zinfandel   PC   T   V
California $$ 24   26

Tasters love the "great fruit and berry flavor" and "kind of chewy texture" that are in fact typical of old vines Zinfandel. Have it with BBQ or a big cheeseburger.

Kitchen Countertop Survivor™ Grade: Avg

Your notes: _____

Cline Zinfandel   PC   T   V
California $ 21   21

Lots of spice and fruit "for a great price" prompted tasters to describe this as "the perfect house wine."

Kitchen Countertop Survivor™ Grade: Avg

Your notes: _____

Clos du Bois Sonoma Zinfandel   PC   T   V
California $$ 23   23

This is Zin in the medium style, with sweet oak in the scent, raspberry fruit, and soft tannins. To me, it tops their more popular Merlot, and it's cheaper.

Kitchen Countertop Survivor™ Grade: B

Your notes: _____

Dancing Bull Zinfandel   PC   T   V
California $ 23   25

This tasty little Zin with "nice fruit and spice" is a great everyday red for sipping, and for pairing with bold foods.

Kitchen Countertop Survivor™ Grade: Avg

Your notes: _____

| **Dry Creek Vineyard Reserve** | PC | T | V |
| **Zinfandel, California** | $$$ | 24 | 26 |

This wine is a perfect introduction to old-vines Zinfandel—"blueberries and chocolate," as one of my sommelier colleagues describes the flavor, with thick and velvety tannins.

Kitchen Countertop Survivor™ Grade: A

Your notes: _____

| **Estancia Zinfandel** | PC | T | V |
| **California** | $$ | X | X |

✗ Hey, Zin fans, here's a textbook one: fig-and-berry fruit, plush tannins, and a licorice scent.

Kitchen Countertop Survivor™ Grade: Avg

Your notes: _____

| **Fetzer Valley Oaks Zinfandel** | PC | T | V |
| **California** | $ | 24 | 21 |

This juicy, spicy Zinfandel has nice cherry flavors and the consistency you can count on from Fetzer's Valley Oaks line.

Kitchen Countertop Survivor™ Grade: B+

Your notes: _____

| **Grgich Hills Sonoma Zinfandel** | PC | T | V |
| **California** | $$$ | 26 | 22 |

In keeping with the Grgich style, this wine's complexity, firm structure, and restraint deliver the power of Zinfandel, with a subtler expression of scent and flavor—the cherry fruit, spice, and oak.

Kitchen Countertop Survivor™ Grade: A

Your notes: _____

| **Joel Gott Zinfandel** | PC | T | V |
| **California** | $$ | 22 | 24 |

The exotic fruit of this wine—blueberry pie filling and licorice—might make you expect a cult-bottling price, but not so, and that's great!

Kitchen Countertop Survivor™ Grade: B+

Your notes: _____

Price Ranges: $ = $12 or less; **$$** = $12.01–20; **$$$** = $20.01–35; **$$$$** = > $35

Kitchen Fridge/Countertop Survivor™ Grades: *Avg.* = a "one-day wine," tastes noticeably less fresh the next day; *B* = holds its freshness for 2–3 days after opening; *B+* = holds *and gets better* over 2–3 days after opening; *A* = a 3- to 4-day "freshness window"; *A+* = holds *and gets better* over 3–4 days

Kendall-Jackson Vintner's Reserve   PC   T   V
Zinfandel, California $$ 20   19

Some mixed reviews here, but most tasters consider it
"solid," as do I. It drinks nicely by itself and with bold
food, especially anything from the grill.

Kitchen Countertop Survivor™ Grade: B

Your notes: _____

Lambert Bridge Zinfandel   PC   T   V
California $$$ 27   24

The wild raspberry-and-licorice scents and flavors and
chewy tannins are textbook Sonoma Zin.

Kitchen Countertop Survivor™ Grade: B

Your notes: _____

Laurel Glen Reds   PC   T   V
California $ 22   24

One taster captured the consensus perfectly: "Fabulous flavor in a Zin 'field blend'. Great with food, great
alone, great value."

Kitchen Countertop Survivor™ Grade: B

Your notes: _____

Montevina Amador Zinfandel   PC   T   V
California $ 24   24

This wine will give you—at a bargain price—a taste
of the Amador Zin style—specifically, a leathery,
savory-spice scent (think cumin and cardamom),
prune and licorice flavors, and a firm tannic grip.

Kitchen Countertop Survivor™ Grade: B+

Your notes: _____

Rabbit Ridge Paso Robles   PC   T   V
Zinfandel, California $$ 21   24

Formerly a Sonoma Zin specialist, whose move to
Paso Robles hasn't hurt quality at all. Look for
"gulpable" wild berry fruit, spice, and smooth tannins.

Kitchen Countertop Survivor™ Grade: Avg

Your notes: _____

Rafanelli Zinfandel   PC   T   V
California $$$ 27   24

Along with Ravenswood and Ridge, one of the famous
"Rs" of CA Zin and one of my favorites, because the
huge chocolate and blueberry flavors and chewy
texture are big yet balanced.

Kitchen Countertop Survivor™ Grade: B+

Your notes: _____

Rancho Zabaco Dry Creek Valley   **PC**   **T**   **V**
Zinfandel, California   **$$**   **27**   **21**

This is my favorite bottling in the Zabaco line, because it's textbook Dry Creek Zin—blueberry compote flavors, sweet spice, thick and juicy texture.

Kitchen Countertop Survivor™ Grade: Avg

Your notes: _____

Rancho Zabaco Heritage Vines   **PC**   **T**   **V**
Zinfandel, California   **$$**   **24**   **21**

This sizzling Zin seems to get better every year, but "the price went up," too. It's got concentrated, rustic flavor that's thick with dried-cherry fruit and tobacco.

Kitchen Countertop Survivor™ Grade: B

Your notes: _____

Ravenswood Sonoma Old Vines   **PC**   **T**   **V**
Zinfandel, California   **$$**   **23**   **23**

Chock-full of "spice," "zest," and fig fruit, this is a "can't go wrong" bottling from one of Cali's best Zin producers.

Kitchen Countertop Survivor™ Grade: B

Your notes: _____

Ravenswood Vintners Blend   **PC**   **T**   **V**
Zinfandel, California   **$**   **22**   **22**

Ravenswood has been a Zin leader for years. It gets high marks for taste and value, with blueberry and spice flavors and a "yummy juiciness" to the texture.

Kitchen Countertop Survivor™ Grade: A

Your notes: _____

Renwood Sierra Zinfandel   **PC**   **T**   **V**
California   **$$**   **23**   **21**

The "flavors of raspberry and spice," meaty-leathery scent, and plump tannins are classic Amador Zin.

Kitchen Countertop Survivor™ Grade: Avg

Your notes: _____

Price Ranges: **$** = $12 or less; **$$** = $12.01–20; **$$$** = $20.01–35; **$$$$** = > $35

Kitchen Fridge/Countertop Survivor™ Grades: *Avg.* = a "one-day wine," tastes noticeably less fresh the next day; *B* = holds its freshness for 2–3 days after opening; *B+* = holds *and gets better* over 2–3 days after opening; *A* = a 3- to 4-day "freshness window"; *A+* = holds *and gets better* over 3–4 days

Ridge Geyserville (Zinfandel)   PC   T   V
California $$$ 28   22

✓ ☺ This happens to be one of my favorite wines, period. Clearly, I am not alone, as this wine continues to garner raves from my tasters. The scent is complex cedar, savory-sweet spice, and dark fruit that's very intense. The texture feels like the finest chamois upholstery for your mouth.

Kitchen Countertop Survivor™ Grade: A+
Your notes: _____

Robert Mondavi Napa Zinfandel   PC   T   V
California $$ 24   24

A "chewy" Zin with plush but gripping tannins, plus lots of red cherry fruit and sweet cinnamon spice.

Kitchen Countertop Survivor™ Grade: Avg
Your notes: _____

Robert Mondavi Private Selection   PC   T   V
Zinfandel, California $ 24   24

The Zinfandel is a standout red in this brand, plump with cherry fruit and balanced.

Kitchen Countertop Survivor™ Grade: Avg
Your notes: _____

Rosenblum Zinfandel Vintner's   PC   T   V
Cuvee, California $ 23   23

The luscious blueberry fruit makes this "slurpable" and a "best under $10 Zin."

Kitchen Fridge Survivor™ Grade: B
Your notes: _____

Seghesio Sonoma Zinfandel   PC   T   V
California $$ 25   24

"What a great deal," say my tasters. This has long been on my list of favorite Zins, because it offers real Sonoma character—wild-berry fruit, dried spices— at an affordable price.

Kitchen Countertop Survivor™ Grade: Avg
Your notes: _____

St. Francis Old Vines Zinfandel   PC   T   V
California $$$ 23   22

This wine's oak and alcohol have gotten too big for my taste, but my panel likes that intensity of licorice-chocolate-boysenberry.

Kitchen Countertop Survivor™ Grade: Avg
Your notes: _____

St. Francis Sonoma Zinfandel   **PC**   **T**   **V**
California   **$$**   **23**   **26**

Some tasters "prefer the Old Vines bottling," but I like the balance of this subtler St. Francis. There's still dark blackberry and fig fruit and lots of American oak.
Kitchen Countertop Survivor™ Grade: B+
Your notes: _____

Woodbridge (Robert Mondavi)   **PC**   **T**   **V**
Zinfandel, California   **$**   **24**   **24**

This is the best varietal in the Woodbridge line, with nice ripe plump fruit. The quality's ramped up of late, and so have the scores.
Kitchen Countertop Survivor™ Grade: Avg
Your notes: _____

DESSERT WINES

Category Profile: No, none of these have major market presence. The "dessert" wines (or at least those sweet enough to qualify) that are statistically the biggest sellers are unfortunately weak commercial products that fulfill purposes other than a fine ending to a meal. There are plenty of great and available dessert wines to choose from, many of them affordable enough to enjoy often, with or instead of dessert (they're fat free!). These are dessert selections written in by my tasters, and by me. I hope you'll try them, because they will really jazz up your wine and food life.

Serve: Serving temperature depends on the wine, so see the individual entries.

When: With dessert, or as dessert; the lighter ones also make nice aperitifs. If you like to entertain, they're

Price Ranges: **$** – $12 or less; **$$** = $12.01–20; **$$$** = $20.01–35; **$$$$** = > $35
Kitchen Fridge/Countertop Survivor™ Grades: *Avg.* = a "one-day wine," tastes noticeably less fresh the next day; *B* = holds its freshness for 2–3 days after opening; *B+* = holds *and gets better* over 2–3 days after opening; *A* = a 3- to 4-day "freshness window"; *A+* = holds *and gets better* over 3–4 days

great. Add fruit, cheese, or some cookies, and you have a very classy end to a meal with very low hassle.

With: Blue cheese, chocolate, or simple cookies (like biscotti or shortbread) are classic. I've given specific matches in the individual entries.

In: An all-purpose wineglass or a smaller wineglass (the standard serving is 3 ounces rather than the traditional 6 for most wines).

Banfi Brachetto d'Acqui	PC	T	V
Italy	$$$	26	26

This "great for a summer afternoon with chocolate" wine is sensational. The fuschia color, fizzy texture, and delicious juicy-berry flavor seem to always surprise and delight. It's pronounced brak-KETT-oh DOCK-we.

Kitchen Countertop Survivor™ Grade: B
Your notes: _____

Baron Philippe de Rothschild	PC	T	V
Sauternes, France	$$$	26	24

This wine has the classic and beautiful honeyed, crème brûlée and peach scent and flavors of true Sauternes, for an affordable price. Serve slightly chilled.

Kitchen Countertop Survivor™ Grade: A
Your notes: _____

Blandy's 10-Year-Old Malmsey	PC	T	V
Madeira, Portugal	$$$$	24	18

Oh, how I love this wine—its flavor is so tantalizingly "out there." There's caramel, burnt sugar, toffee, burnt orange, toasted nuts, spice, and a cut of tangy acidity that keeps your palate on edge. Pair with chocolate!

Kitchen Countertop Survivor™ Grade: A+
Your notes: _____

Bonny Doon Muscat Vin de	PC	T	V
Glaciere (*van duh glahss-YAIR*)	$$	25	23
California			

Dessert wine lovers will be thrilled with the lush passion fruit and peach flavor. It's sold in half bottles.

Kitchen Fridge Survivor™ Grade: A
Your notes: _____

Broadbent 3 Year Fine Rich   PC   T   V
Madeira, Portugal $$ X   X

✗ A great starter Madeira, giving you the candied orange peel–toffee-caramel character at an easy price.

Kitchen Fridge Survivor™ Grade: A+

Your notes: _____

Chambers Rosewood Vineyards   PC   T   V
Rutherglen Muscadelle, Australia $$$ 23   23

"Fig newtons" is how my students, who are nuts for this wine, describe the deep, viscous flavor that finishes nutty and not at all cloying.

Kitchen Fridge Survivor™ Grade: A+

Your notes: _____

Chapoutier Muscat de Beaumes   PC   T   V
de Venise, France $$ 22   20

This wine has an alluring candied orange peel and honeysuckle scent and flavor that's fabulous with creamy cheeses, crème brûlée, or pound cake.

Kitchen Countertop Survivor™ Grade: B

Your notes: _____

Chateau Rabaud-Promis (*shah-TOE*   PC   T   V
***rah-BOW pro-MEE*) Sauternes** $$$$ 24   20
France

"Like honey" is the perfect description for this rich, classic Sauternes with the scent of flowers, honey, peach preserves, and a hint of earth.

Kitchen Fridge Survivor™ Grade: B+

Your notes: _____

Cockburn's Fine Ruby Port   PC   T   V
Portugal $$ X   X

✗ Enjoy this fig-and-spice-flavored dessert wine over many weeks, as the leftovers hold up well.

Kitchen Fridge Survivor™ Grade: A+

Your notes: _____

Price Ranges: **$** = $12 or less; **$$** = $12.01–20; **$$$** = $20.01–35; **$$$$** = > $35
Kitchen Fridge/Countertop Survivor™ Grades: ***Avg.*** = a "one-day wine," tastes noticeably less fresh the next day; ***B*** = holds its freshness for 2–3 days after opening; ***B+*** = holds *and gets better* over 2–3 days after opening; ***A*** = a 3- to 4-day "freshness window"; ***A+*** = holds *and gets better* over 3–4 days

Emilio Lustau Pedro Ximenez   PC   T   V
"San Emilio" (*eh-MEE-lee-oh* $$$ 28   24
LOO-stau Pedro Hee-MEN-ez san
eh-MEE-lee-oh) **Sherry, Spain**

A wonderful dessert-style sherry redolent with fig
flavors that's "lovely with all chocolate desserts." Pros
call Pedro Ximenez "PX" for short.

Kitchen Fridge Survivor™ Grade: A+

Your notes: _____

Ferreira Doña Antonia Port   PC   T   V
Portugal $$$ 24   24

This is a tawny-style Port—all amber-gold color,
toasted nut, cinnamon sugar, cappuccino, and maple
scents and flavors. Serve at room temp. The open
bottle will not go bad.

Kitchen Countertop Survivor™ Grade: A+

Your notes: _____

Ficklin Tinta "Port"   PC   T   V
California $$ 21   23

"Port" is in quotes, because the real thing is from
Portugal. But this is a very worthy version of the style,
with chocolate, nuts, dried figs, and sweet spices
permeating both the scent and the taste.

Kitchen Countertop Survivor™ Grade: A+

Your notes: _____

Fonseca Bin 27 Port   PC   T   V
Portugal $$$ 23   23

This is Port in the ruby style with flavors of ripest figs,
licorice, and allspice. Yum!

Kitchen Countertop Survivor™ Grade: A+

Your notes: _____

Michele Chiarlo Nivole ("Clouds")   PC   T   V
Moscato d'Asti, Italy $$$ 29   23

This delicately sparkling, honeysuckle-scented wine
from the Piedmont region of Italy is low in alcohol,
high in fruit (apricot and tangerine) and refreshment,
and so lovely as an aperitif. Serve chilled.

Kitchen Countertop Survivor™ Grade: B

Your notes: _____

Rivetti Moscato d'Asti La Spinetta   PC   T   V
Italy $$ 23   24

I agree it's the "gold standard by which all others

should be judged" in the category of Moscato d'Asti (the Moscato grape from the town of Asti). The honeysuckle, orange blossom, and apricot scent and flavor are gorgeous, and the light alcohol makes it a "great brunch wine."

Kitchen Countertop Survivor™ Grade: B+

Your notes: _____

St. Supery Moscato	PC	T	V
California	$$	27	21

"A wonderful dessert wine" with the scent of honeysuckles and the flavor of spiced apricots.

Kitchen Fridge Survivor™ Grade: B+

Your notes: _____

Taylor Fladgate 20 Year Tawny	PC	T	V
Port, Portugal	$$$$	X	X

✗ 20-year tawnies are "pricey" due to the decades of aging, but I think still a value because the open bottle holds, and the complexity—toasted walnuts, streusel, and caramel—is awesome.

Kitchen Fridge Survivor™ Grade: Avg

Your notes: _____

Warre 10-Year-Old Otima Tawny	PC	T	V
Port, Portugal	$$$	22	16

The "nut flavor" and "smooth, warming texture" are classic to tawny Port, which is a touch sweet but not at all cloying.

Kitchen Fridge Survivor™ Grade: A+

Your notes: _____

Yalumba Museum Muscat	PC	T	V
Australia	$$$	X	X

✗ Here's an affordable way to experience Australia's "liqueur Muscat" wines—syrupy-textured, nutty-rich from long aging, and plump with mincemeat, fig, and rum-soaked fruitcake flavors.

Kitchen Fridge Survivor™ Grade: A

Your notes: _____

Price Ranges: **$** = $12 or less; **$$** = $12.01–20; **$$$** = $20.01–35; **$$$$** = > $35

Kitchen Fridge/Countertop Survivor™ Grades: *Avg.* = a "one-day wine," tastes noticeably less fresh the next day; *B* = holds its freshness for 2–3 days after opening; *B+* = holds *and gets better* over 2–3 days after opening; *A* = a 3- to 4-day "freshness window"; *A+* = holds *and gets better* over 3–4 days

THE
GREAT WINE MADE SIMPLE
MINI-COURSE:
A WINE CLASS IN A GLASS

How do you go about choosing wine? Many buyers assume the quick answer is to "trade up"—if you spend more, the wine will be better, right? Not necessarily, because price and quality are rarely proportional, meaning you cannot assume that a twenty-dollar bottle is twice as good as a ten-dollar one. And more important, preferences are individual. So the best way to ensure you'll be happy with your wine choices is to learn your taste.

Here are two quick wine lessons, adapted from my book *Great Wine Made Simple,* that will let you do exactly that. You're probably thinking, Will there be a test? In a way, every pulled cork is a test, but for the *wine:* Are you happy with what you got for the price you paid, and would you buy it again? This mini-course will teach you to pick wines that pass muster by helping you learn what styles and tastes you like in a wine and how to use the label to help you find them.

If you want, you can complete each lesson in a matter of minutes. As with food, tasting impressions form quickly with wine. Then you can get dinner on the table, accompanied by your wine picks. Start by doing the first lesson, "White Wine Made Simple," one evening, and then Lesson 2, "Red Wine Made Simple," another time. Or you can invite friends over and make it a party. Everyone will learn a little bit about wine, while having fun.

Setup
Glassware: You will need three glasses per taster. A simple all-purpose wineglass is ideal, but clear disposables are fine, too.

Pouring: Start with a tasting portion (about an ounce of each wine). Tasters can repour more of their favorite to enjoy with hors d'oeuvres or dinner.

Flights: Taste the Lesson 1 whites first and then the Lesson 2 reds (pros call each sequence of wine a *flight*). There is no need to wash or rinse the glasses.

To Taste It Is to Know It

Tasting is the fastest way to learn about wine. My restaurant guests tell me this all the time: they know what wines they like when they try them. The trick is in understanding the style and knowing how to ask for it and get it again: "I'd like a Chardonnay with lots of buttery, toasty oak and gobs of creamy, tropical fruit flavors." If you don't know what it means, you might feel silly offering a description like that when wine shopping. But those words really are in the glass, and these easy-to-follow tasting lessons will help you recognize the styles and learn which ones are your favorites.

The Lessons

What You'll Do:
For Lesson 1, "White Wine Made Simple," you will comparison-taste three major white wine grapes: Riesling, Sauvignon Blancs and Chardonnay. For Lesson 2, "Red Wine Made Simple," you will compare three major reds: Pinot Noir, Merlot, and Cabernet Sauvignon. Follow these easy steps:

1. Buy your wines. Make your choice from the varietal sections of this book. It's best to choose wines in the same price category—for example, all one dollar-sign wines. To make the most of the lesson, choose wines from the region(s) suggested in each grape's "tasting notes."
2. Chill (whites only), pour, and taste the wines in the order of body, light to full, as shown in the tasting notes.
3. Use the tasting notes below as a guide, and record your own if you want.

What You'll Learn:
Body styles of the major grapes—light, medium, or full. You'll see that Riesling is lighter (less heavy) than

Chardonnay, in the same way that, for example, skim milk is lighter than heavy cream.

What the major grapes taste like—When tasted side by side, the grapes are quite distinctive, just as a pear tastes different from an apple, a strawberry tastes different from a blueberry, and so on.

What other wine flavor words taste like—Specifically, you'll experience these tastes: oaky, tannic, crisp, and fruity. Knowing them is helpful because they're used a lot in this book, on wine bottle labels, and by sellers of wine—merchants, waiters, and so on.

Getting comfortable with these basics will equip you to describe the wine styles you like to a waiter or wine merchant and to use the information on a bottle label to find those styles on your own. In the "Buying Lingo" section that follows, I've defined lots of other style words and listed some wine types you can try to experience them.

Tasting Lesson 1
WHITE WINE MADE SIMPLE

Instructions: Taste the wines in numbered order. Note your impressions of:

Color: Which is lightest and which is darkest? Whites can range from pale straw to deep yellow-gold. The darker the color, the fuller the body.

Scent: While they all smell like white wine, the aromas differ, from delicate and tangy to rich and fruity.

Taste and Body: In the same way that fruits range from crisp and tart (like apples) to ripe and lush (like mangoes), the wine tastes will vary along with the body styles of the grapes, from light to full.

Which grape and style do you like best? If you like more than one style, that's great, too!

The White Wines

Grape 1: Riesling (any region)—Light-bodied

Description: Crisp and refreshing, with vibrant fruit flavor ranging from apple to peach.

Brand Name: _____

Your notes: _____

_____

Grape 2: Sauvignon Blanc (France or New Zealand)—
Medium-bodied

Description: Very distinctive! The smell is exotically
pungent, the taste tangy and mouthwatering, like
citrus fruit (lime and grapefruit).

Brand Name: _____

Your notes: _____

_____

Grape 3: Chardonnay (California)—Full-bodied

Description: The richest scent and taste, with fruit flavor
ranging from ripe apples to peaches to tropical fruits.
You can feel the full-bodied texture, too. "Oaky" scents
come through as a sweet, buttery, or toasty impression.

Brand Name: _____

Your notes: _____

_____

Tasting Lesson 2
RED WINE MADE SIMPLE

**Instructions: Again, taste the wines in numbered order
and note your impressions.**

Color: Red wines range in color from transparent ruby,
like the Pinot Noir, to inky dark purple—the darker the
color, the fuller the body.

Scent: In addition to the smell of "red wine," you'll
get the cherrylike smell of Pinot Noir, perhaps plum
character in the Merlot, and a rich dark-berry smell in
the Cabernet. There are other scents, too, so enjoy
them. You can also compare your impressions with
those included in the reviews section of the book.

Taste and Body: Like white wines, red wines range
from light and delicate to rich and intense. You'll note
the differences in body from light to full and the
distinctive taste character of each grape. As you can
see, tasting them side by side makes it easy to detect
and compare the differences.

The Red Wines

Grape 1: Pinot Noir (any region)—Light-bodied

Description: Delicate cherrylike fruit flavor, silky-smooth
texture, mouthwatering acidity, all of which make
Pinot Noir a versatile wine for most types of food.

Brand Name: _____

Your notes: _____

_____

Grape 2: Merlot (California, Chile, or Washington)—
Medium-bodied

Description: More intense than Pinot Noir: rich "red wine" flavor, yet not too heavy. That's probably why it's so popular!

Brand Name: _____

Your notes: _____

_____

Grape 3: Cabernet Sauvignon (Chile or California)—
Full-bodied

Description: The fullest-bodied, most intense taste. Notice the drying sensation it leaves on your tongue? That's tannin, a natural grape component that, like color, comes from the skin. As you can see, more color and more tannin come together. Tasting high-tannin wines with fat or protein counters that drying sensation (that's why Cabernet and red meat are considered classic partners). In reds, an "oaky" character comes through as one or more of these scents: spice, cedar, smoke, toastiness, vanilla, and coconut. No wonder buyers love it!

Brand Name: _____

Your notes: _____

_____

Buying Lingo

Here are the meanings of other major wine style words that you see in this book and on wine bottles.

Acidity—The tangy, tart, crisp, mouthwatering component in wine. It's a prominent characteristic of Riesling, Sauvignon Blanc, and Pinot Grigio whites and Pinot Noir and Chianti/Sangiovese reds.

Bag-in-a-Box—A box with a wine-filled bag inside that deflates as the wine is consumed, preventing oxidation.

Balance—The harmony of all the wine's main components: fruit, alcohol, and acidity, plus sweetness (if any), oak (if used in the winemaking), and tannin (in reds). As with food, balance in the wine is important to your enjoyment, and a sign of quality. But it's also a matter of taste—the dish may taste "too salty" and the wine "too oaky" for one person but be fine to another.

Barrel aged / barrel fermented—The wine was aged or fermented (or both) in oak barrels. The barrels give fuller body, as well as an "oaky" character to the wine's scent and flavor, making it seem richer.

"Oaky" scents are often in the sweet family—but *not* sugary. Rather, *toasty, spicy, vanilla, buttery,* and *coconut* are the common wine words to describe "oaky" character. Other label signals that mean "oaky": Barrel Fermented, Barrel Select, Barrel Cuvee, Cask Fermented.

Bouquet—All of the wine's scents, which come from the grape(s) used, the techniques (like oak aging), the age of the wine, and the vineyard characteristics (like soil and climate).

Bright—Vivid and vibrant. Usually used as a modifier, like "bright fruit" or "bright acidity."

Buttery—Literally, the creamy-sweet smell of butter. One by-product of fermentation is an ester that mimics the butter smell, so you may well notice this in some wines, especially barrel-fermented Chardonnays.

"Corked," "corky"—Refers to a wine whose scent or taste has been tainted by corks or wine-making equipment infected with a bacteria called TCA. While not harmful to health, TCA gives wines a musty smell and taste.

Creamy—Can mean a smell similar to fresh cream or a smooth and lush texture. In sparkling wines, it's a textural delicacy and smoothness of the bubbles.

Crisp—See Acidity.

Dry—A wine without sweetness (though not without fruit; see Fruity for more on this).

Earthy—As with cheeses, potatoes, mushrooms, and other good consumables, wines can have scents and flavors reminiscent of, or owed to, the soil. The "earth" terms commonly attributed to wine include *mushrooms, truffles, flint, dusty, gravelly, wet leaves,* and even *barnyard.*

Exotic—Just as it applies to other things, this description suggests unusual and alluring characteristics in wine. Quite often refers to wines with a floral or spicy style or flavors beyond your typical fruit bowl, such as tropical fruits or rare berries.

Floral—Having scents that mimic flower scents, whether fresh (as in the honeysuckle scent of some Rieslings) or dried (as in the wilted rose petal scent of some Gewurztraminers).

Food-friendly—Food-friendly wines have taste characteristics that pair well with a wide variety of foods without clashing or overpowering— namely, good acidity and moderate (not too heavy) body. The food-friendly whites include Riesling and Sauvignon Blanc; the reds include Chianti, Spanish Rioja, red Rhone, and Pinot Noir wines.

Fruity—Marked by a prominent smell and taste of fruit. In whites the fruit tastes can range from lean and tangy (like lemons and crisp apples) to medium (like melons and peaches) to lush (like mangoes and pineapples). In reds, think cranberries and cherries, plums and blueberries, figs and prunes. Note that *fruity* doesn't mean "sweet." The taste and smell of ripe fruit are perceived as sweet, but they're not sugary. Most wines on the market are at once dry (meaning not sweet) and fruity, with lots of fruit flavor.

Grassy—Describes a wine marked with scents of fresh-cut grass or herbs or even green vegetables (like green pepper and asparagus). It's a signature of Sauvignon Blanc wines, especially those grown in New Zealand and France. *Herbal* and *herbaceous* are close synonyms.

Herbal, herbaceous—See Grassy.

Legs—The drips running down the inside of the wineglass after you swirl it. Not a sign of quality (as in "good legs") but of viscosity. Fast-running legs indicate a low-viscosity wine and slow legs a high-viscosity wine. The higher the viscosity, the richer and fuller the wine feels in your mouth.

Nose—The smell of the wine. Isn't it interesting how wines have a nose, legs, and body? As you've no doubt discovered, they have personalities, too!

Oaky—See Barrel aged.

Off-dry—A lightly sweet wine.

Old vines—Refers to wine from vines significantly older than average, usually at least thirty years old and sometimes far older. Older vines yield a smaller, but often more intensely flavored, crop of grapes.

Regional wine—A wine named for the region where the grapes are grown, such as Champagne, Chianti, Pouilly-Fuisse, etc.

Spicy—A wine with scents and flavors reminiscent of spices, both sweet (cinnamon, ginger, cardamom, clove) and savory (pepper, cumin, curry).

Sweet—A wine that has perceptible sugar, called *residual sugar* because it is left over from fermentation and not converted to alcohol. A wine can be lightly sweet like a Moscato or very sweet like a Port or Sauternes.

Tannic—A red wine whose tannin is noticeable— a little or a lot—as a drying sensation on your tongue ranging from gentle (lightly tannic) to velvety (richly tannic) to harsh (too tannic).

Terroir—The distinctive flavors, scents, and character of a wine owed to its vineyard source. For example, the terroir of French red Burgundies is sometimes described as *earthy*.

Toasty—Wines with a toasty, roasted, caramelized, or smoky scent reminiscent of coffee beans, toasted nuts or spices, or burnt sugar.

Unfiltered—A wine that has not been filtered before bottling (which is common practice). Some say filtering the wine strips out flavor, but not everyone agrees. I think most tasters cannot tell the difference.

Varietal wine—A wine named for the grape used to make it, such as Chardonnay or Merlot.

Handling Wine Leftovers

I developed the Kitchen Countertop Survivor™ and Kitchen Fridge Survivor™ grades to give you an idea of how long each wine stays in good drinking condition if you don't finish the bottle. In the same way that resealing the cereal box or wrapping and refrigerating leftovers will extend their freshness window, you can do the same for wine by handling the leftovers as follows:

All Wines

Cork—At a minimum, close the bottle with its original cork. Most wines will stay fresh a day or two at room temperature. To extend that freshness, purchase a vacuum-sealer (available in kitchen shops and wine shops). You simply cork the bottle with the purchased rubber stopper, which has a one-way valve. The accompanying plastic vacuum pump is placed on top of the stopper; you pump it repeatedly until the resistance tightens, until air has been pumped out of the bottle. Some wine experts don't think rubber stoppers, I've used them for years. In my restaurants,

I have found they extended the life of bottles opened for by-the-glass service at least two days longer than just sealing with the original cork.)

Refrigerate stoppered (and vacuum-sealed) bottles, whether white, pink, or red. Refrigeration of anything slows the spoilage, and your red wine, once removed from the fridge and poured in the glass, will quickly come to serving temperature.

For even longer shelf-life, you can preserve partial bottles with inert gas. I recommend this especially for more expensive wines. Wine Life and Private Preserve are two brands that I have used (sold in wine shops and accessories catalogs). They come in a can that feels light, as if it's empty. Inside is an inert gas mixture that is heavier than air. The can's spray nozzle is inserted into the bottle. A one-second sprays fills the empty bottle space with the inert gas, displacing the air inside, which is the key because no air in contact with the wine means no oxidation. Then you quickly replace the cork (make sure the fit is tight). My experience in restaurants using gas systems for very upscale wines by the glass is that they keep well for a week or more.

Sparkling Wines

Your best bet is to purchase "clam shell" Champagne stoppers, with one or two hinged metal clamps attached to a stopper top that has a rubber or plastic gasket for a tight seal. You place the stopper on top, press down, and then anchor the clamps to the bottle lip. If you open your sparkler carefully and don't "pop" the cork, losing precious carbonation, a stoppered partial bottle will keep its effervescence for at least a few days, and sometimes much longer.

SAVVY SHOPPER: RETAIL WINE BUYING

Supermarkets, pharmacies, price clubs, catalogs, state stores, megastores, dot.coms, and boutiques . . . where you shop for wine depends a lot on the state where you live, because selling wine requires a state license. What many people don't realize is how much the wine laws vary from one state to the next.

In most states, the regulations affect the prices you pay for wine, what wines are available, and how you get your hands on them (ideally, they are delivered to your door or poured at your table, but this isn't always legal). Here is a quick summary of the retail scene to help you make the most of your buying power wherever you live.

Wine Availability The single biggest frustration for every wine buyer and winery is bureaucracy. To ensure the collection of excise taxes, in nearly all states every single wine must be registered and approved in some way before it can be sold. If a wine you're seeking isn't available in your area, this is probably the reason. For many small boutique wineries, it just isn't worth the bother and expense to get legal approval for the few cases of wine they would sell in a particular state. One extreme example is Pennsylvania, a "control state" where wine is sold exclusively by a state-run monopoly that, without competition, has little incentive to source a lot of boutique wines. By contrast, California, New York, and Chicago, with high demand and competition, are good markets for wine availability.

Wine Prices and Discounts Wine prices can vary from one state to the next due to different tax rates. And in general, prices are lower in competitive markets, where stores can use discounts, sale prices, and so on to vie for your business.

Where they are legal, case discounts of 10 to 15 percent are a great way to get the best possible prices for your favorite wines. On the more expensive wines, many people I know coordinate their buying with friends and family so they can buy full cases and get these discounts.

Delivery and Wine-by-Mail In many states, it is not legal for stores or other retailers to deliver wine to the purchaser.

Many catalogs and websites sell wine by mail. Some are affiliated with retail stores or wineries, while others are strictly virtual stores. The conveniences include shopping on your own time and terms, from home or office, helpful buying recommendations and information, and usually home delivery. But the laws governing such shipping are complex, and vary from state to state (in some states it is completely prohibited). When you add in shipping costs, there may not be a price advantage to shopping online, but many people swear by the convenience and buying advice it offers. It is also an easy way to send wine gifts.

Where Should I Shop? That depends on what you're buying. If you know what you want, then price is your main consideration, and you'll get your best deals at venues that concentrate on volume sales—discount stores, price clubs, and so on. If you want buying advice, or are buying rare wines, you're better off in a wine shop or merchant specializing in collectible wines. These stores have trained buyers who taste and know their inventory well; they can help you with your decision. The better stores also have temperature-controlled storage for their rare wines, which is critical to ensure you get a product in good condition. There are also web-based fine and rare wine specialists, but that is a fairly new market. I suggest you purchase fine and rare wines only through sources with a good track record of customer service. In that way, if you have problems with a shipment, you will have some recourse.

Can I Take That Bottle on the Wine List Home with Me? In most states, restaurants' wine licenses allow for sale and consumption "on-premise" only, meaning they cannot sell you a bottle to take home.

Burgundy Buyers, Beware With the exception of volume categories such as Beaujolais, Macon, and Pouilly-Fuissé, buyers of French white and red Burgundy should shop only at fine wine merchants, preferably those that specialize in Burgundy, for two reasons. First, Burgundy is simply too fragile to handle the storage conditions in most stores. Burgundy specialists ensure temperature-controlled storage. Second, selection is a major factor, because quality varies a lot from one winery to the next, and from one vintage to the next. Specialist stores have the needed buying expertise to ensure the quality of their offerings.

Is That a Deal or a Disaster? Floor stacks, "end caps," private labels, and bin ends can be a boon for the buyer, or a bust, depending on where you are shopping. Here's what you need to know about them:

"Floor Stacks" of large-volume categories and brands (e.g., branded varietal wines)—These are a best bet in supermarkets and other volume-based venues, where they're used to draw your attention to a price markdown. Take advantage of it to stock up for everyday or party wines.

"End Cap" wine displays featured at the ends of aisles—A good bet, especially in fine wine shops. You may not have heard of the wine, but they're usually "hidden gems" that the buyer discovered and bought in volume, to offer you quality and uniqueness at a savings.

"Bin Ends"—Retailers often clear out the last few bottles of something by discounting the price. In reputable retail stores, they are usually still good quality, and thus a good bet. Otherwise, steer clear.

Private labels—These are wines blended and bottled exclusively for the retailer—again, good bets in reputable stores, who stake their reputation on your satisfaction with their private labels.

"Shelf-talkers"—Written signs, reviews, and ratings. Good shops offer their own recommendations in lieu of, or along with, critics' scores. If the only information is a critic's score, check to be sure that the vintage being sold matches that of the wine that was reviewed.

Buying Wine in Restaurants

Wine List Strategy Session

A lot of us have a love-hate relationship with the wine list. On the one hand, we know it holds the potential to enhance the evening, impress the date or client, broaden our horizons, or all three. But it also makes us feel intimidated, inadequate, overwhelmed, and . . .

Panicked by prices—That goes for both the cheapest wines *and* the most expensive ones; we're leery of extremes.

Pressured by pairing—Will this wine "go with" our food?

Overwhelmed by options—Can this wine I've never heard of possibly be any good? Does my selection measure up? (Remember, the restaurant is supposed to impress *you*, not the other way around.) This "phone book" wine list makes me want to dial 911.

Stumped by Styles—Food menus are easy because we understand the key terms: appetizer, entree, dessert, salad, soup, fish, meat, and so on. But after *white* and *red*, most of us get lost pretty quickly with wine categories. (Burgundy . . . is that a style, a color, a place, or all three?)

Let's deal with the first three above. For the lowdown on wine list terms, use the decoder that follows to pinpoint the grapes and styles behind all the major wine names.

Wine List Prices

The prices on wine lists reflect three things:

- *The dining-out experience*—The restaurant wine markup is higher than in retail stores because the decor is (usually) nicer, and you get to stay awhile, during which time they open the wine, serve it in a nice glass, and clean up afterward. They also may have invested in the cost and expertise to select and store the wine properly. Consequently those who enjoy drinking wine in restaurants are accustomed to being charged more for the wine than you would pay to drink the same bottle at home. That said, exorbitant markups are, in my opinion, the biggest deterrent to more guests enjoying wine in restaurants (which is both good for the guests and good for business). You can always vote with your wallet and dine in restaurants with guest-friendly wine pricing.

- *Location*—Restaurants in exclusive resorts, in urban centers with a business clientele, or with a star chef behind them, tend toward higher wine markups, because they can get away with it. The logic, so to speak, is that if you're on vacation, it's on the company, or it's just the "in" place, high markups (on everything) are part of the price of admission. However, I don't really think that's right, and I do think these places would sell more wine with lower markups.

- *The rarity of the wine*—Often, the rarer the wine (either because it's in high demand due to critics' hype or because it's old and just a few bottles remain), the higher the markup. It's a form of rationing in the face of high demand/low supply. Food can be the same way (lobsters, truffles, caviar, etc.).

Getting the Most Restaurant Wine for Your Money

Seeking value doesn't make you a cheapskate. Here are the best strategies to keep in mind:

1. Take the road less traveled—Chardonnay and Cabernet Sauvignon are what I call "comfort wines" because they're so well known. But their prices often reflect a "comfort premium" (in the same way that a name-brand toothpaste costs more than the store brand). These spectacular wine styles often give better value for the money, because they're less widely known:

Whites
Riesling
Sauvignon Blanc and Fume Blanc
Sancerre (a French Loire Valley wine made
   from the Sauvignon Blanc grape)
Anything from Washington State or New
   Zealand

Reds
Cotes-du-Rhone and other French Rhone
   Valley reds
Red Zinfandel from California
Spanish Rioja and other reds from Spain
Cabernet Sauvignon from Chile

2. Savvy Splurging—There's no doubt about it:
   nothing commemorates, celebrates, or im-
   presses better than a special wine. Since splurging on wine in a restaurant can mean especially
   big bucks, here are the "trophy" wine styles that
   give you the most for your money on wine lists:

> French Champagne—I think that Cham-
> pagne (the real stuff from France's Cham-
> pagne region) is among the most affordable
> luxuries on the planet, and its wine list
> prices are often among the best of all the
> "badge" wine categories (such as French
> Bordeaux and Burgundy, cult California
> Cabernets, and boutique Italian wines).

> California's Blue Chip Cabernets—I don't
> mean the tiny-production cult-movement
> Cabernets but rather the classics that have
> been around for decades, and still make
> world-class wine at a fair price. Names
> like Beringer, BV, Franciscan, Mt. Veeder,
> Robert Mondavi, Silver Oak, Simi, and
> Stag's Leap all made the survey, and for
> good reason: they're excellent and
> available.

> Italian Chianti Classico Riserva—This
> recommendation may surprise you, but I
> include it because the quality for the price
> is better than ever, and recent vintages
> have been great. I also think that across the

country a lot of people celebrate and do business in steak houses and Italian restaurants, which tend to carry this wine category because it complements their food.

3. The Midprice/Midstyle "Safety Zone"—This is a strategy I first developed not for dining guests but for our *waiters* trying to help diners choose a bottle, usually with very little to go on (many people aren't comfortable describing their taste preference, and they rarely broadcast their budget for fear of looking cheap). The midprice/midstyle strategy is this: in any wine list category (e.g., Chardonnays, Italian reds, and so on), if you go for the midprice range in that section, odds are good the wine will be midstyle. Midstyle is my shorthand for the most typical, crowd-pleasing version, likely to satisfy a high proportion of guests and to be sticker shock free. The fact is that the more expensive the wine is, the more distinctive and even unusual its style is likely to be. If it's not to your taste *and* you've spent a lot, you're doubly disappointed.

4. Ask— With wine more popular than ever, restaurants are the most proactive they've ever been in seeking to put quality and value on their wine lists. So ask for it: "What's the best red wine deal on your list right now?" Or, if you have a style preference, say something like "We want to spend $XX. Which of these Chardonnays do you think is the best for the money?"

Pairing Wine and Food

Worrying a lot about this is a big waste of time, because most wines complement most foods, regardless of wine color, center-of-the-plate protein, and all that other stuff. How well? Their affinity can range from "fine" to "Omigod." You can pretty much expect at least a nice combination every time you have wine with food and great matches from time to time (of course, frequent experimentation ups your odds). The point is, your style preference is a lot more important than the pairing, per se, because if you hate the dish or the wine, you're hardly likely to enjoy the pairing. That said, here is a list of wine styles that are especially favored by sommeliers and chefs for their exceptional food affinity and versatility, along with a few best-bet food recommendations:

Favorite "Food Wines" White	Best-Bet Food Matches
Champagne and Sparkling Wine—So many people save bubbly just for toasts, but it's an amazing "food wine"	Sushi All shellfish Cheeses (even stinky ones) Omelets and other egg dishes Mushroom sauces (on risotto, pasta or whatever)
Riesling from Germany, Alsace (France), America, Australia	Mexican, southwestern, and other spicy foods Shellfish Cured meats and sausages
Alsace (France) White Wines—Riesling, Pinot Gris, and Gewurztraminer	Pacific Rim foods—Japanese, Thai, Korean, Chinese Indian food Smoked meats and charcuterie Meat stews (really!)
Sauvignon Blanc and wines made from it (French Sancerre, Pouilly-Fume, and white Bordeaux)	Goat cheese Salads Herbed sauces (like pesto) Tomato dishes (salads, soups, sauces)
Red	
Beaujolais (from France)	Mushroom dishes
Pinot Noir	Fish (especially rich ones like tuna, salmon, and cod) Smoked meats Grilled vegetables Duck
Chianti, Rosso di Montalcino, and other Italian reds made from the Sangiovese grape	Pizza, eggplant parmigiana (and other Italian-American–inspired tastes) Cheesy dishes Spicy sausages
Rioja from Spain	Roasted and grilled meats

Choosing from the Wine List

You've got the wine list. Unless you know a lot about wine, you now face at least one of these dilemmas:

- You've never heard of any of the wines listed or at least none of those in your price range (OK, maybe you've heard of Dom Pérignon, but let's be real). Or the names you do recognize don't interest you.

- You have no idea how much a decent selection should cost. But you *do* know you want to keep to your budget, without broadcasting it to your guests and the entire dining room.
- The wine list is so huge you don't even want to open it.

Wine List Playbook

Remember, you're the buyer. Good restaurants want you to enjoy wine and to feel comfortable with the list, your budget, and so on. As far as the wine-snobby ones go, what are you doing there anyway? (OK, if you took a gamble on a new place or somebody else picked it, the strategies here can help.)

The basics:

1. *Don't worry if you haven't heard of the names.* There are literally thousands of worthy wines beyond the big brand names, and many restaurants feature them to spice up their selection.
2. *Determine what you want to spend.* I think most people want the best deal they can get. With that in mind, here are some price/value rules of thumb. In most restaurants the wine prices tend to relate to the food prices, as follows:
   - Wines by-the-glass: The price window for good-quality wines that please a high percentage of diners usually parallels the restaurant's mid- to top-priced appetizers. So if the Caesar salad (or wings or whatever) is $5.95, expect to spend that, plus or minus a dollar or two, for a good glass of wine. This goes for dessert wine, too. Champagne and sparkling wines can be more, due to the cost of the product and greater waste because it goes flat.
   - Bottles: This is far more variable, but in general most restaurants try to offer an ample selection of good-quality bottles priced in what I call a "selling zone" that's benchmarked to their highest entree price, plus a margin. That's the variable part. It can range

from $5–10 on average in national chain restaurants and their peers to at least $10–20 in luxury and destination restaurants. So if the casual chain's steak-and-shrimp-scampi combo costs $17.95, the $20–30 zone on their wine list will likely hold plenty of good bottle choices. In an urban restaurant where the star chef's signature herb-crusted lamb costs $28, you could expect a cluster of worthy bottles in the $35–55 range.

We in the trade find it funny, and nearly universal, that guests shy away from the least expensive wines on our lists, suspicious that there's something "wrong" with the wine. But any restaurant that's committed to wine, whether casual chain or destination eatery, puts extra effort into finding top-quality wines at the lowest price points. They may come from grapes or regions you don't know, but my advice is to muster your sense of adventure and try them. In the worst-case scenario, you'll be underwhelmed, but since tastes vary, this can happen with wine at any price. I think the odds are better that you'll enjoy one of the best deals on the wine list.

The wine list transaction: You've set your budget. Now it's time to zero in on a selection. You've got two choices—go it alone or ask for help. In either case, here's what to do:

1. Ask for the wine list right away. It's a pet peeve of mine that guests even *need* to ask (rather than getting the list automatically with the food menus), because that can cause both service delays and anxiety. Many people are scared to request the list for fear it "commits" them to a purchase, before they can determine whether they'll be comfortable with the prices and choices available. As you're being handed the menus, say "We'll take a look at the wine list, too" to indicate you want a copy to review, not a pushy sales job. Tip: I always ask that the wine-by-the-glass list be brought, too. Since many places change them often, they may be on a separate card or a specials board. (I think

verbal listings are the worst, because often key information, like the price or winery, can get lost in translation.)

2. Determine any style particulars you're in the mood for:
   - White or red?
   - A particular grape, region, or body style?

   If the table can't reach a consensus, look at wine-by-the-glass and half-bottle options. This can happen when preferences differ or food choices are all over the map ("I'm having the oysters, he's having the wild boar, we want one wine . . ." is a stumper I've actually faced!).

3. Find your style zone in the list. Turn to the section that represents your chosen category—e.g., whites, the wine-by-the-glass section, Chardonnays, Italian reds, or whatever—or let the server know what style particulars you have in mind.

4. Match your budget. Pick a wine priced accordingly, keeping in mind these "safety zones":
   - The wines recommended in this book
   - Winery or region names that you remember liking or hearing good things about (e.g., Chianti in Italy or a different offering from your favorite white Zinfandel producer)
   - The midprice/midstyle zone (as I explained earlier, many lists have this "sweet spot" of well-made, moderately priced offerings)
   - Featured wine specials, if they meet your price parameters

   You can communicate your budget while keeping your dignity with this easy trick I teach waiters:
   - Find your style zone—e.g., Pinot Grigios —in the wine list
   - With both you and the server looking at the list, *point to the price* of a wine that's close to what you want to spend and then say, "We were looking at this one. What do you think?"
   - Keep pointing long enough for the server to see the price, and you'll be understood

without having to say (in front of your date or client), "No more than thirty bucks, OK?"

I ask my waiters to point to the price, starting at a moderate level, with their first wine suggestion. From there the guest's reaction shows his or her intentions, without the embarrassment of having to talk price.

There's no formula, but the bottom line is this: whether glass or bottle, it's hard to go wrong with popular grapes and styles, moderate prices, the "signature" or featured wine(s) of the restaurant, and/or the waiter's enthusiastic recommendation. If you don't like it, chalk it up to experience—the same could happen with a first-time food choice, right? Most of the time, experimentation pays off. So enjoy!

Wine List Decoder

Wine is like food—it's easy to choose from among the styles with which you're familiar. That's why wines like Pinot Grigio, Chardonnay, Chianti, and Merlot are such big sellers. But when navigating other parts of the list, namely less-common grape varieties and the classic European regional wines, I think many of us get lost pretty quickly. And yet these are major players in the wine world, without which buyers miss out on a whole array of delicious options, from classic to cutting edge.

This decoder will give you the tools you need to explore them. It reveals:

> *The grapes used* to make the classic wines—If it's a grape you've tried, then you'll have an idea of what the wine tastes like.
> *The body styles from light to full* of every major wine category—The waiters and wine students with whom I work always find this extremely helpful, because it breaks up the wine world into broad, logical categories that are easy to understand and similar to the way we classify other things. With food, for example, we have vegetables, meat, fish, and so on.
> *The taste profile,* in simple terms—The exact taste of any wine is subjective (I say apple, you say pear), but knowing how the tastes *compare* is a great tool to help you identify your preferred style.

The names are set up just as you might see them on a wine list, under the key country and region headings, and in each section they are arranged by body style from light to full. (For whites, Italy comes before France in body style, overall. Their order is reversed for reds.) Finally, where applicable I've highlighted the major grapes in italics in the column on the left to help you quickly see just how widely used these grapes are and thus how much you already know about these heretofore mystifying wine names.

Sparkling Wines

- **Italy**

Asti Spumante	Muscat (Moscato)	Light; floral, hint of sweetness
Prosecco	Prosecco	Delicate; crisp, tangy, the wine used in Bellini cocktails

- **Spain**

Cava	Locals: Xarel-lo, Parellada, Macabeo plus Chardonnay	Light; crisp, refreshing

- **France**

Champagne	The red (yes!) grapes Pinot Noir and Pinot Meunier, plus Chardonnay	To me, all are heavenly, but check the style on the label: Blanc de Blancs—delicate and tangy Brut NV, vintage and luxury—range from soft and creamy to rich and toasty

White Wines

- **Italy**

Frascati	Trebbiano, Malvasia	As you've noticed, mostly local grapes are used in Italy's whites. But the style of all these is easy to remember: light, tangy, and refreshing. Pinot Grigio, the best known, is also more distinctive—pleasant pear and lemon flavors, tasty but not heavy. The less common Pinot Bianco is similar.
Soave	Garganega, Trebbiano	
Orvieto	Grechetto, Procanico, and many others	
Gavi	Cortese	
Vernaccia	Vernaccia	
Pinot Grigio		

- **Germany**
  Riesling

	Riesling rules Germany's quality wine scene	Feather-light but flavor-packed: fruit salad in a glass

- **France**
  - ***Alsace—Grape names are on the label:***

	Pinot Blanc	Light; tangy, pleasant
Riesling	Riesling	Fuller than German Riesling but not heavy; citrus, apples, subtle but layered
	Pinot Gris	Smooth, richer texture; fruit compote flavors
	Gewurztraminer	Sweet spices, apricots, lychee fruit

  - ***Loire Valley***

Vouvray	Chenin Blanc	Look for the style name: Sec—dry and tangy; Demi-sec—baked apple, hint of sweetness; Moelleux—honeyed dessert style

Sauvignon Blanc

Sancerre and Pouilly-Fume	Sauvignon Blanc	Light to medium; subtle fruit, racy acidity

  - ***White Bordeaux***

Sauvignon Blanc & Semillon

Entre-Deux-Mers	Sauvignon Blanc and Semillon	Tangy, crisp, light
Graves Pessac-Leognan		Medium to full; ranging from creamy lemon-lime to lush fig flavors; pricey ones are usually oaky

  - ***Burgundy White***

Chardonnay

Macon St.-Veran Pouilly-Fuisse	Every Chardonnay in the world is modeled on white French Burgundy	Light; refreshing, citrus-apple flavors
Chablis		Subtle, mineral, green apple

St. Aubin		
Meursault		Medium; pear, dried apple, nutty; complexity ranging from simple to sublime
Puligny-Montrachet		
Chassagne-Montrachet		
Corton-Charlemagne		

Red Wines

- **France**
  - ***Red Burgundy***

Beaujolais	Gamay	Uncomplicated, light; fruity, pleasant
Beaujolais-Villages		
Beaujolais Cru:		More complex, plum-berry taste, smooth (the wines are named for their village)
Morgon,		
Moulin-a-Vent, etc.		

Pinot Noir

Cote de Beaune	Pinot Noir	Ranging from light body, pretty cherry taste to extraordinary complexity: captivating spice, berry and earth scents, silky texture, berries and plums flavor
Santenay		
Volnay		
Pommard		
Nuits-St.-Georges		
Vosne-Romanee		
Gevrey-Chambertin		
Clos de Vougeot, etc.		

  - ***Red Bordeaux***

Merlot

Pomerol	Merlot, plus Cabernet Franc and Cabernet Sauvignon	Medium to full; oaky-vanilla scent, plum flavor
St. Emilion		

Cabernet Sauvignon

Medoc	Cabernet Sauvignon, plus Merlot, Cabernet Franc, and Petit Verdot	Full; chunky-velvety texture; cedar-spice-toasty scent; dark berry flavor
Margaux		
Pauillac		
St-Estephe		

- **Rhone Red**

Syrah, aka Shiraz

Cotes-du-Rhone	Mainly Grenache, Syrah, Cinsault, Mourvedre	Medium to full; juicy texture; spicy raspberry scent and taste
Cote-Rotie	Syrah, plus a splash of white Viognier	Full; brawny texture; peppery scent; plum and dark berry taste
Hermitage	Syrah, plus a touch of the white grapes Marsanne and Roussane	Similar to Cote-Rotie
Chateauneuf-du-Pape	Mainly Syrah, Grenache, Cinsault, Mourvedre	Full; exotic leathery-spicy scent; spiced fig and berry compote taste

(Red Zinfandel is here in the light-to-full body spectrum)

- **Spain**
  - **Rioja**

Rioja Crianza, Reserva and Gran Reserva	Tempranillo, plus Garnacha, aka Grenache, and other local grapes	Ranging from soft and smooth, juicy strawberry character (Crianza); to full, caramel-leather scent, spicy-dried fruit taste (Reserva and Gran Reserva)

  - **Ribera del Duero**

	Mostly Tempranillo	Full; mouth-filling texture; toasty-spice scent; anise and plum taste

  - **Priorat**

Sometimes Cabernet Sauvignon

Priorat	Varied blends may include Cabernet Sauvignon, Garnacha, and other local grapes	Full; gripping texture; meaty-leathery-fig scent; superconcentrated plum and dark berry taste

- **Italy**

  As you'll notice from the left column, Italy's classic regions mostly march to their own *bellissimo* beat.

  - **Veneto**

Valpolicella	Corvina plus other local grapes	Light; mouthwatering, tangy cherry taste and scent

Amarone della Valpolicella	Corvina; same vineyards as Valpolicella	Full; rich, velvety texture; toasted almond/prune scent; intense dark raisin and dried fig taste (think Fig Newtons)

• *Piedmont*

Dolcetto d'Alba (the best known of the Dolcettos, but others are good, too)	Dolcetto	Light; zesty, spicy, cranberry-sour cherry taste
Barbera d'Alba (look for Barbera d'Asti and others)	Barbera	Medium; licorice-spice-berry scent; earth and berry taste
Barolo Barbaresco	Nebbiolo	Full; "chewy" texture; exotic earth, licorice, tar scent; strawberry-spice taste

• *Tuscany*

Chianti/ Chianti Classico	Sangiovese	Ranges from light, easy, lip-smacking strawberry-spice character to intense, gripping texture; plum, licorice, and earth scent and taste
Vino Nobile di Monte-pulciano	Prugnolo (a type of Sangiovese)	Medium-to-full; velvety texture, earth-spice, stewed plum taste
Brunello di Montalcino	Brunello (a type of Sangiovese)	Very full; "chewy" in the mouth; powerful dark-fruit flavor

Sometimes Cabernet Sauvignon

"Super Tuscans"—not a region but an important category	Usually a blend of Sangiovese and Cabernet Sauvignon	Modeled to be a classy cross between French red Bordeaux and Italian Chianti; usually full, spicy, and intense, with deep plum and berry flavors

The bottom line on restaurant wine lists: In my opinion, it's not the size of the list that matters but rather the restaurant's effort to make enjoying wine as easy as possible for its guests. How? As always, it comes down to the basics:

Top Ten Tip-Offs You're in a Wine-Wise Restaurant

1. You're *never* made to feel you have to spend a lot to get something good.
2. Wine by the glass is taken as seriously as bottles, with a good range of styles and prices, listed prominently so you don't have to "hunt" to find them.
3. The wine list is presented automatically, so you don't have to ask for it (and wait while the waiter searches for a copy).
4. There are lots of quality bottle choices in the moderate price zone.
5. Wine service, whether glass or bottle, is helpful, speedy, and proficient.
6. Waiters draw your attention to "great values" rather than just the expensive stuff.
7. *Affordable* wine pairings are offered for the signature dishes—either on the menu or by servers.
8. You can ask for a taste before you choose a wine by the glass if you're not sure which you want.
9. It's no problem to split a glass, or get just a half-glass, of by-the-glass offerings. (Great for situations when you want only a little wine or want to try a range of different wines.)
10. There's no such thing as no-name "house white and red." (House-featured wines are fine, but they, and you, merit a name or grape and a region.)

IMMER ROBINSON BEST BETS

Sometimes you just need quick recommendations for the buying occasion at hand. Here are my picks.

Best Restaurant Wineries

The following list of wineries probably includes some names that are familiar to you. These wineries are what we in the restaurant wine list business call *anchors*—the core names around which to build a well-balanced, high-quality wine list that pleases a lot of people. It's not a comprehensive anchor list. Rather, it is my personal list of the benchmark names that I've featured on wine lists for years because, in addition to name recognition with guests, they consistently deliver quality and value across their product line and are generally priced at a relative value compared to the competition in their categories. You can choose your favorite grape or style with extra confidence when it's made by one of these producers.

Antinori, Italy
Banfi, Italy
Beringer, California
Cakebread, California
Calera, California
Cambria, California
Chateau St. Jean, California
Clos du Bois, California
Edna Valley Vineyard, California
Estancia, California
Ferrari-Carano, California
Franciscan, California
Geyser Peak, California
Hugel, France
Jolivet, France
Jordan, California

Joseph Phelps, California
Kendall-Jackson, California
King Estate, Oregon
Louis Jadot, France
Moet & Chandon, France
Morgan, California
Penfolds, Australia
Perrier-Jouet, France
Ravenswood, California
Ridge, California
Robert Mondavi, California
Rosemount Estate, Australia
Ruffino, Italy
Sonoma-Cutrer, California
St. Francis, California
Taittinger, France
Trimbach, France
Veuve Clicquot, France

Best Wine List Values

Although wine list pricing varies widely, I regularly see these wines well priced in restaurants around the country and thus offering great value for the money.

White	Red
Bonny Doon Pacific Rim Riesling, USA/Germany	Firesteed Pinot Noir, Oregon
Alois Lageder Pinot Grigio, Italy	Cambria Julia's Vineyard Pinot Noir, California
Burgans Albarino, Spain	Fetzer Valley Oaks Merlot, California
Jolivet Sancerre, France	Franciscan Oakville Estate Merlot, California
Geyser Peak Sauvignon Blanc, California	Markham Merlot, California
Casa Lapostolle Sauvignon Blanc, Chile	Guenoc Cabernet Sauvignon, California
Estancia Pinnacles Chardonnay, California	Penfolds Bin 389 Cabernet/ Shiraz, Australia
Gallo of Sonoma Chardonnay, California	Cline Zinfandel, California
Simi Chardonnay, California	J. Lohr 7 Oaks Cabernet Sauvignon, California
Chateau St. Jean Chardonnay, California	

Best "House" Wines for Every Day— Sparkling, White, and Red

(*House* means *your* house.) These are great go-to wines to keep around for every day and company too, because they're tasty, *very* inexpensive, and go with everything from takeout to Sunday dinner. They're also wines that got high Kitchen Fridge/Countertop Survivor™ grades, so you don't have to worry if you don't finish the bottle right away. (Selections are listed by body style—lightest to fullest.)

Sparkling
Aria Cava Extra Dry Sparkling, Spain
Domaine Ste. Michelle Cuvee Brut Sparkling, Washington

House Whites
Ca' del Solo Big House White, California
Columbia Winery Cellarmaster's Reserve Riesling, Washington
Yellow Tail Chardonnay, Australia
Lindemans Bin 65 Chardonnay, Australia
Gallo of Sonoma Chardonnay, California
Dry Creek Fume Blanc, California

Reds
Echelon Pinot Noir, California
Duboeuf (Georges) Cotes-du-Rhone, France
Montecillo Rioja Crianza, Spain
Rosemount Diamond Label Cabernet, Australia
Los Vascos Cabernet Sauvignon, Chile
Columbia Crest Grand Estates Merlot, Washington

Impress the Date—Hip Wines

White
Bonny Doon Pacific Rim Riesling, USA/Germany
Frog's Leap Sauvignon Blanc, California
Brancott Reserve Sauvignon Blanc, New Zealand
R.H. Phillips Toasted Head Chardonnay, California
Mulderbosch Sauvignon Blanc, South Africa

Red
Firesteed Pinot Noir, Oregon
Two Tone Farm Merlot, California
Joel Gott Zinfandel, California
Escudo Rojo Cabernet blend, Chile
Catena Malbec, Argentina
Penfolds Cabernet/Shiraz Bin 389, Australia

Impress the Client—Blue Chip Wines

Sparkling/White

Taittinger Brut La Française Champagne, France
Cloudy Bay Sauvignon Blanc, New Zealand
Ferrari-Carano Fume Blanc, California
Robert Mondavi Fume Blanc, California
Sonoma-Cutrer Chardonnay, California
Talbott (Robert) Sleepy Hollow Vineyard
    Chardonnay, California

Red

Etude Pinot Noir, California
Domaine Drouhin Pinot Noir, Oregon
Duckhorn Napa Merlot, California
Ridge Geyserville (Zinfandel), California
Stag's Leap Wine Cellars Napa Cabernet Sauvignon,
    California
Jordan Cabernet Sauvignon, California

You're Invited—Unimpeachable Bottles to Bring to Dinner

(You *do* still have to send a note the next day.)

Trimbach Riesling, Alsace, France
Simi Sauvignon Blanc, California
St. Supery Sauvignon Blanc, California
Louis Jadot Pouilly-Fuisse, France
Beringer Napa Chardonnay, California
Calera Central Coast Pinot Noir, California
Ruffino Chianti Classico Riserva Ducale Gold
    Label, Italy
Penfolds Cabernet/Shiraz Bin 389, Australia
St. Francis Sonoma Merlot, California
Franciscan Napa Cabernet Sauvignon, California
Mt. Veeder Napa Cabernet Sauvignon, California

Cellar Candidates

These wines have consistently proven age-worthy throughout my restaurant career. The time window shown for each is the number of years' aging in reasonably cool cellar conditions to reach peak drinking condition. But this "peak" is in terms of *my* taste—

namely when the wine's texture has softened and enriched, the aromas have become more layered, but the fruit remains vibrant. You may need to adjust your cellar regimen according to your taste. Generally, longer aging gradually trades youthful fruit and acidity for a whole new spectrum of aromas, many of which you might not instantly associate with grapes or wine. In whites, aging commonly leads to softened acidity and a nutty/caramel character; in reds, softened tannins and a leathery/spicy character.

White

Trimbach Riesling, France (3–4 yrs)

Trimbach Pinot Gris, France (4–5 yrs)

Didier Dagueneau Silex Pouilly-Fume, France (6–8 yrs)

Edna Valley Vineyard Chardonnay, California (4–5 yrs)

Grgich Hills Chardonnay, California (5–7 yrs)

Chateau Montelena Chardonnay, California (5–7 yrs)

Kistler Durrell Chardonnay, California (5–7 yrs)

Leflaive (Domaine) Puligny-Montrachet, France (5–6 yrs)

Leflaive (Olivier) Puligny-Montrachet, France (2–4 yrs)

Red

Merry Edwards Russian River Pinot Noir, California (3–4 yrs)

Etude Pinot Noir, California (5–6 yrs)

Williams-Selyem Hirsch Pinot Noir, California (5–7 yrs)

Felsina Chianti Classico, Italy (3–4 yrs)

Frescobaldi Chianti Rufina Riserva, Italy (3–5 yrs)

Ruffino Chianti Classico Riserva Ducale Gold Label, Italy (5–7 yrs)

Selvapiana Chianti Rufina, Italy (3–5 yrs)

Banfi Brunello di Montalcino, Italy (6–8 yrs)

Duckhorn Napa Merlot, California (5–7 yrs)

Shafer Merlot, California (4–5 yrs)

Chateau Lynch-Bages Bordeaux, France (6–8 yrs)

Cakebread Napa Cabernet Sauvignon, California (5–7 yrs)

Chateau Gruaud-Larose Bordeaux, France (6–8 yrs)

Groth Napa Cabernet Sauvignon, California (4–5 yrs)

Heitz Napa Cabernet Sauvignon, California
(5–6 yrs)

Mt. Veeder Cabernet Sauvignon, California
(6–8 yrs)

Penfolds Bin 389 Cabernet/Shiraz, Australia
(6–8 yrs)

Silver Oak Alexander Valley Cabernet Sauvignon,
California (6–8 yrs)

Stag's Leap Wine Cellars Napa Cabernet Sauvignon,
California (4–5 yrs)

Muga Rioja Reserva, Spain (7–9 yrs)

Pesquera Ribera del Duero, Spain (7–9 yrs)

Chateau de Beaucastel Chateauneuf-du-Pape,
France (6–8 yrs)

Grgich Hills Sonoma Zinfandel, California (4–5 yrs)

Ridge Geyserville (Zinfandel), California (5–7 yrs)

Would You Drink It on a Plane?

Disregard the package (screw-capped splits)—if you
see these wineries on the beverage cart, you can take
heart. They won't be the greatest wine you ever
drank, but they are often the only redeeming feature
of flying coach.

Glen Ellen Proprietor's Reserve
Sutter Home
Georges Duboeuf

CUISINE COMPLEMENTS

Whether you're dining out, ordering in, or whipping it up yourself, the following wine recommendations will help you choose a wine to flatter the food in question. If your store doesn't carry that specific wine bottle, ask for a similar selection.

Thanksgiving Wines

More than any other meal, the traditional Thanksgiving lineup features a pretty schizo range of flavors—from gooey-sweet yams to spicy stuffing to tangy cranberry sauce and everything in between. These wines are like a group hug for all the flavors at the table and the guests around it. My tip: choose a white and a red, put them on the table, and let everyone taste and help themselves to whichever they care to drink. (Selections are listed by body style—lightest to fullest.)

	White	Red
S T E A L	Cavit Pinot Grigio, Italy Bonny Doon Riesling, Germany/Calif./ Washington Geyser Peak Sauvignon Blanc, California Pierre Sparr Alsace One, France Fetzer Valley Oaks Gewurztraminer, California Gallo of Sonoma Chardonnay, California	Louis Jadot Beaujolais-Villages, France Falesco Vitiano, Italy Duboeuf Cotes-du-Rhone, France Marques de Caceres Rioja Crianza, Spain Cline Zinfandel, California Rosemount Diamond Label Shiraz, Australia
S P L U R G E	Martin Codax Albarino, Spain Trimbach Riesling, France Robert Mondavi Napa Fume Blanc, California Hugel Gewurztraminer, France Cuvaison Chardonnay, California	Morgan Pinot Noir, California Chateau de Beaucastel Chateauneuf-du-Pape, France Penfolds Bin 389 Cabernet/Shiraz, Australia Pesquera Ribera del Duero, Spain Ridge Geyserville (Zinfandel), California

Barbecue

Folie a Deux Menage a Trois, California
Ca' del Solo Big House White, California
Dry Creek Fume Blanc, California
Black Opal Shiraz, Australia
Hill of Content Grenache-Shiraz, Australia
Jaboulet Cotes-du-Rhone, France
Montevina Amador Zinfandel, California

Chinese Food

Hugel Pinot Blanc, France
Jolivet Sancerre, France
Navarro Gewurztraminer, California
Echelon Pinot Noir, California
Marques de Caceres Rioja Crianza, Spain
Ravenswood Zinfandel, California
Louis Jadot Beaujolais-Villages, France
Allegrini Valpolicella, Italy

Nuevo Latino (Cuban, Caribbean, South American)

Freixenet Brut de Noirs Rose Sparkling, Spain
Robert Mondavi Private Selection Pinot Grigio, California
Marques de Riscal White Rueda, Spain
Dallas Conte Merlot, Chile
Los Vascos Cabernet Sauvignon, Chile
Woodbridge (Robert Mondavi) Zinfandel, California

Picnics

Cavit Pinot Grigio, Italy
Domaine Ste. Michelle Cuvee Brut Sparkling, Washington
Beringer White Zinfandel, California
Lindemans Bin 65 Chardonnay, Australia
Citra Montepulciano d'Abruzzo, Italy
Duboeuf (Georges) Beaujolais-Villages, France

Sushi

Moet & Chandon White Star Champagne, France
Trimbach Riesling, France
Burgans Albarino, Spain
Jolivet Sancerre, France
Villa Maria Sauvignon Blanc, New Zealand
Frog's Leap Sauvignon Blanc, California

Louis Jadot Pouilly-Fuisse, France
B&G Beaujolais-Villages, France
Beringer Founders' Estate Pinot Noir, California
Calera Central Coast Pinot Noir, California

Clambake/Lobster Bake
Kendall-Jackson Vintner's Reserve Sauvignon Blanc,
    California
Murphy-Goode Fume Blanc, California
Gallo of Sonoma Chardonnay, California
Beringer Napa Chardonnay, California
Cambria Chardonnay, California
Louis Jadot Beaujolais-Villages, France
Firesteed Pinot Noir, Oregon

Mexican Food
Ecco Domani Pinot Grigio, Italy
King Estate Pinot Gris, Oregon
Meridian Sauvignon Blanc, California
Hugel Gewurztraminer, France
Beringer White Zinfandel, California
Dry Creek Fume Blanc, California
Duboeuf (Georges) Cotes-du-Rhone, France
Cline Zinfandel, California
Ravenswood Vintners Blend Zinfandel, California

Pizza
Citra Montepulciano d'Abruzzo, Italy
Salice Salentino, Taurino, Italy
Montecillo Rioja Crianza, Spain
D'Arenberg The Footbolt Shiraz, Australia
Montevina Amador Zinfandel, California
Woodbridge (Robert Mondavi) Zinfandel,
    California
Penfolds Koonunga Hill Shiraz/Cabernet Sauvignon,
    Australia

The Cheese Course
Frescobaldi Chianti Rufina Riserva, Italy
Penfolds Bin 389 Cabernet/Shiraz, Australia
Chateau de Beaucastel Chateauneuf-du-Pape,
    France
Muga Rioja Reserva, Spain
Pesquera Ribera del Duero, Spain
St. Francis Sonoma Zinfandel, California

Ridge Geyserville (Zinfandel), California
Rosemount GSM (Grenache-Shiraz-Mourvedre),
  Australia
Grgich Hills Sonoma Zinfandel, California
Mt. Veeder Cabernet Sauvignon, California
Chateau Gruaud-Larose Bordeaux, France
Banfi Brunello di Montalcino, Italy
Alvaro Palacios Les Terrasses Priorat, Spain

Steak

Ferrari-Carano Chardonnay, California
Talbott (Robert) Sleepy Hollow Vineyard
  Chardonnay, California
Morgan 12 Clones Pinot Noir, California
Domaine Drouhin Pinot Noir, Oregon
Ruffino Chianti Classico Riserva Ducale Gold
  Label, Italy
Pio Cesare Barolo, Italy
Shafer Merlot, California
Cakebread Napa Cabernet Sauvignon,
  California
Beringer Knights Valley Cabernet Sauvignon,
  California
Robert Mondavi Napa Cabernet Sauvignon,
  California
Groth Napa Cabernet Sauvignon, California
Stag's Leap Wine Cellars Napa Cabernet Sauvignon,
  California
Joseph Phelps Napa Cabernet Sauvignon,
  California
St. Francis Old Vines Zinfandel, California

Salad

Ruffino Orvieto, Italy
Hugel Pinot Blanc, France
Trimbach Riesling, France
Ceretto Arneis, Italy
Henri Bourgeois Pouilly-Fume, France
Louis Jadot Macon-Villages Chardonnay, France
Allegrini Valpolicella, Italy
Calera Central Coast Pinot Noir, California

Vegetarian

Folonari Pinot Grigio, Italy
Gallo of Sonoma Pinto Gris, California

Hess Select Chardonnay, California
Estancia Pinnacles Pinot Noir, California
Castello di Gabbiano Chianti, Italy
Jaboulet Cotes-du-Rhone Parallele 45, France

WINERY INDEX

Au Bon Climat, California
    Rincon & Rosemary's Pinot Noir **$$$$**   97
    Santa Barbara Chardonnay **$$$**   66
    Santa Barbara Pinot Noir **$$**   98
    Talley Vineyard and Pinot Noir **$$$$**   98

Aveleda, Portugal
    Vinho verde **$**   83

Babcock, California
    7 Oaks Sauvignon Blanc **$$$**   56

Babich Marlborough, New Zealand
    Sauvignon Blanc **$$**   56

Ballatore, California
    Gran Spumante **$**   37

Banfi, Italy
    Brachetto d'Acqui **$$$**   174
    Brunello di Montalcino **$$$$**   112

Baron Philippe de Rothschild, France
    Sauternes **$$$**   174

Barton & Guestier (B&G), France
    Beaujolais **$**   94
    Merlot **$**   117

Becker, Texas
    Viognier **$$**   84

Beaulieu Vineyard (BV), California
    Carneros Pinot Noir **$$**   98
    Coastal Cabernet Sauvignon **$**   128
    Coastal Chardonnay **$**   67
    George de Latour Private Reserve Cabernet   128
      Sauvignon **$$$**
    Napa Valley Zinfandel **$$**   168
    Rutherford Cabernet Sauvignon **$$$**   128

Bella Sera, Italy
    Pinot Grigio **$**   46

Benton Lane, Oregon
    Pinot Noir **$$**   98

Benziger, California
    Fume Blanc **$$**   56

Beringer, California
    Bancroft Ranch Merlot **$$$$**   117
    Chenin Blanc **$**   84
    Founders' Estate Cabernet Sauvignon **$**   129
    Founders' Estate Chardonnay **$**   67
    Founders' Estate Merlot **$**   118
    Founders' Estate Pinot Noir **$$**   98
    Founders' Estate Sauvignon Blanc **$**   56
    Gewurztraminer **$**   84

Buena Vista, California
  Carneros Pinot Noir **$$**   99

Burgans (Bodegas Vilarino-Cambados), Spain
  Albarino **$$**   84

Burgess, California
  Merlot **$$$**   118

Byron, California
  Santa Maria Valley Pinot Noir **$$**   99

Ca'del Solo, California
  Big House Red **$$**   153
  Big House White **$**   85

Cain, California
  Cain Cuvee Bordeaux Style Red **$$$**   130

Cakebread, California
  Chardonnay Reserve **$$$$**   68
  Napa Cabernet Sauvignon **$$$$**   130
  Napa Chardonnay **$$$$**   67
  Sauvignon Blanc **$$$**   57

Calera, California
  Central Coast Pinot Noir **$$$**   99

Cambria, California
  Julia's Vineyard Pinot Noir **$$$**   99
  Katherine's Vineyard Chardonnay **$$**   68

Camelot, California
  Chardonnay **$**   68

Campo Viejo, Spain
  Rioja Reserva **$$**   150

Canyon Road, California
  Sauvignon Blanc **$**   57

Casa Lapostolle, Chile
  Classic Merlot **$**   118
  Cuvee Alexandre Cabernet Sauvignon **$$**   130
  Cuvee Alexandre Chardonnay **$$**   68
  Sauvignon Blanc **$**   57

Castello di Brolio, Italy
  Chianti Classico **$$**   113

Castello di Gabbiano, Italy
  Chianti **$$**   113
  Chianti Classico Riserva **$$$**   113

Castello di Volpaia, Italy
  Chianti Classico Riserva **$$$**   113

Catena, Argentina
  Chardonnay **$$**   68
  Zapata Alamos Malbec **$$$**   153

Chateau Montelena, California
Cabernet Sauvignon **$$$$** 132
Chardonnay **$$$** 69

Chateau Prieure-Lichine, Bordeaux, France **$$$** 132

Chateau Rabaud-Promis, France
Sauternes **$$$$** 175

Chateau Simard, Bordeaux, France **$$$$** 118

Chateau Souverain, California
Alexander Valley Cabernet Sauvignon **$$$** 133
Alexander Valley Merlot **$$** 119

Chateau Ste. Michelle, Washington
Cold Creek Chardonnay **$$** 69
Cold Creek Merlot **$$** 118
Columbia Valley Cabernet Sauvignon **$$** 133
Columbia Valley Chardonnay **$$** 69
Columbia Valley Gewurztraminer **$** 85
Columbia Valley Merlot **$$** 118
Columbia Valley Sauvignon Blanc **$** 57
Indian Wells Chardonnay **$$** 70
Indian Wells Merlot **$$** 118
Johannisberg Riesling **$** 50

Chateau St. Jean, California
Cinq Cepages Cabernet Blend **$$$$** 133
Fume Blanc **$** 57
Robert Young Chardonnay **$$$** 70
Sonoma Chardonnay **$$** 70
Sonoma Pinot Noir **$$** 100

Christian Moueix, France
Merlot **$** 118

Citra, Italy
Montepulciano d'Abruzzo **$** 156

Cline, California
Red Truck **$** 155
Syrah **$** 161
Zinfandel **$** 168

Clos du Bois, California
Marlstone **$$$$** 133
Sonoma Cabernet Sauvignon **$$** 134
Sonoma Chardonnay **$$** 70
Sonoma Merlot **$$** 120
Sonoma Pinot Noir **$$$** 100
Sonoma Sauvignon Blanc **$$** 58
Sonoma Zinfandel **$$** 168

Cloudy Bay, New Zealand
Sauvignon Blanc **$$$** 58

Cockburn's, Portugal
Fine Ruby Port **$$** 175

Fetzer, California
  Sundial Chardonnay $ 72
  Valley Oaks Cabernet Sauvignon $ 136
  Valley Oaks Chardonnay $$ 72
  Valley Oaks Gewurztraminer $ 86
  Valley Oaks Johannisberg Riesling $ 51
  Valley Oaks Merlot $ 121
  Valley Oaks Zinfandel $ 169

Ficklin, California
  Tinta "Port" $$ 176

Firesteed, Oregon
  Pinot Noir $ 102

Five Rivers Ranch, California
  Pinot Noir $ 102

Flowers, California
  Pinot Noir $$$$ 103

Folie a Deux, California
  Menage a Trois White $ 86

Folonari, Italy
  Pinot Grigio $ 46

Fonseca, Portugal
  Bin 27 $$$ 176

Foppiano, California
  Petite Sirah $ 154

Franciscan, California
  Magnificat $$$$ 136
  Napa Cabernet Sauvignon $$$ 137
  Oakville Chardonnay $$ 72
  Oakville Estate Merlot $$$ 121

Francis Coppola
  See Coppola

Frei Brothers Reserve, California
  Cabernet Sauvignon $$ 137
  Merlot $$ 122
  Pinot Noir $$ 103

Freixenet, Spain
  Brut de Noirs Sparkling Cava Rose $ 40
  Cordon Negro Brut $ 40

Frescobaldi, Italy
  Chianti Rufina Riserva $$$ 114

Frog's Leap, California
  Cabernet Sauvignon $$$ 137
  Merlot $$$ 122
  Sauvignon Blanc $$ 59

Gallo of Sonoma, California
  Cabernet Sauvignon $$ 137
  Chardonnay $ 72
  Merlot $ 122

Honig, California
  Sauvignon Blanc $$ 60

Hugel, Alsace, France
  Gewurztraminer $$ 87
  Pinot Blanc $$ 87

Indaba, South Africa
  Chenin Blanc $ 88

Iron Horse, California
  Pinot Noir $$$ 103
  Wedding Cuvee Brut $$$ 40

Jaboulet, France
  Parallele 45 Cotes-du-Rhone $ 163

Jacob's Creek, Australia
  Cabernet Sauvignon $ 139
  Chardonnay $ 73
  Shiraz/Cabernet $ 163

Jade Mountain, California
  Syrah $$ 163

Jean-Luc Colombo, France
  Les Abeilles, Cotes-du-Rhone $ 163

Jekel, California
  Riesling $ 52

J.J. Prum, Germany
  Wehlener Sonnenuhr Riesling Kabinett $$ 52

J. Lohr, California
  7 Oaks Cabernet Sauvignon $$ 139
  Bay Mist White Riesling $ 52
  Hilltop Cabernet Sauvignon $$$ 139
  Riverstone Chardonnay $ 73

Joel Gott, California
  Sauvignon Blanc $$ 60
  Zinfandel $$ 169

Jolivet (Pascal), France
  Sancerre $$ 61

Jordan, California
  Cabernet Sauvignon $$$ 139
  Chardonnay $$$ 73

Joseph Drouhin, France
  Pouilly-Fuisse $$ 73

Joseph Phelps, California
  Insignia $$$$ 140
  Le Mistral $$$ 164
  Napa Cabernet Sauvignon $$$$ 140
  Pastiche Rouge $ 164
  Sauvignon Blanc $$ 61

Justin, California
  Isosceles $$$$ 140

Marques de Riscal, Spain
Rioja Reserva **$$** 151
Rueda White **$** 88

Marquis Phillips, Australia
Sarah's Blend (Syrah/Merlot) **$$** 164

Martin Codax, Spain
Albarino **$$** 88

Mason, California
Sauvignon Blanc **$$** 62

Matanzas Creek, California
Chardonnay **$$$** 76

Meridian, California
Cabernet Sauvignon **$** 141
Chardonnay **$** 77
Merlot **$$** 123
Pinot Noir **$** 105

Merry Edwards, California
Russian River Valley Pinot Noir **$$$$** 105

Merryvale, California
Profile Cabernet blend **$$$$** 142
Sauvignon Blanc **$$** 62
Starmont Chardonnay **$$** 77

Mer Soleil, California
Chardonnay **$$$$** 77

MezzaCorona, Italy
Pinot Grigio **$** 47

Michele Chiarlo, Italy
Le Orme Barbera d'Asti **$** 156
Moscato d'Asti Nivole (Clouds) **$$$** 176

Michel Laroche, Burgundy, France
Chablis St. Martin **$$$** 77

Miguel Torres, Spain
Vina Sol White **$** 88

Mionetto, Italy
DOC Prosecco **$$** 42

Mirassou, California
Chardonnay **$** 77
Pinot Noir **$** 105

Moët & Chandon, Champagne, France
Brut Imperial **$$$$** 42
White Star **$$$$** 42

Mondavi (Robert), California
See Robert Mondavi

Monkey Bay, New Zealand
Sauvignon Blanc **$** 62

Monte Antico, Italy
  Toscana Red **$**   114

Montecillo, Spain
  Rioja Crianza **$**   151
  Rioja Reserva **$$**   151

Montes, Chile
  Alpha "M" **$$$$**   123
  Merlot **$**   123

Montevina, California
  Amador Zinfandel **$**   170
  Pinot Grigio **$**   47
  Sauvignon Blanc **$**   62

Morgan, California
  Metallico Chardonnay **$$**   78
  12 Clones Pinot Noir **$$**   105

Miguel Torres
  Vina Sol **$**   88

Morgante, Italiy
  Nero d'Avola **$**   157

Mt. Veeder, California
  Napa Cabernet Sauvignon **$$$$**   142

Mulderbosch, South Africa
  Sauvignon Blanc **$$**   62

Muga, Spain
  Rioja Reserva **$$$**   152

Mumm Cuvee, Napa, California
  Brut Prestige Sparkling **$$**   42

Murphy-Goode, California
  Fume Blanc **$**   63

Navarro, California
  Gewurztraminer **$$**   89

Navarro Correas, Argentina
  Malbec **$**   154

Nobilo, New Zealand
  Sauvignon Blanc **$**   63

Nozzole, Italy
  Chianto Classico Riserva **$$**   114

Opus One, California
  Cabernet Sauvignon Blend **$$$$**   142

Ornellaia, Italy
  Super Tuscan **$$$$**   114

Osborne, Spain
  Solaz Tempranillo **$**   152

Pahlmeyer, California
  Meritage **$$$$**   142

Panther Creek, Oregon
  Pinot Noir **$$$** 106

Papio, California
  Chardonnay **$** 78

Paraduxx, California
  Red Blend **$$$$** 142

Paul Blanck, France
  Gewurztraminer "Classique" **$$** 89

Pavillon Blanc du Chateau Margaux, France
  Bordeaux Blanc **$$$$** 63

Pedroncelli, California
  Pinot Noir **$$** 106

Penfolds, Australia
  Bin 389 Cabernet/Shiraz **$$$** 142
  Coonawarra Shiraz Bin 128 **$$$** 164
  Grange **$$$$** 165
  Kalimna Shiraz Bin 28 **$$$** 165
  Koonunga Hill Cabernet/Merlot **$$** 143
  Koonunga Hill Chardonnay **$** 78
  Koonunga Hill Shiraz/Cabernet **$** 165
  Rawson's Retreat Chardonnay **$** 78
  Rawson's Retreat Merlot **$** 124
  Semillon/Chardonnay **$** 89

Pepperwood Grove, California
  Pinot Noir **$** 106
  Viognier **$** 89

Perdrix, France
  Mercurey **$$$** 106

Perrier-Jouët, Champagne, France
  Flower Bottle **$$$$** 42
  Grand Brut **$$$$** 43

Pesquera, Spain
  Ribera del Duero **$$$** 152

Pierre Sparr, France
  Alsace-One **$** 89
  Carte D'Or Riesling **$** 53
  Pinot Blanc **$** 89

Pine Ridge, California
  Cabernet Sauvignon Stag's Leap
    District **$$$$** 143

Pio Cesare, Italy
  Barolo **$$$$** 157

Piper-Heidsieck, Champagne, France
  Brut Cuvee **$$$$** 43

Piper-Sonoma, California
  Brut Sparkling **$$** 43

Smoking Loon, California
  Cabernet Sauvignon $ — 146
  Chardonnay $ — 80
  Pinot Noir $ — 109
  Viognier $ — 90

Sokol-Blosser, Oregon
  Evolution $$ — 90
  Reserve Pinot Noir $$$$ — 109

Solaris, California
  Pinot Noir $ — 109

Solorosa, California
  Rose $$ — 93

Sonoma-Cutrer, California
  Russian River Ranches Chardonnay $$$ — 80

Spy Valley, New Zealand
  Sauvignon Blanc $ — 64

Staglin Family, California
  Cabernet Sauvignon $$$$ — 146
  Chardonnay $$$$ — 80

Stag's Leap Wine Cellars, California
  Napa Cabernet Sauvignon $$$$ — 147
  Napa Merlot $$$$ — 125

Steele, California
  Mendocino Pinot Noir $$$ — 109

Sterling Vineyards, California
  Napa Cabernet Sauvignon $$$ — 147
  Napa Merlot $$$ — 125
  Napa Sauvignon Blanc $ — 64
  North Coast Chardonnay $$ — 80

Stonestreet, California
  Alexander Valley Cabernet Sauvignon $$$ — 147

Straccali, Italy
  Chianti $ — 116

Strub, Germany
  Niersteiner Paterberg Riesling Spatlese $$ — 54

Sutter Home, California
  Chardonnay $ — 81
  Gewurztraminer $ — 90
  Merlot $ — 125
  White Zinfandel $ — 93

Swanson Vineyards, California
  Merlot $$$ — 126

Taittinger, Champagne, France
  Brut La Française $$$$ — 44

Talbott (Robert), California
  Sleepy Hollow Vineyard Chardonnay $$$$ — 81

Wild Horse, California
  Pinot Noir **$$$**   110

Willakenzie, Oregon
  Willamette Valley Pinot Noir **$$$**   110

Willamette Valley Vineyards, Oregon
  Pinot Gris **$$**   48
  Pinot Noir **$$**   110
  Reserve Pinot Noir **$$$**   110

Williams-Selyem, California
  Hirsch Pinot Noir **$$$$**   110
  Sonoma Coast Pinot Noir **$$$$**   111

Wolf Blass, Australia
  President's Selection Shiraz **$$**   166

Woodbridge (Robert Mondavi), California
  Chardonnay **$**   82
  Merlot **$**   126
  Pinot Grigio **$**   48
  Zinfandel **$**   173

Wyndham, Australia
  Bin 555 Shiraz **$**   166

Wynn's Coonawarra Estate, Australia
  Cabernet Sauvignon **$$**   148

Yalumba, Australia
  Museum Muscat **$$$**   177

Yellow Tail, Australia
  Cabernet Merlot **$**   148
  Cabernet Shiraz **$**   148
  Chardonnay **$**   82
  Merlot **$**   126
  Shiraz **$**   166
  Shiraz Cabernet **$**   166

Zemmer, Italy
  Pinot Grigio **$$**   48

Zenato, Italy
  Amarone della Valpolicella Classico **$$$$**   157

Zind-Humbrecht, France
  Gewurztraminer "Wintzenheim" **$$**   91

THANKS TO . . .

The tasting panel! You've made buying and drinking wine better and more fun for everyone who picks up this book. Thanks for sharing your hidden gems, and for telling it like it is. Keep tasting!

Cindy Renzi, for culling all the wine ratings from the database; and Katie McManus, for wordsmithing many of the new wine reviews.

Broadway Books, especially Jennifer Josephy and Steve Rubin, for believing in the book.

DEDICATED TO . . .

My husband, John Robinson, and my children, Lucas and Jesse.

In loving tribute to the memory of the missing from Windows on the World, where wine really was for everyone.

PLEASE JOIN MY TASTING PANEL

To share your comments on wines you like (or dislike), visit www.andreawine.com. While you're there, you can get wine and food pairings, download delicious wine-worthy recipes, and check out my new *Complete Wine Course* DVD, and my wine club:

The A-List™ is my wine club of discoveries that are limited, and really amazing for the price. These are wines you won't find in most stores (or buying guides!), delivered to your door (where legal) and paired with recipes I've created to perfectly showcase the wines. Visit www.alistwine.com for more info.

More great wines and superb recipes from **Andrea Immer Robinson**

© John McJunkin

Great Wine Made Simple
REVISED EDITION
Now available in a revised and updated edition, the book that introduced Andrea's commonsense approach to selecting the perfect wine every time.

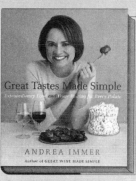

Great Tastes Made Simple
Enhance the flavor of even the most casual meals with winning wine selections. Includes 20 original recipes.

Everyday Dining with Wine
Make everyday meals special by enjoying them with the perfect wine. Features 125 wonderful recipes.

Andrea's Complete Wine Course for Everyone
Andrea's new DVD features 10 interactive tasting lessons you can follow along at home with your friends and family.

 Broadway Books • Available wherever books are sold
www.andreawine.com